LINCOLN & CALIFORNIA

LINCOLN
and
CALIFORNIA

The President, the War, and the Golden State

BRIAN MCGINTY

Potomac Books
An imprint of the University of Nebraska Press

All rights reserved. Potomac Books is an imprint of the
University of Nebraska Press.
Manufactured in the United States of America.

Library of Congress Cataloging-in-Publication Data
Names: McGinty, Brian, author.
Title: Lincoln and California: the President, the war, and the
Golden State / Brian McGinty.
Description: Lincoln: Potomac Books, an imprint of the
University of Nebraska Press, 2023. | Includes bibliographical
references and index.
Identifiers: LCCN 2023012289
ISBN 9781640126060 (hardcover)
ISBN 9781640126077 (epub)
ISBN 9781640126084 (pdf)
Subjects: LCSH: Lincoln, Abraham, 1809–1865. | Lincoln,
Abraham, 1809–1865—Friends and associates. | California—
History—Civil War, 1861–1865. | United States—Politics
and government—1861–1865. | BISAC: HISTORY / United
States / Civil War Period (1850–1877) | BIOGRAPHY &
AUTOBIOGRAPHY / Presidents & Heads of State
Classification: LCC E457.2 .M4756 2023 | DDC 973.7092
[B]—dc23/eng/20230425
LC record available at https://lccn.loc.gov/2023012289

Set in Minion Pro by K. Andresen.

To the memory of the Californians who helped Abraham Lincoln become president, preserve the Union, and bring about the eventual extinction of slavery.

Contents

Illustrations

Acknowledgments

IT WOULD BE IMPOSSIBLE FOR ME TO NAME EVERYONE WHO offered me help, ideas, and inspiration for the writing of this book. My interest in Lincoln and his connection with California began many years ago, motivated by members of my own family, who shared their interest in Lincoln and directed me to my first sources of information about his life and accomplishments. My own studies in the History Department at the University of California in Berkeley helped to increase that interest and to direct it particularly toward Lincoln's connections with California, as did the research and writing that led to my previously published books about important aspects of his life and career. Scholars and authors who offered me encouragement for my previous work include, among many others, Harold Holzer and Frank J. Williams, prize-winning Lincoln scholars, authors, and officers of the Lincoln Forum; James M. McPherson, Pulitzer Prize–winning historian and distinguished Lincoln scholar and author; and Michael Burlingame, acclaimed Lincoln scholar, author, and president of the Abraham Lincoln Association in Springfield, Illinois. Paul Finkelman, author of important books and scholarly articles relating to Abraham Lincoln's legal career, and Richard W. Etulain, prolific and prize-winning historian whose main interest is the history and literature of the American West, offered encouragement and valuable suggestions for improvement of the text. At the University of Nebraska Press, my work was encouraged by Bridget Barry, editor in chief; Thomas F. Swanson, editor for Potomac Books; Leif

Milliken, the Press's rights and contracts director; Taylor Rothgeb, acquisitions editor; and Natalie Taylor Jones, copyeditor, whose careful, precise, and thorough copyediting was beautifully done. Kevin Waite, distinguished scholar of the Civil War era and author of *West of Slavery: The Southern Dream of a Continental Empire* (2021), provided insights into the cotton states' goal of western expansion and Lincoln's efforts to avoid that result by opposing secession. Libraries in which I conducted my research include the U.S. National Archives; the Library of Congress; the California State Archives; the California State Library; the Bancroft Library at the University of California in Berkeley; the Los Angeles Public Library; the San Francisco Public Library; the library of the California Historical Society; and the Lincoln Memorial Shrine and Library in Redlands, California, whose curator, Nathan Gonzales, provided insights that helped me hone my research and writing. At the Lincoln Presidential Library in Springfield, Illinois, I received valuable guidance from James J. Cornelius, the library's curator and the secretary of the Abraham Lincoln Association, and other staff members. To all these people, and those whose names I have failed to include here, many thanks and my sincere appreciation.

Introduction

THE TIES THAT BOUND ABRAHAM LINCOLN TO CALIFORNIA, and California to Abraham Lincoln, have been ignored by too many writers and historians. The great Civil War president has been the subject of thousands of books, yet his important relationship with the western state both before and during the war, the key part it played in bringing on the conflict, and the vital help it gave him in winning it, have been little described and only imperfectly understood.

Lincoln never set foot in California. He never spent a day visiting it. He did, however, often speak of his hope that he could one day go there. He did repeatedly say that he might like to make it his and his family's home after he left the White House. He was never able to do that, of course, because another tragic event intervened. But the connections between Lincoln and California were not merely hopes or desires.

Lincoln had been drawn to the West since his birth in 1809. He had moved with his family from the then western state of Kentucky into western Indiana, then farther west into Illinois, and looking even farther west across the Mississippi toward the plains and the mountains that extended to the distant horizon. While serving in Congress in the 1840s, he had described himself as a "western free state man" and ardently championed the construction of railroads that would stretch across the continent as far as California's Pacific coast. When Oregon, California's northern neighbor, sought to become a state, Lincoln was offered important official positions there, which he declined, and one that he sought but did not receive. His legendary debates with senator Stephen Douglas in 1858 had focused on his opposition to the threatened westward spread of slavery into Kansas and Nebraska and the even further spread of slavery wherever the voters (whites, not blacks, and men, not women) wanted it to spread. The slaveholders in the South hoped to expand slavery westward as far as California, making their slave empire one that would grow in size, strength, and power and become sustainable into the indefinite future. Without California, the great Civil War might never have been fought. Led by the slave-owning president James Knox Polk, Congress had declared war with Mexico, authorizing the U.S. Army and navy to invade the country and seize California, hoping to incorporate all or part of it into the South's slaveholding empire. The threat that Lincoln might prevent them from doing so gave rise to the secession led by the slave-owning Confederate president Jefferson Davis and the fearsome combat that followed.

Lincoln had opposed the war with Mexico—the war that his political hero Henry Clay called a "most unnecessary and horrible war" and that Ulysses S. Grant, the man he chose to lead the Union army to victory in the Civil War, more tersely described as a "wicked war." After it was fought and won, however, Lincoln was willing to accept California as one of the states, to pay close attention to it when he was president, and to eagerly make use of the many and important strengths it brought to the nation as the Civil War was being fought: vast quantities of gold and silver that helped finance the Union war effort, and volunteer troops and professional soldiers who helped keep the secessionist slave power from capturing the state. So, at the end of the terrible conflict, California emerged dramatically as a symbol of the life, liberty, and pursuit of happiness that Lincoln cherished and sought to preserve.

This book describes important people who, beginning early in Lincoln's life, drew his attention to the West and to California. Among them were Charles Maltby, the one-time store clerk who shared his life with Lincoln in New Salem, Illinois, in 1832 and, after crossing the plains to begin a new life in California in 1849, sought (and received) appointments to federal offices in the state from Lincoln, then wrote the first California-published biography of the deceased president; James Short, a man who farmed land a few miles north of New Salem and became one of Lincoln's friends, eventually receiving an appointment from him as an Indian agent in California; and James A. McDougall, a twice-elected attorney general of Illinois who participated in court cases there in which Lincoln was also an attorney, but went to California in 1849 and was there elected as its attorney general, as one of its U.S. congressmen, and in 1861 as one of its U.S. senators, communicating duly with Lincoln. John Hanks, a cousin of Lincoln's mother who lived and worked with Lincoln in both Indiana and Illinois, was largely responsible for Lincoln's popular reputation as a "rail-splitter," and in the early 1850s spent three years in the gold fields of California. Richard J. Oglesby, an Illinois-based lawyer and politician who helped John Hanks make Lincoln known to millions as the "rail-splitter" but later joined the California gold rush, returned to Illinois where he supported Lincoln's rise to the presidency and served as a major general in the Civil War, as a U.S. senator from Illinois, and as a three-time governor of the state. The legendary western explorer John C. Frémont, popularly called "The Pathfinder," was one of the first two United States senators representing California, the first presidential nominee of the newly formed Republican Party, and, by appointment of Lincoln, the tragic commander of the Union army in war-torn Missouri. James Shields, the Irish-born attorney who in 1842 challenged Lincoln to a duel that was never fought, served in many official positions, including as a U.S. senator representing three states (Illinois, Minnesota, and Missouri); after moving to California in 1861, Shields was commissioned by Lincoln as a brigadier general of U.S. volunteers. Ulysses S. Grant, William Tecumseh Sherman, Henry W. Halleck, Joseph Hooker, and Winfield Scott Hancock were all West Point graduates who served the nation in prewar California and struggled to achieve victory as Union generals under Lincoln's command after the conflict began. Edward D. "Ned" Baker, whom Lincoln described as his "dearest personal friend," was a fierce fighter and eloquent orator who helped establish the Republican Party in California before becoming a U.S. senator from Oregon. Baker campaigned in 1860 for Lincoln's election as president in both Oregon and California, personally introducing Lincoln to the gathered crowd at the U.S. Capitol when he was inaugurated president in March 1861; in October 1861 Baker met a tragic death in the Civil War battle of Ball's Bluff, causing Lincoln to sob bitterly. Leland Stanford was one of the founders of the Republican Party in California, governor of the state during the Civil War, and president of the Central Pacific Railroad, which was preparing to build the transcontinental railroad that Lincoln and other Republicans so vigorously supported. John Conness, an Irish-born U.S. senator representing California, helped raise the funds necessary to fight the war and introduced the bill that Lincoln signed making California's magnificent Yosemite Valley the first national park set aside under federal law for the permanent benefit of the public. Noah Brooks, the California-based journalist who became one of Lincoln's closest friends in war-torn Washington and, using the pen name "Castine," sent 258 fact-filled "Letters from Washington" to Sacramento before returning to finish his writing career in the Pacific Coast state.

The book also includes an important discussion of the suffering that California's Native Americans endured after Europeans first appeared in their midst and of President Lincoln's failure to do anything to better their conditions—partly because of his preoccupation with the Civil War then threatening the dissolution of the nation, and partly because he did not really understand their plight. He did say more than once that he hoped he could help them after the war concluded, but whether he would in fact have done so remains a subject of disagreement among historians who have studied the subject.

The book includes recollections of Lincoln's oft-stated wish that he could visit California after he left the White House, perhaps even make a home there for himself and his family, climb to the top of Lone Mountain, where Edward Baker's body was buried, and look out over the Golden Gate and the Pacific Ocean. It concludes with a description of the fascinating ways in which California and Californians have remembered Lincoln, including notable sculptures erected to honor his memory; the building of the Lincoln Memorial Shrine in Redlands, California, the only museum and research center dedicated to Abraham Lincoln west of the Mississippi; the planning and construction of the Lincoln Highway, the first transcontinental automobile road, built between New York City and Lincoln Park in San Francisco, honoring the deceased president and providing the nation's first coast-to-coast vehicular travel route; the creation of the Lincoln-Roosevelt League, a political organization that promoted the enactment of many of the political reforms inspired by Lincoln; the creation of the Progressive (or Bull Moose) political party that nominated California's governor Hiram Johnson as the vice-presidential candidate to run with presidential candidate Theodore Roosevelt in 1912; and the inspiration that California's three time-elected governor and U.S. Supreme Court Chief Justice Earl Warren derived from the memory of Lincoln as in 1954 he led the nation's highest court to make its monumental decision ending racial segregation in the United States.

This book has its roots in my deep and abiding fascination with both Lincoln and California. My interest in Lincoln's life and work was kindled by his early life as a lawyer and his experiences helping men and women in mid-nineteenth-century Illinois solve their legal problems. My interest in California grew out of my birth and long life in the western state and my own experience as a practicing lawyer there. As I studied Lincoln's life, I developed more respect and sympathy for the issues he faced and the gifts he brought to the presidency in the time of its greatest crisis. As I studied California's history, I learned more about Lincoln's growing interest in the state, what it did to help him preserve the Union, and ultimately to kindle his hope to visit there, or perhaps even make his home there.

Although this book focuses on only one of the United States, it is no more a local or regional history than my previous books about Lincoln may be described as merely legal history, judicial history, or transportation history. It includes important information about other western states that had an important effect on Lincoln's efforts to save the Union: Arizona, Nevada, Idaho, and, quite importantly, Oregon, where some of his friends settled and kept him advised about developments there and where he received invitations to assume key federal positions. It is a story of the powerful ties that bound an important state and region together with an important president, and the historic contributions that all of them made to the beginning—and the conclusion—of the Civil War.

April 14, 1865

APRIL 14, 1865, BEGAN AS ONE OF THE HAPPIEST DAYS IN one of the happiest weeks in Abraham Lincoln's life. It was Good Friday, and news of the end of the war that had so cruelly racked the nation for the previous four years was elevating the president's feelings and those of the people who lived in Washington. He arose at seven o'clock, put on a faded dressing gown and a pair of well-worn slippers, and walked down the hall to the family sitting room on the second floor of the White House. There he read a chapter or two of the Bible, as was his habit, before moving on to his office, where he tended to some correspondence. At about eight o'clock, he went downstairs to the family dining room, where he joined his wife, Mary, his twenty-one-year-old son, Union army captain Robert T. Lincoln, and his twelve-year-old son, Tad, for breakfast. Robert had witnessed the surrender of Confederate general Robert E. Lee to Union lieutenant general Ulysses S. Grant at Appomattox Courthouse, Virginia, on Palm Sunday, April 9, and brought details of it to his father. He also brought a portrait of General Lee, which Lincoln scanned thoughtfully before saying, "It is a good face; it is the face of a noble, brave man. I am glad the war is over at last."[1]

Lincoln met with his cabinet from eleven o'clock until two in the afternoon, discussing a myriad of issues relating to the upcoming reconstruction of the rebellious Southern states. General Grant attended the meeting, advising Lincoln and his cabinet secretaries of the details of Lee's surrender.[2] When the meeting concluded, the cabinet members commented on the president's happy mood. "That's the most satisfactory Cabinet meeting I have attended in many a long day," said secretary of war Edwin M. Stanton. "Didn't our chief look grand today?"[3]

Many members of Congress came to the White House to congratulate Lincoln on the successful conclusion of the war and to discuss other business that concerned them.[4] One was Indiana's Schuyler Colfax, Speaker of the House of Representatives, who was planning to leave the next day for a trip to California. Another was Cornelius Cole, a congressman from California who was planning to return to his home state and meet with his constituents.[5] Colfax's journey would be overland, while Cole would be going to New York to board a steamship that would take him south to Panama, where he would cross the isthmus by train and then board another steamer for a voyage north to San Francisco.

Meeting Lincoln together, Colfax and Cole asked Lincoln if he was planning to convene a special session of Congress to deal with reconstruction issues.[6] If he was, they would call off their California journeys so they could attend. Lincoln told them he was not. They then asked him about controversial announcements made by Maj. Gen. Godfrey Weitzel, the acting military governor of Richmond, regarding public prayers in that city's churches. They did not want the preachers there to be allowed to perpetuate secessionist sentiment. Lincoln assured them that he had communicated with Weitzel regarding that matter and that he was satisfied with what the general was permitting.[7]

The president was in a talkative mood and spoke happily with Colfax and Cole about their California travel plans. "You are going to California, I hear," he said to Colfax. "How I would love to make that trip, but public duties chain me down here, and I can only envy you its pleasures." He continued, "Now, I have been thinking over a message I want you to take from me to the miners where you visit. I have very large ideas of the mineral wealth of our Nation. I believe it practically inexhaustible. During the war, when we were adding a couple of million dollars every day to our national debt, I did not care about encouraging the increase in the volume of our precious metals. We had the country to save first. But now that the rebellion is overthrown and we know pretty near the amount of our national debt, the more gold and silver we mine makes the payment of that debt so much the easier."

Lincoln was thinking of the hundreds of thousands of soldiers who would be looking for work after the fighting concluded, and of the immigrants who were then pouring into the country, who would also need jobs. "I intend to point them to the gold and silver that waits for them in the west," he said. "Tell the miners from me, that I shall promote their interests to the utmost of my ability; because their prosperity is the prosperity of the nation, and we shall prove in a very few years that we are indeed the treasury of the world."[8]

Lincoln told Colfax and Cole that he was thinking of taking up his residence in California after his term of office was over. He had often spoken to friends of this possibility, for he thought that California would afford better opportunities for his sons than any of the older states. He hoped that Colfax would bring him back "a good report of what his keen and practiced observation would note in the country he was about to see for the first time."[9]

At about three in the afternoon, Lincoln and his wife, Mary, left the White House for a carriage ride. Mrs. Lincoln later remembered that April 14, 1865, was "the happiest day" of the president's life. The president was "funny" and "in high spirits." He told her that, when his presidency ended, he intended to take her and their family to Europe and, upon his return, to "go to California" over the Rocky Mountains and see their soldiers "digging out gold to pay [the] national debt."[10]

After supper, the president had a second visit with Speaker Colfax, who found Lincoln still in high spirits.[11] As he and Mrs. Lincoln walked out the White House door on their way to attend a play at Ford's Theatre, he turned to the Speaker and said, "Don't forget, Colfax, to tell those miners that that is my speech to them—a pleasant journey to you. I will telegraph you at San Francisco—good bye."[12]

Schuyler Colfax had not yet left Washington when he learned

that Lincoln had been shot at Ford's Theatre. He rushed to the room in which the president's body lay in its death throes, and when the lifeless body was sent back to Illinois he accompanied it there. He delivered a eulogy of the president in Chicago before leaving for the West, and when he reached Salt Lake City, he gave another eulogy before a crowd of six thousand persons assembled in the Mormon Tabernacle.[13]

Cornelius Cole was in a sleeping car in a train on its way to New York when he was awakened with the news of the shooting. In his memoirs, Cole said that he had "always looked upon this unexampled crime as the culmination of a spirit engendered by slavery and the legitimate offspring of man's inhumanity to man."[14]

April 14, 1865, would be remembered as a tragic day in the history of the United States and in the life of the Lincoln family. It was also a momentous day in the minds and hearts of Californians, many of whom had hoped to welcome the president into their midst but now realized that they never would. In the days and weeks and years that followed, their memories of him grew. Men and women and children who had known him, and who had played important roles in the history of the western state as he served in the White House, were collected, assembled, reviewed, and recorded for history—a history that forms a fascinating but little-known part of the story of the great president, and that will be told in the pages that follow.

2

A Western Free State Man

WHEN LINCOLN WAS A MEMBER OF THE U.S. HOUSE OF Representatives in 1848, he declared that he was "a Northern man, or rather, a Western free state man."[1] George Ashmun, a member of the same Congress who also presided over the political convention that nominated Lincoln for president in 1860, described him as "a man of Western origin and growth, who has grown with the marvelous growth of that marvelous region."[2] In October 1864 Henry Bellows, a Unitarian clergyman and president of the U.S. Sanitary Commission, a private organization created to provide physical and spiritual comfort for sick and wounded soldiers, presented Lincoln with a box containing gold crystals sent to him from California. Lincoln was thankful for it—not because of the money it was worth (he never cared inordinately for money) but because it aroused in him images of the beautiful western state he was more than ever anxious to visit, a state "which produces such wonderful things and such a generous people."[3] On March 21, 1865, only weeks before his tragic death, he told his California-based friend Charles Maltby: "I have long desired to see California; the production of her gold mines has been a marvel to me, and her stand for the Union, her generous offerings to the Sanitary Commission, and her loyal representatives have endeared your people to me; and nothing would give me more pleasure than a visit to the Pacific shore."[4]

Lincoln's western roots and outlook influenced his life from beginning to end, inspiring his interest in the vast expanses of land that stretched off to the Pacific Ocean. Importantly, it caused him to look to the western state for support during the Civil War, and inspired the immense gratitude he expressed for the gold and silver it sent to help finance the Union war effort and the military support it gave to his efforts to end the Confederate rebellion. California was, after all, a "Western free state"—western in its geography, culture, and politics, and "free," at least in theory, as the Civil War engulfed the nation.

Lincoln's life as a "Western Free state man" began on February 12, 1809, when he was born in Hardin (now LaRue) County in the then-western state of Kentucky. It continued when his father moved his family in the fall of 1816 to Perry (later part of Spencer) County in Indiana, another western state, and continued in 1830, when the family moved farther west to Macon County, Illinois. When he reached the age of twenty-one, Lincoln moved by himself yet farther west to the frontier town of New Salem, Illinois, where he began life as a part-time postmaster and store clerk. In 1832 he volunteered for military service in the Black Hawk War, a short but historically important conflict with the Sauk and Fox native peoples, who sought to return from west of the Mississippi to the territory in Illinois that had been taken from them by the white settlers. He began his career as an attorney in the western frontier town of Springfield, Illinois, where he married the Kentucky-born Mary Todd in 1842 and became a father. His first son, Robert Todd Lincoln, was born in 1843. His second, named Edward Baker Lincoln in honor of his close friend and fellow lawyer Edward D. Baker, was born in 1846. Baker was eventually to draw his attention even farther west to California.

When, where, and how Lincoln first learned of California is not perfectly clear, although it was very probably when he met men who had visited there, settled there, or entered into its political life. John Hanks was one of the earliest such men. A first cousin of Lincoln's mother, Nancy Hanks Lincoln, he was born in Beardstown, Kentucky, in 1802, and lived with the Lincoln family in Kentucky for four years, working with young Abraham farming corn, leveling trees, and building fences. Hanks moved westward

6

to Macon County, Illinois, in 1828, and helped persuade Lincoln's father to bring the Lincoln family to Illinois in 1830. When Lincoln's father soon returned to Indiana, Abraham remained with Hanks. In 1831 the two young men piloted a flatboat down the Ohio and Mississippi Rivers to New Orleans, where Lincoln saw black slaves being cruelly abused. In 1832 both Hanks and Lincoln served in the Black Hawk War. Responding to news of the discovery of gold in California in 1849, Hanks joined a wagon train that traveled westward across the plains and mountains to the gold fields. He worked there as a gold miner for three years before returning to Illinois with little more than the clothes on his back. There he could, and almost certainly did, tell Lincoln of his experiences in the West and in California.[5]

Charles Maltby was another such man. He had been born in Vermont in 1811 but came west to Illinois with his father in 1828 and began work as a farmer. After Lincoln came west to New Salem, Maltby and Lincoln became close friends there. They worked together during the day in a log storehouse that a man named Denton Offutt had retained Lincoln to manage and visited the townspeople in the evening. Lincoln occasionally indulged in sports and games—wrestling, jumping, and pitching quoits—but Maltby recalled that those activities "were never allowed to interfere with his duties or studies."[6] Starting at about eight o'clock in the evening, Lincoln read voraciously, studying grammar, reading law books (he was already thinking about becoming a lawyer), and enjoying poetry. Around eleven o'clock, Lincoln and Maltby spread blankets on the store counter and made themselves as comfortable as they could to go to sleep. When he was president, Lincoln told a reporter from San Francisco who was in Washington, "I know Maltby, for I slept with him six months."[7] Maltby confirmed the statement years later, remembering that when he and Lincoln lived in New Salem "blankets were spread upon the counter" after they finished their evening reading, and they then "retired to rest on their hard couch, which prepared them for the labors and duties of the coming day."[8] Like Lincoln, Maltby served briefly in the Black Hawk War.[9] When Offutt's storehouse failed in early 1832,

Lincoln and Maltby bought a large log storehouse on the banks of the Sangamon River and made preparations to accept products delivered there by a steamer. The steamer came to the storehouse with a good delivery, but on its return they found it had been badly damaged by the twisting river and gave up the project. Maltby moved to a nearby county but maintained his friendship with Lincoln until he left for California in the gold rush year of 1849, traveling with his wife in a wagon train.

Another of Lincoln's earliest western friends was James Frazier Reed, who served with him in the Black Hawk War and became one of his early legal clients. He was one of the executors of the estate of Jacob M. Early, a man who was killed in 1838 in a violent political dispute, and called on Lincoln to help him sell off some land that Early had owned. Lincoln did this and continued to represent Reed in other matters in the early 1840s.[10] In 1845 Reed became the U.S. pension agent for Springfield, but on April 14, 1846, he led a train of covered wagons that left Springfield to head west across the plains. It included a family known as the Donners, who would later become famous for the tragedy that struck them. On October 5, at a place called Iron Point in what later became the state of Nevada, Reed intervened in a fight between two of the wagon drivers, and when one of them attacked him, Reed stabbed him in the chest. The stabbed man's death so enraged the other travelers that they threatened to kill Reed if he didn't leave them, so he and a teamster named Walter Herron headed out through increasing mounds of freezing snow, eventually making it to Sutter's Fort in California's Sacramento Valley. They tried to return to help the Donners avoid freezing death and hunger but were not able to make it through the snow, and the Donners resorted at last to the grisly offense of cannibalism. Remaining in California, Reed spent some time in the Napa Valley recovering from his mountain ordeal before serving in minor political offices, trying his hand at mining gold, and finally settling in San Jose in 1874. While traveling to California, he carried some documents relating to Lincoln and the service they shared in the Black Hawk War. Discovered years later in the California State Library, they are muster rolls in Lincoln's own writing recording details of his, Reed's, and other men's militia service in the 1832 conflict. They had been left to Reed by his Black Hawk War commander and were considered important enough by Reed that he carried them all the way to California, where they still survive—historical documents treasured by Lincoln students and California historians.[11]

Another western traveler was William Levi Todd, a first cousin of Mary Todd Lincoln, who grew up near the Lincolns in Springfield and in April 1845 joined a man named William F. Swasey in a wagon train headed for the Oregon Territory. When he and Swasey became involved in arguments with the other travelers, they changed their destination to California. Todd was in the town of Sonoma in June 1846, when a party of Americans led by a man named William Ide (and furtively supported by John C. Frémont, the western explorer Lincoln would later appoint as one of his Civil War generals) attempted to make California an independent republic. Todd and three other men painted a crude picture of a grizzly bear along with a star and the words "California Republic" on a sheet of unbleached cotton attached to two strips of red flannel, then joined with other men to raise it high on a flagpole, thus creating what later became recognized as the California state flag. But the "republic" only lasted twenty-five days, ending when U.S. naval commander John Drake Sloat flew the American flag over California's capital at Monterey, declaring the territory an American possession. Todd continued to live in California until his death in Los Angeles in 1876.[12]

Edward D. Baker may have been the man who most excited Lincoln's interest in California—in fact, in all the West. Born in London in 1811, he left England with his family when he was only five years old, first spending time in Philadelphia, then moving on to Indiana, where the family joined the utopian community of New Harmony, which was only fifty miles distant from the Pigeon Creek home where Lincoln grew up. Two years later, the Baker family moved again to Belleville, Illinois, located just across the Mississippi from St. Louis, Missouri, where they met a lawyer and politician named Ninian Edwards. He was a prominent man who had formerly been chief justice of the Kentucky Court of Appeals, governor of the territory of Illinois, United States senator from Illinois, and, after 1826, governor of Illinois. Young Baker's intellectual curiosity drew him into Edwards's law library, which aroused legal and political ambitions in him and inspired a political sympathy with Henry Clay, Lincoln's "beau ideal" of a statesman. It also drew Baker and Lincoln together, after Edwards's son Ninian W. Edwards married Elizabeth Todd in Kentucky in 1832 and in 1835 moved to Springfield, Illinois, where Lincoln met Elizabeth Todd's younger sister, Mary, and married her on November 4, 1842.

Baker's biographers believe that the two men probably met for the first time when they both volunteered for service in the Black Hawk War in 1832. After that conflict, they began to practice law in Springfield and soon became fast friends.[13] They joined Henry Clay's Whig Party and opposed the Democrats, who rallied in support of Tennessee's president Andrew Jackson. Beginning in 1837, they served in the Illinois General Assembly, which held its meetings in the southwestern Illinois town of Vandalia. Their law practices were busy, combining all sorts of cases, criminal as well as civil. Baker spent much of his leisure time with Lincoln and his wife, Mary, winning the admiration and affection of both and inspiring them to name their second son, Edward Baker Lincoln, in his honor.[14] He was called "Eddie" for his short life, which ended on February 1, 1850, probably as the result of tuberculosis.[15]

Both Baker and Lincoln were ambitious to be elected to Springfield's seat in the U.S. Congress, but because only one Whig could win in Illinois (the Democrats controlled most of the state), they reached an informal agreement with another Springfield aspirant named John J. Hardin to take turns in occupying the seat. Hardin was elected in 1843, Baker in 1844, and Lincoln in 1846. Lincoln did not take his seat until December 6, 1847.

When the Democratic president and slaveholder James Knox Polk persuaded Congress to declare war against Mexico, Congressman Baker volunteered to lead a regiment of soldiers into the Southern country. When other members of Congress raised a storm of criticism because Baker was serving both as a congressman and as an active military officer, he resigned his congressional seat.[16] By June 1847, however, the war was for practical purposes over, so he made his way back to Springfield.[17] But because Lincoln had won election as his successor in Congress, Baker sensed that his political opportunities in Springfield were dimming and moved north to Galena, where he was quickly elected to another seat in Congress.[18]

Lincoln used his seat in Washington to vigorously attack the war with Mexico. His previous political views had been mostly about economic development, but they now acquired a geographical focus, looking toward the West—California in particular—and the significance of the war with Mexico and the western spread of slavery. His opposition to Polk's aggression did not affect his support of the American soldiers who were sent into the conflict, however. He voted in favor of appropriations to pay them for their service and provide them with arms, equipment, and supplies. He did not blame the fighting men (certainly not Edward Baker) for the conflict—only the political leaders who followed Polk's lead into the aggression.

Lincoln and Baker were both determined Whigs. In 1848 Clay made a weak attempt to regain the party's presidential nomination, but after he failed in 1848, they urged their fellow Whigs to nominate the Mexican War hero Zachary Taylor for president. After Taylor was nominated and defeated his opponents (the Democrat Gen. Lewis Cass, and the candidate of the newly established Free Soil Party, former president Martin Van Buren), the Free Soilers suggested that Baker should become Taylor's vice-presidential running mate. Taylor did not choose him for that position nor select him to become a member of his cabinet, which Lincoln warmly suggested that he do, so Baker returned to Washington where, on December 5, 1849, he took his seat in the House of Representatives as a representative from Galena.

Lincoln hoped that Taylor would appoint him to the position of commissioner of the U.S. General Land Office, which paid a good salary of $3,000 a year and included authority over federal land sales in Ohio, Indiana, Illinois, and, in his own words, "the whole Northwest."[19] He soon threw his support to other aspirants for the job, however, and declined two more offers: one as secretary to the governor of the Oregon Territory and a second as governor of the territory. The reasons for Lincoln's decisions to decline these offers are not clear. Some historians have noted reports that Mary told him he would be forgotten out in the territories and never have an opportunity to become involved in mainstream politics. Yet others think he believed his political future would be dim—or even nonexistent—in Oregon because of the preponderance of Democrats there. One report notes that when a White House visitor asked him about his refusal of the Oregon governorship, the visitor said, "How fortunate that you declined. If you had gone to Oregon, you might have come back as senator, but you would never have been President," and Lincoln replied, "Yes, you are probably right."[20]

When, on July 9, 1850, President Taylor unexpectedly died, Baker responded by delivering a moving eulogy of him in the House of Representatives, where he continued to serve until Congress adjourned on September 28, 1850.[21] Lincoln's short term as a representative from Springfield had ended, but he went to Chicago, where he delivered another eulogy of Taylor, praising his battlefield courage but not extolling his political acumen, saying simply that he had "the confidence and devotion of the people."[22]

Baker was restless—and ambitious. News of the gold that had been discovered in the foothills of California's Sierra Nevada had unleashed a massive rush of men and women from all corners of the world, so he accepted a well-paying job recruiting construction workers to come to Panama and join in the construction of a railroad that would transport gold seekers who were on their way to California across the isthmus.[23] After recovering from a bad bout of tropical fever, he returned for a short recovery in Springfield, then gathered his wife and two of his daughters and set out for California. Again crossing Panama to make the journey, he arrived in San Francisco on June 28, 1852, and, while scouting out political opportunities among California's Whigs, quickly began his work there as a lawyer.[24]

Lincoln had in the meantime begun to think seriously about returning to an active political life in Illinois. His thoughts were stimulated by a new law called the Kansas-Nebraska Act, which had been sponsored and largely pushed through Congress by Illinois's U.S. senator Stephen A. Douglas. Finally passed on May 30, 1854, the law authorized residents of the Nebraska Territory (soon to be divided into Kansas and Nebraska) to decide for themselves whether they would permit slavery in their midst or oppose it. Douglas believed that the law, called "popular sovereignty," would end the national argument about the future of slavery and the threats of Southern secession by simply letting local voters decide whether they would or would not have slavery. Lincoln strongly disagreed with the law and Douglas's defense of it, believing that it would promote the western spread of slavery and effectively repeal the Compromise of 1850, which had barred slavery in northern territories. He delivered impassioned speeches expressing his opposition to the Kansas-Nebraska Act. One was delivered in Bloomington, Illinois, on September 26, 1854; another in Springfield on October 4 of the same year; and a third in Peoria, Illinois.[25]

Lincoln won a seat in the Illinois House of Representatives in 1854 but declined to accept it when he contemplated the greater challenge of being elected the following year to the U.S. Senate. Many others were seeking the same senatorial seat, seeking to defeat the Irish-born incumbent James Shields who had, in 1842, challenged Lincoln to a duel that had not been fought after Lincoln expressed regrets for disparaging remarks he had made about Shields in an Illinois newspaper. Lincoln made a strong effort to win the Whig Party's nomination for the U.S. Senate in 1855. On the first ballot (U.S. senators were then chosen by votes in the state legislature), he received forty-five of the fifty votes needed for election. But when on subsequent ballots a proslavery Democrat named Joel Matteson seemed close to winning, he threw his support to Lyman Trumbull, a Democrat who opposed the westward spread of slavery. Trumbull was then elected.[26]

Lincoln was active in 1856, the first year in which the Republican Party was able to take part in the presidential election. Its first presidential nominating convention met in Philadelphia on June 17 and named California's John C. Frémont as the party's presidential nominee.[27] Lincoln was not personally present in Philadelphia, but many of the delegates there knew him and wanted him to be the nominee for vice president, believing that he would help the party win the important state of Illinois. On an informal ballot, fifteen names were put forth, and Lincoln received 110 votes to 259 for William L. Dayton, a former U.S. senator from New Jersey. On the formal ballot, Dayton clearly prevailed, and Lincoln promptly withdrew his name. He took to the hustings, however, delivering many speeches in favor of Frémont and Dayton in Illinois. Unfortunately, they did not prevail, as the Democratic presidential nominee, Pennsylvania's James Buchanan, and the Democratic vice-presidential nominee, Kentucky's John C. Breckinridge, were elected.

Lincoln was discouraged but not defeated. He made another attempt to win a Senate seat in 1858, campaigning directly against Senator Douglas. His goal was in part to redeem himself from his 1855 defeat, in part to make his opposition to the western spread of slavery perfectly clear. Now a member of the newly founded Republican Party, he challenged Douglas to a series of debates. Reluctant at first to accept the challenge, Douglas finally agreed. Meeting in seven towns up and down Illinois and speaking to enormous crowds, some numbering more than ten thousand people, the two men plumbed the depths of the slavery issue and its western spread. When Republicans outpolled Democrats in the popular vote for members of the legislature who would select the senator, Lincoln was encouraged. But when the legislature itself voted, malapportionment of the legislative districts gave the Democrats more seats than the Republicans. Douglas was thus reelected and Lincoln defeated.

In far-off California, Baker quickly learned that the state's politics were dominated by Democrats, most of whom were followers of U.S. senator William M. Gwin, a Tennessee-born medical doctor who owned slaves in Mississippi and headed up the "Chivalry" or "Chiv" faction of the party in California. Baker opposed the slave interests, which had a near stranglehold on California's public offices. He also opposed the men who formed the controversial Vigilance Committee in San Francisco in 1856, claiming that their purpose was to rid the city of thugs and criminals and restore "law and order" to its streets. Most of the vigilantes' venom was actually directed against immigrants of Irish and German descent who were members of the Catholic Church. Baker was not a Catholic, but he was more than willing to fight for Catholics when he saw that they were victims of kangaroo courts. His most celebrated case was his defense of a mild-mannered Italian gambler named Charles Cora, who was charged with the murder of the Southern-sympathizing U.S. marshal William Richardson. After nine days of trial and forty-one hours of deliberation in San Francisco, the members of Cora's jury were unable to agree on a verdict.[28] A new trial was then scheduled. The vigilantes decided, however, that a hanging was more appropriate. Their victims were Cora and an Irish gambler named Charles Casey, who had shot a crusading newspaper editor named James King of William (William was his father's name) in a quarrel. Both Cora and Casey were hauled to a public scaffold and lynched. Baker shared the outrage expressed by other defenders of due process but realized that all he could effectively do was fight for it in courtrooms and on political rostrums.

In 1858 Baker agreed to represent a young black man from Mississippi named Archy Lee, who had come to California the year before with a white man named Charles Stovall, who now sought to take him back to Mississippi. Lee had been a slave on a plantation owned by Stovall's father. But California's Constitution, adopted by the state's constitutional convention in 1849 and approved by Congress and president Millard Fillmore when the state was admitted to the Union, explicitly provided that "all men are by nature free and independent" and "neither slavery nor involuntary servitude, unless for the punishment of crimes, shall ever be tolerated" in the state.[29] Archy's friends thus argued that he was not a slave. Stovall's attorney claimed, however, that he could take Archy Lee back to Mississippi under the terms of the onerous United States

Fugitive Slave Act, which had been adopted in 1850 by the same Congress that admitted California to the Union. When Lee and the black residents of California opposed Stovall's attempt, a series of highly explosive trials followed, finally resulting in a hearing before United States Commissioner George Pen Johnston in San Francisco.

Baker was Archy Lee's principal lawyer in the hearing. He mounted an impassioned defense of the black man's freedom and California's prohibition of slavery. San Francisco's leading newspaper, the *Daily Alta California*, described Baker's speech as "one of the most eloquent efforts that we have ever heard" and told its readers that "more than one eye in the room was moist with tears."[30] It resulted in George Pen Johnston's bold decision to declare Archy Lee a free man and order the United States marshal to release him from custody.[31] The legal struggle of Archy Lee was one of the most important battles over the future of slavery fought anywhere in the United States. A black newspaper published a few years later in San Francisco remembered it as "the famous Archy case which agitated California to its very centre [*sic*], and was the first triumph for freedom."[32] Historian Philip J. Ethington has described it as "California's Dred Scott case."[33]

Lincoln was keenly aware of the *Dred Scott* case decided in 1857 and Supreme Court Chief Justice Roger Taney's provocative assertion in the case that African Americans had "no rights which the white man was bound to respect."[34] Lincoln's outrage over *Dred Scott* spurred his renewed interest in politics and helped propel him into the national debate over the future of slavery in the United States.

Baker's opposition to slavery brought him close to David C. Broderick, the leading Democrat who opposed slavery in California. A former New Yorker of Irish immigrant descent, Broderick had come to California to seek economic opportunity and political office. After he was elected in 1857 to one of California's two U.S. Senate seats, he gave a powerful speech against slavery in the national Capitol.[35] When he returned to California, David S. Terry, a combative lawyer, judge, and politician from Texas with strongly racist and proslavery views, challenged Broderick to a duel. Baker was Broderick's second in the duel with Terry that was fought on September 13, 1859, and, after Broderick fell with a bullet in his chest, Baker took him to a friendly house where he watched over him as he attempted to recover. After Broderick finally died, Baker delivered a long and impassioned eulogy over his body in downtown San Francisco's Portsmouth Plaza, preparing it for burial on an eminence west of San Francisco called Lone Mountain.[36]

Baker tried to win elective office in California. He had helped to form the new Republican Party in California, which was pledged to halt the spread of slavery into states where it did not already exist. In 1859 he received the Republican nomination for a seat in the U.S. House of Representatives and campaigned vigorously for it, but when the votes were cast on September 7 of that year, he was badly defeated. California still had too many proslavery Democrats and too few antislavery Republicans for him to win an election.

Lincoln had failed to win election to the Senate in Illinois, and Baker had failed to win election to the House of Representatives in California. The two men were widely separated by geography but not by their political views or personal affection. They were friends and, as events would soon prove, their friendship was soon to loom large in the history of the United States; it would powerfully strengthen the ties that drew Abraham Lincoln to the West, and to California.

Honest Old Abe

LINCOLN WAS DISCOURAGED BY HIS FAILURE TO DEFEAT Douglas in 1858. He stated his feelings in a letter to Anson G. Henry, a medical doctor who had been one of his Illinois friends before moving to the Oregon Territory in 1852: "I am glad I made the late race. It gave me a hearing on the great and durable question of the age, which I could have had in no other way; and though I now sink out of view, and shall be forgotten, I believe I have made some marks which will tell for the cause of civil liberty long after I am gone."[1]

Lincoln's feeling changed when, in October 1859, he received an invitation from leaders of New York's state Republican Party to come east and deliver an address at the Reverend Henry Ward Beecher's famous Plymouth Church in Brooklyn. They were searching for a good candidate to run for the presidency the following year and wanted to learn more about Lincoln. New York's senator William Seward seemed to many of them their best choice. He had served both as governor and as senator, earning a kind of national fame when in October 1858 he spoke of an impending "collision" between the North and the South. "Shall I tell you what this collision means?" he asked his audience in Rochester. "They who think that it is accidental, unnecessary, the work of interested or fanatical agitators, and therefore ephemeral, mistake the case altogether. It is an irrepressible conflict between opposing and enduring forces, and it means that the United States must and will, sooner or later, become either entirely a slaveholding nation or entirely a free-labor nation."[2] Seward's remarks were widely reported, but many of New York's Republicans felt that they were too extreme to win national approval and wanted to consider other candidates.

After giving the New York invitation serious thought, Lincoln accepted and made the journey to New York in February 1860. When he arrived there he found that the venue of his address had been changed to the Great Hall of Manhattan's Cooper Institute, informally called Cooper Union. He was escorted to the speaker's rostrum there on February 27, 1860, by David Dudley Field, brother of California's Supreme Court Chief Justice Stephen J. Field. William Cullen Bryant, editor of the *New York Post*, introduced him to the audience as an "eminent citizen of the West."[3] Among those in the audience were California's former senator John C. Frémont; his wife, Jessie Benton Frémont, and Horace Greeley, editor of the influential and widely read *New York Tribune*, who had made a long stagecoach trip to California the previous summer and was often credited with originating the famous phrase "Go west, young man"; and many influential Republicans.

Lincoln's speech revealed that he had done considerable research in preparing for it. Reviewing the early history of the United States, he refuted the controversial views that Supreme Court Chief Justice Roger Taney had expressed in his *Dred Scott* opinion and argued forcibly against Stephen Douglas's defense of the theory of popular sovereignty. He condemned slavery as "an evil not to be extended," and described Southern threats of secession as a "rule or ruin" philosophy.[4] At the end of his two-hour speech, Horace Greeley wrote in the *Tribune* that "Lincoln is one of Nature's orators, using his powers solely and effectively to elucidate and convince, though their inevitable effect is to delight and electrify as well."[5] When reports of the speech reached California, the widely read *Sacramento Daily Union* published the full text and commented that the opinions put forth by Lincoln were "of more consequence than those which he will utter during the campaign and under the excitement of an active Presidential contest."[6]

As the leaders of the Illinois state Republican Party were preparing for their convention in the town of Decatur in 1860, a young lawyer and rising politician named Richard J. Oglesby became interested. Born in Kentucky in 1824, Oglesby had been orphaned at the age of eight but brought to Illinois by an uncle. He served in the Mexican War and returned with an interest in Whig politics. When news of the discovery of gold reached Illinois in late 1848, he headed to California, where he mined gold for a while and then operated a successful store in the California mining town of Nevada City. When a fire leveled his store, he headed back to Illinois, taking the steamship route through Central America and carrying the substantial sum of $5,000 dollars in California gold with him. A Republican by choice, he asked Lincoln's cousin John Hanks about Lincoln's early life west of Decatur. When Hanks told him that Lincoln had cleared some land there, the two men went to the site of the clearing and picked up two split logs that Hanks said Lincoln had cut. They took them to Decatur, and after the convention opened on May 9, 1860, Hanks and a friend named Isaac Jennings took them into the newly erected wood and canvas hall they called the Wigwam because it resembled a Native American log house. They had flags and streamers attached to the logs and an inscription describing Lincoln as "The Rail Candidate for President in 1860." Lincoln did not claim to have split the logs, but he was pleased with the excitement that engulfed the three-thousand-delegate convention, which chose him as the Illinois state candidate for the Republican presidential nomination.

Baker had in the meantime received an invitation from Republicans in Oregon to come north and explore the possibility of running for a U.S. Senate seat there. They were interested in him, of course, because he was an eloquent speaker and a Republican. But his earlier statements about the acquisition of the Oregon Territory by the United States also helped. Lincoln was not an expansionist— not anxious for the United States to acquire western territory to expand its domain and its population. Baker was. When Baker was in the House of Representatives, he rebutted a colleague from Massachusetts by stating that the United States should go "for the whole of Oregon; for every grain of sand that sparkled in her moon-light, and every pebble on its wave-worn strand." He argued that Oregon "was ours—all ours! Ours by treaty—ours by discovery!"[7] Baker thought seriously about the Republican invitation, which came in a letter from Lincoln's Oregon-based friend Anson G. Henry, and he may even have boarded a northbound steamship that was leaving San Francisco for the northern territory. But he abruptly decided not to go. After the territory was finally admitted to the Union on February 14, 1859, however, he received another invitation—possibly again from Henry. And this time he decided to go, finally leaving in December. Arriving there, he renewed his friendships with former Illinoisans he already knew and became acquainted with others. He then traveled widely through the state, giving impassioned speeches and impressing listeners with his oratorical powers.[8]

California's Republicans held a state convention in Sacramento in February 1860, where they selected eight delegates to attend the Chicago convention. They instructed the delegates to vote for Seward's nomination or, if it became clear that the convention could not agree on him, to support another suitable candidate. Leland Stanford was chosen as one of the delegates, but business pressures prevented him from attending.[9]

When the convention opened in Chicago on May 16, 1860, Republicans adorned the entrance to their newly built convention hall—called the Wigwam like the one in Decatur—with a portrait of California's late senator David Broderick. Broderick had been a supporter of Stephen Douglas before he was killed—or, as the California-based Western historian Hubert Howe Bancroft said, "removed from earth."[10] But many believed that Broderick's opposition to slavery and support for the Union would have drawn him into the Republican Party, as it did many of his Democratic colleagues. And when Republican newspapers in California learned of Broderick's honored place in Chicago's convention hall, they exulted. "Nothing more appropriate could be conceived," wrote the influential *Sacramento Daily Union*, "than that the portrait of such a man should adorn the walls of a Republican Convention."[11]

The platform adopted by the convention on May 17, 1860, declared its support for the Declaration of Independence's historic statement that "all men are created equal." It denounced "threats of disunion" as an "avowal of contemplated treason." It denounced the theory expounded in Chief Justice Roger Taney's *Dred Scott* opinion that the Constitution demanded the expansion of slavery into the territories but defended the right of every state "to order and control its own domestic institutions according to its own judgment exclusively." It branded the recent reopening of the African slave trade "under the cover of our national flag, aided by perversions of judicial power," as "a crime against humanity and a burning shame to our country and age." And it opposed any change in the naturalization laws that would "abridge or impair" the rights of immigrants to enter the country. Evidencing its westward vision, the platform also declared that a railroad to the Pacific Ocean was "imperatively demanded by the interests of the whole country" and that the federal government "ought to render immediate and efficient aid in its construction."[12]

Lincoln was an impassioned proponent of the construction of railroads—and, most significantly, the importance of building one that would extend across the continent to the Pacific Ocean. Railroads had come over the Appalachians from the Atlantic Seaboard when he was beginning his career as a lawyer and politician, and he quickly became familiar with the iron rails and steam locomotives that sped across the prairies spouting clouds of black smoke. The rivers, which were the most important avenues of traffic before the railroads, were often impassable when the water was low, and when winter turned the upper reaches of the streams to ice, navigation came to a screeching halt. Even when the waters were running free, there were many obstructions— hidden rocks, treacherous rapids, trees that hung over the riverbeds, sandy shoals, snags (fallen trees that anchored themselves to the river bottoms), and islands that appeared unexpectedly in one season and disappeared as unexpectedly in the next. Railroads, in contrast, could move wherever rails could be laid, and they were as passable in the depths of winter as in the summer. In

1832, in his first campaign for elective office, Lincoln publicly proclaimed his support for railroad construction. "No other improvement that reason will justify us in hoping for," he said then, "can equal in utility the rail road. It is a never failing source of communication, between places of business remotely situated from each other. Upon the rail road the regular progress of commercial intercourse is not interrupted by either high or low water, or freezing weather, which are the principal difficulties that render our future hopes of water communication precarious and uncertain."[13] Lincoln became a railroad attorney of sorts in the 1840s and 1850s (he never worked exclusively for railroads, but took cases both for them and against them). In one case, he represented the powerful Illinois Central Railroad in a difficult tax case, saving the corporation about half a million dollars in county taxes. For his work in that case, he received a fee of $5,000—an enormous sum in that time—which he promptly divided with his junior partner, William H. (Billy) Herndon.

In 1857 Lincoln was one of the attorneys in a trial that tested the legal ability of railroads to cross the Mississippi River. From its home base in Chicago, the Chicago and Rock Island Railroad had in 1851 and 1853 crossed northern Illinois to the town of Rock Island, Illinois, and built a bridge that extended from Rock Island to Davenport, Iowa, all the while hoping to extend its railroads into Iowa and beyond. Their hopes were opposed by owners of the enormously profitable steamboats that plied the river and by Jefferson Davis, who would soon become the president of the Confederate States of America. Davis favored railroads, even one that would reach the Pacific coast, but he wanted it to be built on a Southern route that would facilitate the movement of people, freight, and slaves from the South into the land recently acquired from Mexico. Serving then as secretary of war under president James Buchanan, he denied the Chicago and Rock Island Railroad's requested right-of-way across the Mississippi. The Chicago and Rock Island Railroad nevertheless continued its construction, and the bridge opened to traffic on April 21, 1856. It seemed to work well until May 6 of that year, when a Cincinnati-based steamboat named the *Effie Afton* crashed into it at high speed, badly damaging its river supports and causing it to erupt in flames and tumble into the river. The bridge was quickly rebuilt and opened again to traffic, but the *Effie Afton* remained a total loss, so its owners filed suit for damages in the U.S. Circuit Court in Illinois. The case came on for trial in Chicago in September 1857 with United States Supreme Court Justice John McLean presiding. Lincoln was one of six lawyers who participated in the trial, which continued for nearly three weeks.

When it came time for Lincoln to deliver his argument to the jury, he left no doubt in the jurors' minds that he was defending the bridge against the damage claims of the steamboat owners and not attacking the steamboats or the steamboat men. "The last thing that would be pleasing to me," he said, "would be to have one of the great channels extending almost from where it never freezes to where it never thaws blocked up. . . . But there is a travel from east to west whose demands are not less important than that of those of the river. It is growing larger and larger, building up new countries with a rapidity never before seen in the history of the world."[14]

One of the plaintiffs' attorneys ominously warned that the bridging of the Mississippi might lead to "a dissolution of the Union," for it arrayed competing interests against each other: steamboats versus railroads, East versus West, potentially even North versus South. The verdict that came at the end of the trial was not completely pleasing to Lincoln and the owners of the Rock Island Bridge, but it was even less pleasing to the steamboat owners. The jurors favored Lincoln's side in the lawsuit, but not unanimously: The final vote was nine to three in favor of the bridge. The decision meant that the bridge owners did not have to pay damages to the steamboat owners, and the bridge did not have to be torn down. The *Chicago Daily Democrat* editorialized that the hung verdict was "virtually a triumph for the bridge," although it left open the possibility of a new trial.[15] But the steamboat owners decided not to take their chances a second time with Chicago jurors.[16]

The Wigwam was crowded as the voting for a presidential nominee began on May 18, 1860. Seward led off the first ballot with a healthy lead, while Lincoln took second place. Salmon P. Chase of Ohio, Edward Bates of Missouri, and Simon Cameron of Pennsylvania, all notable Republicans in their home states, trailed behind. John C. Frémont drew a single vote. Frémont had become famous in the 1830s and 1840s by leading exploring expeditions through much of the West and publishing the results of his discoveries with the assistance of his influential father-in-law, senator Thomas Hart Benton of Missouri. He was credited, too, with having coined the name that was given to the deep channel that connected San Francisco Bay to the Pacific Ocean. He called it the "Golden Gate," and the name was soon applied to the state itself.[17] Then, in 1850, he won additional recognition when California's legislature chose him to be one of the new state's first U.S. senators.

Frémont's Senate term ended after only two years, and he was replaced by John Weller, a proslavery Democrat and future governor. Frémont had in 1847 purchased one of the largest Mexican ranchos in California, a grant in the foothills of the Sierra Nevada named Las Mariposas by the Mexicans but called Mariposa by the Americans. When valuable gold deposits were discovered on the rancho, it became the subject of an intense legal struggle, first fought in the U.S. Land Commission in San Francisco and then continued in the federal courts in San Francisco and Washington DC.[18] Frémont eventually lost Mariposa and the gold on it, but not before he had become the Republican Party's 1856 presidential candidate. Lincoln had campaigned for Frémont in 1856, but without real enthusiasm, feeling that the American people were not yet ready to elect a Republican president. In the election of 1856, Pennsylvania's pro-Southern Democrat, James Buchanan, received 1,836,072 popular votes while Frémont received 1,342,345 and New York's ex-Whig-turned-Know-Nothing, former president Millard Fillmore, received 873,053. Although Buchanan did not win a majority of the popular votes, he took 174 electoral votes to Frémont's 114 and Fillmore's 8. In California, Frémont did even more poorly than he did nationally. Buchanan won 53,342 votes in the state, Fillmore received 36,195, and Frémont received only

20,704. Frémont did not receive a single one of California's electoral votes—all four of them went to Buchanan.[19]

As the voting continued in the 1860 Chicago convention, Lincoln gained on Seward in the second ballot, and by the third he was within one and a half votes of securing the nomination. Sensing that victory was near, one of his supporters convinced the chairman of the Ohio delegation to shift four votes to Lincoln. As other delegates rushed to add their votes to his total, Lincoln was acclaimed as the winner.

The *New York Times* revealed how little it knew about the Illinoisan when it reported his nomination, telling its readers: "The work of the Convention is ended, . . . and ABRAM [sic] LINCOLN, of Illinois, is declared its candidate for President by the National Republican Party."[20] Senator Hannibal Hamlin of Maine was chosen as Lincoln's running mate. Lincoln was advised of his nomination by a letter that George Ashmun, a former Whig congressman from Massachusetts who now served as the convention's president, sent to him in Springfield. Lincoln accepted readily, advising Ashmun that "the declaration of principles and sentiments, which accompanies your letter, meets my approval; and it shall be my care not to violate, or disregard it, in any part."[21]

News of Lincoln's nomination made it back to California via the Pony Express, a private mail-carrying service recently established to carry mail to the Pacific coast more quickly than the ocean-going steamboats that carried the U.S. mail. The Express was a picturesque symbol of America's westward tilt, a rough-riding chain of horseback riders who plunged bravely through Native American country and massive buffalo herds. But it was also an effective service that would continue for some eighteen months until even faster telegraph lines were completed all the way to California.

Most Californians knew that Lincoln had debated Illinois's senator Stephen Douglas in 1858 and lost the election that followed. But they knew little else about him. Democratic politicians in California and elsewhere were calling him a "Black Republican" because of his opposition to the spread of slavery. Others were falsely charging that he was an abolitionist and wished to immediately put slavery to an end. Real abolitionists—those who argued that the peculiar institution should not only be condemned but promptly and irrevocably extinguished—charged that he was a Southern sympathizer, a man who said that slavery was wrong but had no intention of doing anything about it. But many newspaper reports, nationally as well as in California, were calling him "Honest Old Abe" because his reputation for steadfast honesty was what most people knew about him.[22] There were lots of different opinions about the gentleman from Illinois in 1860. So "Honest Old Abe" seemed to be a satisfactory label to apply to him as he began to be considered as a possible presidential nominee of the Republican Party.

When Baker received the news of Lincoln's nomination in Chicago, he took to the hustings, eagerly campaigning for his Illinois friend in both Oregon and California. Meanwhile, his own hopes for political recognition in Oregon were warming.

Joseph Lane, a proslavery, pro-secessionist Democrat who was then serving as one of Oregon's first U.S. senators, had just been nominated to run for vice president by the proslavery, pro-secessionist Democratic Party then meeting in Charleston, South Carolina. John C. Breckinridge of Kentucky was that party's presidential candidate. Lane's Oregon Senate term was expiring, as was that of a minor Democratic politician named Delazon Smith. Baker made it clear that he was willing to seek not just Republican votes for a Senate seat from Oregon but also those of friendly Democrats. His bedrock principle, like Lincoln's, was preservation of the Union. Going back and forth between Oregon and California, he campaigned for Lincoln for president and himself for U.S. senator. His speeches were so widely admired and his charm so evident that he managed to win the approval of a bare majority of Oregon's legislators who, on October 2, 1860, elected him as one of their state's new U.S. senators. The other was Democrat James W. Nesmith, who was elected on the same day.[23] Baker wrote his mother in Illinois (then past eighty) to tell her the good news. He also wrote to Lincoln, expressing hopes for his victory in the coming November. "I hope to see you President," he wrote

Lincoln, "and if I do not mistake you will feel that you have a true and warm friend at your side, who will feel for you all the attachment in prosperity which was nurtured in adversity."[24]

On his way to take his seat in Washington, Baker stopped in San Francisco where, on October 26, he spoke to a crowd of several thousand supporters who had gathered in San Francisco's American Theatre. He spoke there for more than two hours, demonstrating once again his eloquence and his passionately pro-Republican opinions. He explained his opposition to slavery, telling the crowd: "In the presence of God,—I say it reverently,—freedom is the rule, and slavery the exception." He affirmed the Republican Party's strong support for the building of a transcontinental railroad and told the audience that Lincoln would work hard to facilitate the railroad if he was elected president. And, of course, he *would* be elected president![25] It was a "great speech," San Francisco's *Daily Alta California* told its readers, and the theater was "crowded from pit to dome."[26] John C. Frémont and his wife, Jessie Benton Frémont, were in the audience. She was impressed by Baker's powerful speech.[27] California historian Theodore Henry Hittell later called this address "the greatest speech ever delivered in California."[28] The popular respect that Baker received was from Oregon, of course, but also from California. And many of the Union supporters in the Golden State continued to regard him as more a representative of their own state than of Oregon.[29]

The political environment of California was not favorable to "Honest Old Abe" in 1860. Most of the voters were Democrats, as they had proved in election after election. Three men occupied the governor's chair in 1860, and all were Democrats. John B. Weller finished his gubernatorial term on January 9, 1860, when his successor, Milton S. Latham, took office. Latham served only five days as governor until the Democrat-controlled legislature sent him to the U.S. Senate as successor to David C. Broderick. Democratic lieutenant governor John G. Downey succeeded Latham in the governorship, taking office on January 10, 1860.

William M. Gwin left office on March 4 of that year and was succeeded by James A. McDougall, another Democrat, one who had served as attorney general of Illinois, had met Lincoln in the courtroom there, and had remained loyal to the Union. In California's last statewide election, conducted in October 1859, the Democrats had trounced their opponents, electing both of their candidates for the U.S. House of Representatives (California had only two House seats then, although it was expected that the 1860 census would increase that number to three) and Latham, their candidate for governor. Latham received 61,455 votes to the Republican Leland Stanford's only 10,139.[30]

The Democratic Party still dominated California's political life. The newly founded Republican Party had not yet won an important election in the state, and as the presidential election of 1860 approached, their prospects for doing so did not seem good. Broderick's death had been lamented by Republicans but accepted with satisfaction by Gwin's "Chivalry" Democrats, who hoped that a presidential candidate sympathetic to their proslavery views would be elected to succeed the outgoing president James Buchanan. Gwin kept the slaves he owned, numbering about two hundred, on a plantation in Mississippi and did not bring them to California. Republicans, still hungering for some victory in California, hoped that the Chivalry domination of the state could be ended and that they could somehow win more voters in California than their opponents. The African Americans who remained in the state were fearful that their hopes for some basic human rights would not be realized for many years.[31]

Despite their dim prospects for victory, California's Republicans were not inconsequential. Some were former Democrats; some had been Know-Nothings, a short-lived party dedicated to excluding unwanted immigrants (mostly Irish and German Catholics) from the United States; but most had been Whigs. Some advocated the abolition of slavery while others merely opposed its spread into western territories, believing that if it could not expand it would eventually shrivel and die. All, however, were firm supporters of the Union, and all opposed senator Stephen Douglas of Illinois, who was asserting national leadership of the Democratic Party with his argument that the voters of each state or territory should decide for themselves whether they did or did not want to have slavery. Douglas's popular sovereignty doctrine was supported by some of California's so-called Lecomptonite Democrats, who believed that the proslavery constitution adopted in Lecompton, Kansas, should be accepted by Congress and that Kansas should be admitted to the Union as a slave state. Douglas was critical of the process by which slavery had been approved by the Kansas voters and backed away from the Lecompton constitution, prompting some of its supporters to join voters who looked to senator Jefferson Davis of Mississippi and senator John Breckinridge of Kentucky, both proslavery Democrats, for leadership.

Seward's supporters were disappointed that their man had not been successful in the Chicago nominating convention, but they joined in their support of Lincoln, if for no other reason than that he was so much more acceptable than the opposition. George Ashmun celebrated the nomination. "I know Abraham Lincoln well," Ashmun said. "I sat with him in Congress, and a truer or more loyal man never held a seat in the House of Representatives. You may say he is not the handsomest man in the world, but we did not nominate him for ball-room purposes. We wanted a man of loyal heart, and we found him in Abraham Lincoln. And another reason," Ashmun said (making a statement quoted earlier in this book). "He is a man of Western origin and growth, who has grown with the marvelous growth of that marvelous region."[32] Ashmun and many of the other Republicans made it clear that Lincoln's ties with the West were an important reason for his nomination. Other observers did not agree. The *Philadelphia Evening Journal* told its readers that Lincoln used "coarse language" and that his "vulgar vituperative" personality reflected his early experience as a "flatboatman [*sic*] and a rail-splitter." Southern newspapers were even more negative in their descriptions of him. In Richmond, Virginia, the *Enquirer* dismissed Lincoln as "an illiterate partisan without talents, without education."[33]

There were two Democratic candidates: Illinois's Stephen Douglas and Kentucky's John Breckinridge. Neither man was nominated at the party's regular convention in Charleston, South Carolina, which erupted in a bitter dispute over the slavery question, but both eventually went to Baltimore, where new conventions were held. There Douglas became the candidate of the Democrats who opposed the Lecompton constitution in Kansas but were content to let each state decide for itself if it should have slavery. Breckinridge became the candidate of the Democrats who supported Lecompton and slavery wherever states approved it. A fourth group of delegates, refugees from the Whig and Know-Nothing parties, also met in Baltimore to name John Bell of Tennessee, a former senator and secretary of war, as the candidate of the newly named Constitutional Union Party. Bell's running mate was Edward Everett of Massachusetts, a scholar, educator, and veteran politician who, on November 19, 1863, would earn a kind of fame by delivering a two-hour speech at Gettysburg, Pennsylvania, before Lincoln delivered the brief remarks in which he promised Americans "a new birth of freedom."

California's Democrats were confused. Should they support Breckinridge, signaling their sympathy for the secessionist threats emanating from the South, or Douglas, the man who supported the Union but said that the voters in each state should decide whether they wanted slavery? Republicans had only one choice, and that was Lincoln. The state's newspapers reflected the division of opinion. Twenty-four of them favored Douglas and twenty-two Breckenridge. Only seven favored Lincoln, and three Bell.[34] Republicans campaigned enthusiastically for Lincoln and Hamlin. Stanford stumped the state, hoping to win supporters for his own political ambitions while he helped Lincoln.[35]

Edward Baker may have been the most effective campaigner for Lincoln. Not only did he have personal ties to Lincoln, but he was also generally recognized as the best political speaker in either California or Oregon. He also opposed slavery, favored the preservation of the Union, and ardently hoped that Lincoln would become president. On the day the Oregon legislature chose him as their U.S. senator, California's Democrats were not as anxious as Baker to support Lincoln, and their public statements indicated their ill feelings. In his outgoing annual message, Governor Weller said that in the event of secession, California "will not go with the South or the North, but here upon the shores of the Pacific found a mighty Republic which may in the end prove the greatest of all."[36] In his capacity as U.S. senator, William Gwin expressed similar thoughts, prompting the *Sacramento Daily Union* to condemn him for supposing that California was not wholly in favor of the perpetuation of the Union. The Sacramento paper said that Gwin would soon find that Californians not only supported the Union but also wanted "Union men—staunch and open advocates of the Union as it is—to represent them in Congress," adding, "Well may they consider themselves misrepresented and disgraced by the sentiments avowed by the Senator."[37] Gwin later tried to modify his remarks. He said that he was not advocating secession but merely explaining what would happen if it occurred. Newly elected Senator Latham said he hoped the Union would be "imperishable" but added that if it was ever broken up "the eastern boundary of the Pacific republic will be, in my opinion, the Sierra Madre and the Rocky Mountains" (far to the east of California's existing border).[38] Talk of a "Pacific republic"—mainly coming from Southern sympathizers—was alarming to the Republicans, who stoutly defended the Union.

Campaigning in California was spirited. There were mass meetings and huge parades. One of the most colorful group of campaigners called themselves the Wide Awakes. They were young men in their teens, twenties, and thirties who enthusiastically supported Lincoln and vehemently opposed slavery. They gathered in large halls to hear speakers and engage in debates, but most notably paraded in military style through the streets of towns and cities wearing black oilskin capes and black caps and carrying large torches. The *New York Times* described them as "young men of character and energy, earnest in their Republican convictions and enthusiastic in prosecuting the canvass on which we have entered."[39] Accompanied by marching bands equipped with fifes and drums, the Wide Awakes in California most often appeared in San Francisco and Sacramento, although they also entered smaller cities and towns. They had been formed early in 1860, after Cassius M.

Clay, a Kentucky politician who, like Lincoln, had been a Whig but had abandoned that party for the Republicans, gave a speech in Hartford, Connecticut, expressing his strong antislavery opinions. Their name was derived from the name that the supporters of John Brown had used to support his antislavery crusade in Kansas.[40] After Lincoln was nominated by the Republicans, the number of Wide Awakes grew and their parades through the streets of cities extending from Maine in the Northeast to California in the Far West excited more attention. In the Southern states where slavery was defended, the Wide Awakes were objects of contempt and derision, and rigorously excluded. In California, their parades were supported by those who condemned slavery but bitterly opposed by those who defended it.[41] As they marched through the streets, arguments between them and their opponents often erupted, quickly escalating into physical fights, and even some attacks with stones and knives. On August 23, 1860, a mass meeting of Republicans convened in San Francisco's new Music Hall where, shortly after dusk, a contingent of some fifty Wide Awakes marched into the hall and were greeted by loud and enthusiastic cheers.[42] On September 1 a large group of Wide Awakes joined a Republican meeting in Oakland, adding to the fervor of the assembly.[43] On September 28 a Republican meeting in San Francisco's Music Hall included an enthusiastic group of Wide Awakes who, after the meeting was over, accompanied Edwin Bryant Crocker, a Sacramento-based Republican politician and future executive of the Central Pacific (soon to be the Southern Pacific) Railroad, to his hotel.[44] On October 13 some four hundred Wide Awakes met at the corner of California and Montgomery Streets in San Francisco and, with their torches ablaze and a band accompanying them, began a colorful parade through the city's streets.[45] A little later in the same month, another group of Wide Awakes went from Sacramento to the town of Folsom in the foothills of the Sierra Nevada carrying six hundred torches, which they lit and carried through the town's streets, and yet another group marched through the streets of Petaluma, north of San Francisco Bay.[46]

Lincoln was aware of the groups who supported his candidacy, including the Wide Awakes, but as it was traditional for presidential candidates to stay at home and not travel about the country seeking votes, he remained in Springfield as the election day approached. He took a temporary office in the Illinois State House not far from his law office and his nearby family home. There, with the help of John Nicolay, a young German immigrant who worked as his secretary, he welcomed visitors who wanted to ask him questions. And he wrote letters. When answering questions, he was characteristically cautious and restrained. He had already made his positions on the key issues of the election quite clear. He had stated that he supported the Republican Party platform, and when asked what his position was on a particular issue, he felt no need to come up with a new answer. He was cordial, courteous, and humorous. But he had no wish to stir up new controversies. His opponents would be happy to find something they could use against him. So he avoided making new statements.

Campaign biographies were published, some based on interviews with people who knew Lincoln and others based on information about him that was already in print. The most informative were those written by William Dean Howells and John L. Scripps.[47] Howells was an Ohio journalist who later became a famous American novelist and critic, while Scripps was then editor of the *Chicago Press and Tribune*, soon to become one of the most powerful newspapers in the country as the *Chicago Tribune*.

Election day was November 6. Lincoln was in the Springfield State House until the early evening, when he went to the telegraph office with some friends to learn about early returns. He was pleased by reports that he had drawn more votes in Illinois than Douglas, but expressed concern about early returns from New York and New Jersey that appeared shaky. He continued to receive good reports, however, and soon learned that he had carried Illinois but also Pennsylvania, New York, and Massachusetts. Lincoln's supporters were anxious as the votes in California were cast. Early voting in Sacramento favored Douglas, with Lincoln running second and Breckinridge third.[48] Support for Breckinridge dominated Los Angeles County, with enthusiasm for Douglas waning and that for Lincoln almost nonexistent.

In San Francisco, the sun was bright and the sky cloudless as voters lined up early to cast their votes. There were a few fistfights at the polls, most caused by men who had imbibed too much whiskey, but they did not seem to interfere with the quietness of the voting. When Senator Gwin appeared at his polling place, he was challenged on two grounds: first, that he was not really a resident of California, but of Texas (his "home" in San Francisco was a hotel room), and second, that he was opposed to the Pacific Railroad. Both challenges were quickly dismissed, and he was permitted to cast his vote.[49]

When all the California votes were counted, it was apparent that the votes for the major presidential candidates were painfully close. None received a majority. Lincoln took 38,733, Douglas 37,999, and Breckinridge 33,969. John Bell trailed with only 9,111. The percentages were just over 32 percent for Lincoln, just under 32 percent for Douglas, a little more than 28 percent for Breckinridge, and only 7.6 percent for Bell. The split on the Democratic side had clearly benefited the Republicans. If the Douglas and Breckinridge votes were counted together, the Democrats would have won. They did not, however, for the decisive votes were the four electoral votes that would go to Lincoln. His opponents would receive none.[50]

The Democratic split had also helped the Republicans in Oregon. Lincoln won 5,329 votes in that state, or 36.1 percent of the total, to Breckinridge's 5,075 (34.4 percent) and Douglas's 4,136 (28 percent). Not even the presence on the Breckinridge ticket of the vice-presidential nominee, Oregon's dominant political leader and U.S. senator Joseph Lane, prevented the state's three electoral votes from going to Lincoln.[51] When the national votes were all tallied, Lincoln received 1,865,908 (39.9 percent), Douglas 1,380,202 (29.5 percent), Breckinridge 849,018 (18.1 percent), and Bell 590,901 (12.6 percent). Lincoln carried all of the slave-free states except New Jersey, but not a single one of the slave states. His electoral vote total was one hundred eighty. Breckinridge's was seventy-two, Bell's thirty-nine, and Douglas's twelve.[52] California's four votes added a little to his total, but they were not necessary to his victory. He was a minority president, but one who had clearly won.

After winning the presidency, Lincoln told a visitor: "All through the campaign my friends have been calling me 'Honest Old Abe,' and I have been elected mainly on that cry."[53] When an old farmer approached him and said, "Uncle Abe, I didn't vote for yer, but I am mighty glad yer elected just the same," Lincoln responded: "Well, my old friend, when a man has been tried and pronounced not guilty he hasn't any right to find fault with the jury."[54]

The jury had rendered its verdict. Lincoln found no fault with it. "Honest Old Abe" would be president.

4

California's Future

AS LINCOLN SURVEYED THE NATION HE HAD BEEN ELECTED to lead, he knew that California was not the location of the most virulent conflict then pervading it. It was, however, the scene of an important struggle. A vast expanse of land separated from the rest of the United States by nearly two thousand miles of sparsely populated plains, mountains, rivers, valleys, and deserts, California was far distant from the principal population centers of the United States and also from those of Mexico, the nation from which the Americans had pried it in the war of 1846–1848. Persuaded by that separation, the Spanish settlers of what was then called Alta (or Upper) California had in 1836 declared their independence from Mexico, proclaiming Alta California a "free and sovereign state" and continuing to assert its independence for a short time before accepting the authority of a new governor sent from Mexico City. Dissatisfied with Mexico's seeming neglect of California, the local leaders had contemplated the possibility that they would be taken over by a European power. Would it be England? Loyal subjects of Queen Victoria already occupied the northern reaches of the Pacific coast, soon to be declared British Columbia and become part of the Dominion of Canada. Would France claim the right to govern California? It already occupied many islands in the South Pacific and in a couple of years would send the newly designated Emperor Maximilian into the heart of Mexico to erect a French-dominated empire there. Nobody doubted that the powerful European nations were still colonial powers and eager to capture desirable territories around the world. When rebellious Americans who had migrated to California raised the legendary Bear Flag over the plaza in Sonoma in 1846 and declared an independent "California Republic," the threat of separation was once again recognized. Some Spanish-speaking Californios were comfortable with the idea of an independent republic, although they would prefer to have ruled over it themselves rather than to have handed it over to hard-drinking American invaders. But the Bear Flag idea died when the American flag rose over Monterey on July 7, 1846, and California was proclaimed an American possession.[1]

After California's acquisition by the United States, there were rumblings of an effort, not to declare the state independent but to divide it, with one part embracing slavery and the other excluding it. Some of the American residents argued that slavery could not be maintained in California because the terrain and the weather were unsuited to it, but this argument was not seriously considered by many. Southern California and the vast reaches of California's Central Valley invited productive agriculture like that practiced in the American South. Who was to say that cotton and wheat could not be grown in California? Or other crops that would contribute to the health and wealth not only of the state but of the rest of the nation as well? California's eventual recognition as the greatest agricultural state in the United States proved that it could provide good fields in which African American slaves could be put to work.

Lincoln was aware of the hopes—and even some efforts—of many supporters of slavery to divide California. In 1855, in the midst of his unsuccessful effort to be elected to the U.S. Senate from his home state, he prepared a list of resolutions he hoped the Illinois legislature would adopt that took strong stands against the expansion of slavery. He urged the state's legislators to oppose efforts to permit the territories of Kansas or Nebraska from becoming slave states, to oppose efforts to establish slavery "in any country, or place, where it does not now legally exist," and to resist "the now threatened attempt to revive the African slave-trade." In the same list, he turned his attention to California, urging Illinois legislators to "resist, to their utmost, the now threatened attempt to divide California, in order to erect one portion thereof into a slave-state."[2]

Most Americans believed that "manifest destiny" had led them to California and guaranteed their occupation of it. It was free land for the taking, they thought, but once taken, the land could not be given back. Others believed that manifest destiny had led them to California but that it had not decreed that it should remain an inseparable part of the United States.

"Manifest destiny" was an expression most famously (and perhaps first) used by an American lawyer, diplomat, and journalist named John L. O'Sullivan in an article he wrote for *The United States Magazine and Democratic Review* in 1845.[3] The annexation of Texas was then a controversial issue facing the American people (it was originally part of Mexico), and manifest destiny was a doctrine that many felt entitled them to do it. O'Sullivan wrote:

> Away, then, with all idle French talk of balances of power on the American Continent. . . . There is no growth in Spanish America! Whatever progress of population there may be in the British Canadas, is only for their own early severance of their present colonial relation to the little island three thousand miles across the Atlantic; soon to be followed by Annexation, and destined to swell the still accumulating momentum of our progress. And whosoever may hold the balance, though they should cast into the opposite scale all the bayonets and cannon, not only of France and England, but of Europe entire, how would it kick the beam against the simple, solid weight of the two hundred and fifty, or three hundred millions [*sic*]—and American millions—destined to gather beneath the flutter of the stripes and stars, in the fast hastening year of the Lord 1945!

"Americans" lived in the Confederate states as well as in the United States, did they not? Where was it decreed that only the United States could rule over the western half of the continent? Union loyalists explained, as Lincoln had, that the Constitution of the United States had formed "a more perfect union" out of the ruins left by the Articles of Confederation.[4] How, they asked, could a "more perfect union" be sliced into parts by conventions or leg-islatures in individual states? Confederates answered this question by saying that the Constitution permitted states to go their own way if they were provoked to do so by other states. Lincoln's elec-tion, and his oft-repeated condemnation of slavery, they argued, were provocations enough, so they were well within their rights to leave. Since Lincoln would take away their slaves, denying them the right to enslave Africans for the production of magnificent crops like cotton, they maintained that they could go their own way.

Slavery, of course, was the precipitating cause for secession, and the threat to forbid it from spreading and to decree its ulti-mate death in the passage of time, was the unfairness. However much the proponents of secession denied this, it was true. Con-federate vice president Alexander Stephens made the point clear in a speech he delivered in Savannah on March 21, 1861, when he stated that the controversy was over whether "African slavery as it exists amongst us" was "the proper *status* of the negro in our form of civilization." He declared affirmatively: "This was the immedi-ate cause of the late rupture and present revolution. Jefferson in his forecast, had anticipated this, as the 'rock upon which the old Union would split.' He was right. What was conjecture with him, is now a realized fact."[5]

California had been roiled by controversies over slavery from its beginning. The Constitution adopted in Monterey in 1849 had banned slavery from the state.[6] But that had not calmed the efforts of proslavery forces to impose discriminatory laws on African Americans, to expel them from the state, and even to change the state constitution to enslave them.

Lincoln's victory in the presidential election of 1860 quickly renewed interest in the creation of a Pacific Republic. Breckinridge supporters talked about where the boundaries of such a republic would be, suggesting that its territory would extend all the way from the Pacific Ocean to the Rocky Mountains and include not only California but also Oregon, New Mexico, Washington Terri-tory, and Utah, and that it could even continue southward into the Mexican State of Sonora. (What later became Nevada was then a part of the territory of Utah, and what later became Arizona was a part of the territory of New Mexico.) John C. Burch, one of California's two U.S. congressmen, as well as a Democrat and fervent Breckinridge supporter, published an open letter in which he said that the people of the West would "raise aloft the 'flag of the Bear,'" which had been raised over the short-lived "California Republic" at Sonoma in 1846, and seek refuge from disunion and Civil War in a "prosperous, happy and a successful Republic on the Pacific Slope."[7] Charles L. Scott, the state's other congressman and also a Democrat, published another letter in which he said that he "would make any sacrifice to preserve our Union with the hallowed and sacred associations that cluster around it," but added that in his "hearts of hearts" he warmly sympathized with the South, and if the Union was divided, he would "strenuously advocate the secession of California and establishment of a separate republic on the Pacific slope."[8]

The *Sacramento Daily Union* described the arguments of the Breckinridge men for a Pacific Republic. They began by "apologizing for secession," the *Union* said, and "denying the right of the General Government to make war on a State." They would clearly have preferred California to join the Southern states in secession but knew there was not enough political support for that, so they wanted to break the state and its neighbors off from the Union. The *Union* explained:

> The Breckinridge leaders are to a man immigrants from Southern States. . . . They are not men, as a general rule, who engage in any of the useful or industrial enterprises of the day. Outside of the learned professions, they are rarely found employed in anything except politics, the discharge of the duties of a political office or exhibiting themselves as loud talkers on the corner of the streets and partisans of Southern ideas and policy, which they would force upon California. The last election destroyed the future prospects of this class of politicians by profession. . . . They are, therefore, in a condition so hopeless as to render them desperate enough to undertake the advocacy of a Pacific Republic.[9]

The *San Jose Mercury* expressed similar thoughts, telling its readers that in the surrounding county there were a large number of men (nearly all Breckinridge supporters, and some who had voted for Douglas) who favored the formation of a Pacific Republic. "They do not attempt to conceal their opinions," the *Mercury* said. The newspaper conceded that they had a right to their opinions, but when they tried to "make use of improper influences for the promotion of their wishes," it was "time to expose and denounce them." Interestingly, the *Mercury* found that a significant number of "squatters" (settlers who wanted to take the large Spanish and Mexican land grants away from their owners and open them to free American settlement) hoped that the formation of a Pacific Republic would nullify the Treaty of Guadalupe Hidalgo, which had brought a formal conclusion to the war between Mexico and the United States in 1848—and, with it, federal laws upholding the grants. The *Mercury* scoffed, arguing that the creation of a Pacific Republic was "utterly impracticable," that it would cause "general disorder and utter lawlessness," and that it would lead to the establishment in California of a kind of slavery, or, as the correspondent called it, "a system of labor destructive to the interests of the working men." This system would benefit "none except some of southern birth, who, too indolent to work, and too arrogant to admit the equality of the laborer, would form an antagonistic class in society, claiming for themselves the privilege of rulers, and grasping for their own use the proceeds of other people's labor. In no way could the people of California more effectually destroy their highest interests than by joining in such a wicked and desperate scheme."[10]

Lincoln's election victory persuaded Senator Latham that he should not strongly advocate a Pacific Republic. Speaking to his Senate colleagues in Washington in early 1861, Latham admitted that he might personally favor an independent state in the West but that he was not sure that his constituents agreed. "There is but one thing which will or can alienate the affections of the people of the Pacific from the Union as it is, or as it may be," Latham said, "and that is a failure to give them a Pacific Rail road, and, until this is completed, overland mail facilities. Upon this question they are clamorous, urgent, unanimous."[11]

As news of Lincoln's election spread through the state, there were street demonstrations in some California cities—among them Oakland, San Jose, Marysville, Placerville, and San Francisco. News reports from the Southern states—particularly one brought on April 27 by the Pony Express advising Californians that Fort Sumter had surrendered to Confederate attack—persuaded many Union supporters that action was needed. Outrage, and a sense of anxiety, was increasing.[12]

The issue seemed to many Californians to be expressed in the argument over "states' rights." In April 1861 the *Sacramento Daily Union* issued an editorial explaining—and condemning—many of the arguments being made by the Breckinridge supporters, and in California by proponents of the Pacific Republic: "For years past a certain class of Southern politicians have constantly been proclaiming their devotion to States' rights, and been warning the people of the danger to their liberties which the consolidation of power in the Federal Government threatened. . . . This class of men acknowledge no National allegiance; they have no country beyond the limits of their State, and sneer at all intimations that they owe any obligations to the National Union."[13] Opposition to secession—and very clearly to the Pacific Republic—was gathering steam. At the end of May, a United States Union Club was formed in the state's far-northern Siskiyou County by men who considered any attempt to form an independent republic "traitorous in the extreme." Using florid language (with obvious references to the raising of the Bear Flag at Sonoma in 1846), they adopted a resolution declaring that they considered "all attempts to form a Pacific Confederacy under the Bear flag as nothing less than barefaced treason" and that they as Californians would "*bear* [sic] no flag but that which *bears* [sic] upon its folds the thirty-four stars and thirteen stripes of the Union."[14]

The California legislature met in Sacramento on January 7, 1861, still dominated by Democrats, some who supported Stephen Douglas in the presidential campaign and others who were unabashed Breckinridge men, but with a growing number of Republicans mixed in. The first task facing the legislators was the selection of a successor to Senator Gwin, whose term was about to expire and who, after Lincoln's victory and the secession of the Southern states, had little support among the voters. The legislative balloting was furious and at times angry, but on April 2 a choice was announced.[15] It was Democrat James A. McDougall, a hard-hitting lawyer and powerful orator (Bancroft said he was "distinguished for wit, sarcasm, and classicism") who had twice served as attorney general of Illinois, before going to California in 1849 and there becoming its attorney general and one of its U.S. congressmen.[16] Born in New York in 1817, he had moved to Illinois in 1837, where he sometimes took part in cases in which Lincoln was also an attorney. In 1856 he joined Edward Baker in the courtroom defense of the accused murderer Charles Cora. McDougall was elected to Gwin's Senate seat in 1861 not solely because of his Democratic Party membership but also, and perhaps most importantly, because he was a strong Union supporter.[17] During his election battle, McDougall wrote Lincoln saying, "I will stand by the government" and "I only desire to know when where and how I may render the best service to our common country. Permit me to say further *that I have faith in you*."[18]

The second issue facing the legislature in 1861 was the one that politicians all over the United States were confronted with—and that many dreaded. What, if anything, should (or could) be done about the secession of the Southern states? Some of the Democrats who had supported Breckinridge in the 1860 election argued that, of course, they supported the Constitution; but they did not agree with the Republican reaction to the Southern secession, nor did they believe that the seceding states could be "suppressed" without violating the Constitution. They pointed out (quite correctly) that the Constitution says absolutely nothing about secession. It neither authorizes nor condemns it, and it gives the president no explicit power to fight against it. Some politicians called for a resolution of the legislature affirming its support of the Constitution. Others countered that such a resolution was intended by "Black Republicans" to embarrass Democrats, to force them to declare their faith in the Constitution and suggest that if they did not do so they must be disloyal. The debates in Sacramento were noisy, raucous, and often angry. But the political tides were changing. It was no longer acceptable for a Democrat to argue with a straight face that he did not have to prove that he was loyal, or that he supported the Constitution. He had to make that declaration. And so on May 17 the legislature approved the following resolution: "Resolved, by the Senate, the Assembly concurring, That the people of California are devoted to the Constitution and Union of the United States, and will not fail in fidelity and fealty to that Constitution and Union, now in the hour of trial and peril; that California is ready to maintain the rights and honor of the National Government, at home and abroad, and at all times to respond to any requisition that may be made upon her to defend the Republic against foreign or domestic foes."[19] The resolution was signed on the next day by Democratic governor and erstwhile Breckinridge supporter John G. Downey.[20]

Despite the legislature's resolution, there were Californians who still believed that the state could be broken off from the Union and who were willing to do what they could to bring about that result. The Confederate states had military power that could be used not only to oppose Union forces in the East but also to harass them along the Pacific coast, if given the opportunity. Some prominent Californians left the state to join Southerners who advocated secession. Former state supreme court chief justice David S. Terry, congressman Charles Scott, state controller Samuel H. Brooks, and former state assemblyman Daniel Showalter, who had recently killed one of his adversaries in a duel, were three men with rabidly secessionist views who left the state to join the Southerners. Some Californians claimed a defiant loyalty to the Union but secretly carried on disloyal activities. Two groups, one calling itself the Knights of the Golden Circle and another calling itself the Knights of the Columbian Star, claimed they had ties with the Confederates, although proof of those ties was never very clearly established.[21]

Statewide and local elections were scheduled for 1861. People who favored the preservation of the Union seemed to be in the ascendancy, although the enthusiasm with which they advocated that position varied widely. Many shared the opinion of president James Buchanan that the Union should not be divided but that the Union government could do nothing to "coerce" secessionist states back into the fold. Most of these people now gathered under the Breckinridge fold, even though they had announced that they were the regular Democrats. Other Democrats made it clear that they believed that the federal government could properly resist any military attempt to secede, even on the battlefield if necessary, and thus called themselves Union Democrats. A large number of people who opposed secession preferred to be known as Republicans. They were followers of Abraham Lincoln. They supported him in the 1860 election and celebrated when he emerged as the victor. They advanced the candidacy of three men for the office of governor that would be vacated by John Downey early in 1862.

The Breckinridge Democrats nominated John R. McConnell, the Union Democrats John Conness, and the Republicans Leland Stanford. San Francisco's *Daily Alta California* ridiculed McConnell, a former state attorney general, and the convention that nominated him, noting that the Breckinridge Democrats did not explicitly favor staying in the Union but simply disapproved efforts to get out of it. The convention delegates adopted a resolution that, according to the *Alta*, said only that since they could not take the state of California out of the Union they should do "something in return for the benefit which it derives from the General Government." The *Alta* added that the convention "adopted the resolution with about as much cordiality as a party of convicts might show, in declaring that, while in the State Prison, they would continue to make bricks."[22]

Stanford was not an inspiring speaker, but he was a determined campaigner, and he stumped the northern part of the state (where most of the Republicans were found) with the Sacramento district attorney, Cornelius Cole.[23] Stanford favored the preservation of the Union, without question, but whether he favored it for constitutional reasons or because he wanted the federal government to support the construction of a transcontinental railroad connecting California to the rest of the country was not very clear. The Central Pacific Railroad, which would soon become the corporate home of the western portion of the transcontinental road, was legally organized on June 28, 1861, and Stanford was its president.[24] Southern California was less densely populated than the North, and everybody knew that Democrats outnumbered their opponents there.

When election day came, Stanford won with a total of nearly fifty-six thousand votes. His two opponents, however, won a total of nearly sixty-four thousand, clearly more than Stanford.[25] He was a minority winner, as Lincoln had been in 1860, but he realized that victory was better than defeat, even if only by a plurality. Stanford was formally inaugurated in Sacramento on January 10, 1862. In his inaugural address, he spoke on a variety of subjects, including land settlement (he favored giving American settlers the right to occupy parts of the very large Spanish and Mexican land grants that had been preserved in different parts of the state); Chinese immigration (he believed that the settlement in California of what he called an "inferior race" of people should be discouraged); the establishment of steamship lines to China (he believed this would be good for business); the Pacific Railroad (as a businessman who was already president of the Central Pacific Railroad, he strongly favored government subsidies to encourage the building of a transcontinental railroad); the fiscal economy (he advocated limits on government spending, but not any that would exhibit "a mean and narrow spirit"); and the promotion of education (which he believed would help more people understand the proposals of both the state and federal governments and why they were in the people's best interests). But he closed with a stirring passage in which he declared that the struggle then being waged in the United States between those who favored the Union and those who wanted to secede from it indicated that the Republican Party was the "real democratic party." He said:

> Political parties will always exist in all free Governments. There they have always been recognized by the wisest, the ablest, and best; while in despotic governments, they have little or no existence. Recognizing these facts, while the party, to whose confidence and partiality I am mainly indebted for the high position, the duties of which I have this day solemnly sworn to discharge, remains true to the cause of the people—I shall not ignore or forget its existence, but rather ask that all who agree with its cardinal and truly conservative principles shall unite to put down the enemies of free government, and bear aloft the emblem of our nationality, and of the hope of the freedom loving throughout the world.[26]

It was a wordy conclusion, but an inspiring one, to be sure.

5

The War Begins

LINCOLN REMAINED IN SPRINGFIELD AFTER THE PRESIDENTIAL
election votes were tabulated. There he met men who wished to
join his administration as members of his cabinet or other federal officers. He made no significant public statements but, aware
of the turmoil that was sweeping across the nation as Southern
states threatened secession, he began to prepare the speech he
would give at his inauguration.

Baker made it back to Washington DC, where he took his Senate seat on December 5. He eagerly participated in official business but managed to make a short trip to Springfield, where he
arrived on December 24. Learning that Baker was in town, Lincoln eagerly walked down the street to welcome him and, when
they met, said that he "he would rather see Baker elected Senator
than any man alive." "I was coming to call on you, Mr. President,"
Baker answered. "None of that between us, Baker," Lincoln countered. They were friends, as both understood—warm and loyal
friends. Lincoln asked Baker to personally introduce him when
he gave his inaugural address in Washington, and Baker eagerly
agreed to do so.

South Carolina was the first state to announce its secession
when, on December 20, 1860, its legislature unanimously adopted
an ordinance declaring that "the union now subsisting between
South Carolina and other States, under the name of 'The United
States of America,' is hereby dissolved." After the beginning of
1861, conventions assembled in other slaveholding states to follow

South Carolina's example. Mississippi did so on January 9, Florida on January 10, Alabama on January 11, Georgia on January 19, Louisiana on January 26, and Texas on February 1.

Lincoln left Springfield on February 11, boarding a train with his son Robert, his secretaries John G. Nicolay and John Hay, a number of army officers, and some friends and relatives. The trip was slow, going from Illinois through Indiana, Ohio, Pennsylvania, New York, New Jersey, and Maryland, with stops along the way where Lincoln made conciliatory remarks. Jefferson Davis of Alabama was at the same time making his way to Montgomery, Alabama, where, on February 18, he appeared before the State Capitol and was inaugurated provisional president of the Confederate States of America. Lincoln escaped a threatened assassination attempt as he passed through Baltimore and on February 23 finally arrived in Washington.[1] He took up rooms there in Willard's Hotel, where he continued to meet political associates and friends.

On March 4, the date set for Lincoln's inauguration, outgoing president James Buchanan left the White House in an open carriage and, under partly cloudy skies, headed for Willard's, where Lincoln joined him for the trip to the Capitol. Riding with the two men were Democratic senator James A. Pearce of Maryland and Republican senator Edward Baker of Oregon. Troops under the command of Army Chief of Staff Brevet Lt. Gen. Winfield Scott lined the streets, watched the carriage from windows along Pennsylvania Avenue, and stationed themselves on the roofs of buildings overlooking the east steps of the Capitol. The Senate was convened to welcome Lincoln as he arrived at the Capitol. There Lincoln's newly elected vice president, Hannibal Hamlin of Maine, took his oath of office before Baker stepped out onto the east front of the Capitol, surveyed the thousands of spectators who had gathered there, and addressed the crowd in his best stentorian tones: "Fellow citizens, I introduce to you Abraham Lincoln, the President-elect of the United States."[2]

Lincoln's address was long and carefully worded. He tried to assure Southerners that he would make no effort to interfere with slavery in their own states, but added that the spread of slavery into western territories was of concern to him. He declared that his principal goal was the preservation of the Union, stating that "in contemplation of universal law and of the Constitution the Union of these States is perpetual. . . . Continue to execute all the express provisions of our National Constitution, and the Union will endure forever." He said that he had no wish to amend the Constitution to guarantee that slavery would never be abolished in the states where it was now located, but that he would not oppose an effort to propose and adopt such an amendment. His closing remarks, suggested by William Seward (his designated secretary of the treasury), were conciliatory. "We are not enemies, but friends," he said. "We must not be enemies. Though passion may have strained it must not break our bonds of affection. The mystic chords of memory, stretching from every battlefield and patriot grave to every living heart and hearthstone all over this broad land, will yet swell the chorus of the Union, when again touched, as surely they will be, by the better angels of our nature."[3]

The people in California learned what Lincoln had said when the text of his address was brought there by the Pony Express.[4] The text inspired responses, some that were approving, others that were outraged; some that urged peaceful consideration of all he had said; and some that predicted war would soon erupt between the North and the South. The *Marysville Express*, which had supported Breckinridge in the election, thought the address was a declaration of war against the South. In an article titled "The Last Hope Destroyed," it told its readers that "with the stolid madness of his party," Lincoln declared he would collect the public revenues and hold the Federal forts and arsenals in the Southern states "even though the people in those states would regard this as a declaration of war." "The people there united can never be conquered," it said. The *Express* believed that Lincoln would attempt to invade the Southern states but that the attempt would fail, saying: "Ten millions [*sic*] of people—brave people as the Southern people are— can never be successfully invaded by any power." It added that the first Federal guns fired "will unite the South and bring on civil war." The *Marysville Democrat*, which had supported Stephen Douglas in the presidential election, told its readers that Lincoln's address was not a "war cry" but that it breathed "the utmost moderation and forbearance," adding that it was "quite clear that there can be no war, unless the rebellious States take the initiative."[5]

The rebellious states did take the initiative. They declared that Federal forts located in their boundaries now belonged to the Confederate states and could not be maintained by Lincoln's government. Fort Sumter, in the harbor of Charleston, South Carolina, became the focus of immediate attention. After Lincoln made efforts to resupply the Federal troops then holding it, and Davis sent troops under the command of Louisiana's Gen. P. G. T. Beauregard to force its surrender, shelling ordered by Beauregard forced the Federal commanding officer, Maj. Robert Anderson, to formally surrender on April 14. Lincoln responded by calling for seventy-five thousand militia volunteers to come to Washington to defend the capital. Virginia, which had not yet decided whether to secede, adopted an ordinance of secession on April 17, after which Davis invited applications for "commissions or letters of marque and reprisal," which would authorize privately owned vessels to be armed and sent to sea to attack Northern ships. Two days later, Lincoln responded by declaring a naval blockade of the Confederate coast.[6]

On April 20 U.S. Army colonel Robert E. Lee submitted his resignation and prepared to join the Confederate forces. On April 25 Lincoln ordered Gen. Winfield Scott to suspend the writ of habeas corpus in Maryland to facilitate the passage of militia troops through that state to Washington, triggering a fierce rebuke from Supreme Court Chief Justice Roger Taney, who agreed with Lincoln that secession was wrong but believed, as had James Buchanan, that the federal government had no power to oppose it.[7] In May the provisional Confederate Congress voted to move its capital from Montgomery, Alabama, to Richmond, Virginia, which was closer to the expected battlefields separating the North and the South, and Jefferson Davis arrived there on May 29.

In June Confederate forces under General Beauregard began to assemble around an important rail center at Manassas, Virginia, near the banks of the sluggish Bull Run River. Lincoln sent Brig. Gen. Irvin McDowell and thirty-five thousand troops south to challenge the Confederate troops under Beauregard. Unknown to McDowell, Beauregard's twenty-two thousand troops were being reinforced by twelve thousand additional soldiers from the northern Shenandoah Valley under Gen. Joseph E. Johnston. The men on both sides were inexperienced in major fighting and poorly trained. But one of the commanders in Johnston's force was a former professor from the Virginia Military Institute recently appointed to the rank of brigadier general under Johnston. He was Thomas Jonathan Jackson, soon to be acclaimed as "Stonewall" Jackson after another officer watched him in conflict and reportedly exclaimed, "There is Jackson standing like a stone wall."[8]

Fighting broke out on the morning of Sunday, July 21, and continued almost all day. In the closing moments of the battle, the Union troops fled in panic. One of the Union soldiers wounded was a young man from Massachusetts named Oliver Wendell Holmes Jr., son of the celebrated poet Olive Wendell Holmes Sr., who would later win fame as a justice of the United States Supreme Court. The *New York Tribune*'s Horace Greeley wrote Lincoln: "The gloom in this city is funereal for our dead at Bull Run were many, and they lie unburied yet. On every brow sits sullen, scorching, black despair."[9]

While the fighting raged on the border between Northern and Southern states, it was clear that the eyes of both Northerners and Southerners were aimed farther west. Lincoln's opposition to the spread of slavery into the western territories had enraged Southern defenders of slavery, who wanted to expand their territory beyond the Mississippi, beyond Texas, even to the Pacific coast and California. Jefferson Davis had made that point clear when he was serving as U.S. secretary of war in the 1850s, stating that "the country on the Pacific is in many respects adapted to slave labor, and many of the citizens desire its introduction." If a railroad could be built across the country, connecting the Pacific with states east of the Mississippi, "future acquisitions to the South would insure to our benefit."

Reports of the surrender of Fort Sumter and the Union defeat at Bull Run were carried by steamships from New York to Panama, then transported across the isthmus, where more steamships were waiting to take them north to San Francisco. The steamships were slow, while stagecoaches driven across the plains and mountains were faster. But the fastest of all was the Pony Express, which continued to be the major route for sending war news to California until October 24, 1861, when completion of the overland telegraph made it possible for news to be transmitted more rapidly.

War reports were being carried not only across the country but also abroad. There they reached John C. Frémont, the former western explorer and U.S. senator from California who had gone to England, hoping to raise money he needed to pay off debts he had incurred on his Mariposa land grant in California. Frémont's attention was now focused on Missouri, a key battleground state that had not joined the other slave states in secession but was widely perceived as in imminent danger of doing so. It was the state that had so long been represented in the U.S. Senate by Frémont's formidable father-in-law, Thomas Hart Benton, and to which his strong-minded wife, Jessie Benton Frémont, was tied by warm friendships. Missouri's newly elected governor Claiborne F. Jackson was one of the most dangerous Southern sympathizers in the state. After a training camp on the outskirts of St. Louis was garrisoned by Confederate sympathizers, Union army captain Nathaniel Lyon seized it, and Jackson responded by calling out fifty thousand volunteers to "repel the invasion." Frémont was on his way to New York and, from there, to Washington DC. He was still a Californian—his wife, Jessie, remained in her home in San Francisco—but he was a Republican, a defender of the Union, and an ambitious warrior yearning for a fight.

Mrs. Frémont hurried to New York to meet her husband. They both intended to communicate with Lincoln. Lincoln had campaigned in 1856 for Frémont's election as president and had briefly considered appointing him secretary of war, before resolving instead to name Simon Cameron of Pennsylvania to that position. (He would soon rue that decision.) Lincoln did not know, however, how potentially disastrous his appointment of Frémont would soon prove to be.

Responding to Frémont's invitation to join the fight on the Union side, Lincoln appointed him as a major general in May 1861 and sent him to St. Louis as commander of the Department of the West, a vast area that included Illinois and the land spreading west from the Mississippi all the way to the Rocky Mountains. Once he had arrived in St. Louis, Frémont began to reveal many of the faults that had caused him so much trouble in California during the Mexican War. He gave orders recklessly, spent money foolishly, isolated himself from experienced advisers, and made critical decisions without proper reflection. He complained about a lack of supplies and backup troops to successfully pursue Confederate troops and guerrillas. And, most critically, he assumed powers that Lincoln believed he did not have. One of the orders that troubled Lincoln was Frémont's order for the arrest of Frank Blair, one of the leading politicians in Missouri, a member of Congress, a brother of Lincoln's postmaster general, Montgomery Blair, a son of Francis Preston Blair, one of Lincoln's most trusted advisers, and himself the holder of a major general's commission in the Union army. Frémont ordered Blair's arrest for "insidious & dishonorable efforts" to undermine Frémont's authority. It outraged Blair and disturbed Lincoln when he heard about it.[10]

Another of Frémont's orders, however, soon dwarfed even that. On August 30 he declared the whole of Missouri's slave population forever free. When Lincoln learned of this declaration, he asked Frémont to modify it so that it would apply only to slaves used by Confederates in the war effort, in conformity with the Confiscation Act that Congress had just passed.[11] Lincoln feared that a more sweeping order would forcefully drive Missouri out of the Union and possibly carry Kentucky with it. Mrs. Frémont, who liked always to be at her husband's side, left St. Louis for Washington, where she demanded an "immediate interview" with Lincoln. He granted her request, but in a curt and unfriendly way, arousing incredible anger on her part and arousing his own dissatisfaction with Frémont. The general declined to honor Lincoln's order for modification. The president responded by conferring with General Scott and members of his cabinet, who all agreed that Frémont would have to go. On October 24 Lincoln penned a letter dismissing the general from his Missouri command and had it personally delivered nine days later.[12]

Although Frémont was no longer in command in Missouri, he retained his military commission. He spent some time in New York, then received an order commanding the newly created Mountain Department, which included western Virginia, eastern Kentucky, and part of Tennessee. He took up his headquarters in the town of Wheeling, but soon found himself in combat with the redoubtable "Stonewall" Jackson at the battle of Cross Keys, Virginia. He tried but was unable to destroy Jackson's army, and Jackson successfully escaped. After the battle, Frémont's Corps was put under the overall command of Gen. John C. Pope, whom Frémont bitterly resented. He then resigned his command and never received another.

Lincoln now had to decide who would lead Union military forces in the combat with the Confederates. Lt. Gen. Winfield Scott was too old (seventy-four) and physically unable to lead troops in battle (he weighed more than three hundred pounds and suffered from dropsy, rheumatism, vertigo, and gout), so Lincoln looked for young and more able officers. On July 27 he placed George B. McClellan at the head of the army that had been defeated at First Bull Run. McClellan was a young man (only thirty-four years old) and short (he stood only five feet eight) but he had impressed observers with his military skill. A West Point graduate, he had fought in the Mexican War, then built forts, improved harbors, and even designed a comfortable military saddle that was named for him. He had resigned his captain's commission in 1857 to accept prestigious employment with railroads, serving as chief engineer and vice president of the Illinois Central Railroad and then president of the Ohio and Mississippi railroads. Lincoln was impressed both by his military record and his involvement with the railroads, which Lincoln favored highly. It did not take long for "Little Mac" to turn the Army of the Potomac into a strong fighting force. But his political views—he was a strongly anti-Republican and pro-slavery Democrat—caused him to move his troops so slowly and cautiously that confidence in his ability to engage in actual combat with Confederate troops soon began to vanish. As historian James M. McPherson has written, he had "an alarmist tendency to inflate enemy strength and intentions."[13] Lincoln was hopeful at first that McClellan would boldly attack Confederate forces. His hope, however, began to wane as McClellan continued to lead them into cautious military maneuvers that did not actually confront the Rebels.

Men with military experience from all over the North shared Lincoln's concern about the progress of the war. And some of the most important came from California. One who would soon become a prominent member of Lincoln's military forces was a Californian named Henry Wager Halleck. Born on a farm in Westernville, New York, in 1815 Halleck had attended West Point, where he studied military engineering and graduated third in the class of 1839. He had come to California during the Mexican War aboard the USS *Lexington*, a sloop of war that was loaded with artillery for the military force then occupying California.[14] Because the artillery was too heavy to be carried across the isthmus of Panama, the *Lexington* was sent all the way around Cape Horn, a voyage that took some six months to complete. Two other West Point graduates came aboard the same ship with Halleck: Edward Otho Cresap Ord and William Tecumseh Sherman, both of whom were to attract Lincoln's attention and play important roles in the Civil War.

Halleck and Sherman were put to work under the military governor, Col. Richard B. Mason, who was stationed in Monterey.[15] Mason named Halleck as his secretary of state, a position that authorized him to delve into California's provincial records and land titles and soon made him something of an expert on California's laws.[16]

Brig. Gen. Bennet Riley became California's military governor in April 1849. Frustrated by the federal government's failure to organize a civil government in California, he acted on his own authority and called a constitutional convention that met in Monterey in September and October 1849 and adopted the constitution that led to California's admission to the Union in September 1850. Halleck attended the convention as a delegate from Monterey while Sherman acted as Riley's military representative. A state government was organized, with Peter H. Burnett soon elected as the first governor and John C. Frémont and William M. Gwin chosen as the first two U.S. senators. General Riley then left California, while Halleck headed north to San Francisco, where he began a busy career as a lawyer and land manager, representing clients before the U.S. Land Commission established by Congress in 1851 and overseeing the construction of the largest commercial building in San Francisco, a five-story structure that occupied a full block on San Francisco's main commercial thoroughfare, Montgomery Street. Opened in 1853, it was initially called the Washington Block but eventually became known as the Montgomery Block, the largest commercial structure west of the Mississippi. Halleck also supervised the planning and construction of fortifications. He revealed his background as an army engineer by supervising the construction of a looming military fort on the bayshore guarding the entrance to San Francisco Bay, and lighthouses along the Pacific coast, including a massive fort, called Fort Point, on the rocky shore of the Golden Gate, the maritime entrance into San Francisco Bay.

Halleck also became involved in the management of one of the most valuable—and controversial—mines in California. Located in coastal hills fifty or so miles south of San Francisco, it was named New Almaden after the legendary Almadén mine in the Sierra Morena of south-central Spain, where rich deposits of an ore called cinnabar produced mercury (also known as quicksilver) that had been mined since Roman times. (*Almadén*, in Spanish, is an obsolete word for "mine" or "mineral.")[17] New Almaden was generally regarded as not only California's oldest mine (the indigenous natives had mined it for hundreds, perhaps even thousands, of years) but also its richest for, although it did not produce gold, the quicksilver it yielded was essential to refining gold.

Halleck was a devoted military man, but he realized that the reduced size of the U.S. Army diminished opportunities for advancement. In 1854 he had resigned his army commission and left for a trip to New York, where in 1855 he married Elizabeth Hamilton, granddaughter of the American founding father Alexander Hamilton and sister of Schuyler Hamilton, Halleck's best friend from West Point. The two then returned to San Francisco, where Halleck resumed his legal practice and busy business life.

Litigation surrounding ownership of New Almaden Quicksilver Mine provided Halleck with additional income, for he acted as supervising manager of the company that controlled the mine and was making fabulous profits from its mercury production. In 1858 president James Buchanan's attorney general, Jeremiah Black, sent an attorney named Edwin M. Stanton to California to try to obtain federal control over the property and the mine. As manager of the mine, Halleck was Stanton's opponent. Stanton's combative legal efforts contributed to a judicial injunction that was issued in 1858 to shut down the mine, at least for the time being. Halleck's management of the mine ended about the same time. The struggle between the two men aroused bitter animosities between them that continued well into the Civil War, when Stanton was Lincoln's secretary of war and Halleck was commanding general of the Union armies.[18]

Halleck was also busy as a writer and translator. He worked for several years on an English translation of the four-volume biography of Napoleon by Antoine Henri Jomini that was published in New York in 1864. Before his arrival in California, he published technical reports on the varieties and uses of bitumen (a kind of asphalt used for paving), on the elements of military organization, and on the elements of national defense. People who knew Halleck—or just knew of him—had no doubt that he was a scholarly man who often had his face buried in a book or collection of manuscripts. If troops gave Zachary Taylor the nickname of "Old Rough and Ready" and Winfield Scott "Old Fuss and Feathers," nobody doubted why the men who fought under Halleck in the Civil War called him "Old Brains."

As the threat of a sectional conflict between the North and the South grew in intensity, Halleck became concerned. He did not particularly care about the fate of the slaves, for he had moderate racial views, believing that some reforms were necessary to improve the lot of the men and women held in bondage but that full abolition of slavery was not yet called for.[19] He was deeply distressed, however, by the looming threat of secession and anxious to play a part in suppressing it. Shortly after Lincoln won the presidential election, Halleck received an appointment as a major general of the California militia from governor John G. Downey. In the meantime, however, he let it be known that he was anxious to join the Federal army. A friend in Washington let Commanding Gen. Winfield Scott know of Halleck's wishes, and in 1860 Scott "directed" him to come to Washington. When he arrived there, Lincoln was president, and the two met together.

The telegraph line connecting California with the eastern states had been completed, so news reports from the East were promptly received there and sent on to readers. On November 8 the pro-Union *Sacramento Daily Union* reported that Halleck had just arrived in Washington.[20] On November 12 San Francisco's *Daily Alta California*, also pro-Union, reported that Halleck had been assigned to the army's Department of the West.[21] On November 29 the *Red Bluff Independent* told its readers that Halleck was one of only four major generals in the United States Army and that he was "regarded by good Judges as next to McClellan in military science. . . . He is just the man for the West, as McClellan is the man for the East."[22] Halleck was quickly sent to St. Louis, which was still reeling from the tumult created by the abortive leadership there of Frémont, and was promptly installed as commander of the Department of Missouri.[23]

Edward Otho Cresap Ord was another military figure with a California background who soon joined Lincoln's military force. Born in Cumberland, Maryland, in 1818 but raised in Washington DC, he had attended West Point, graduating seventeenth in his class in 1839, the same year as Halleck. Coming to California with both Halleck and Sherman, he was assigned the duty of drafting maps of the new city of Sacramento, the adjoining mining district, and the Southern California community of Los Angeles. Military assignments led him back to the East, then back to California, Oregon, and Washington Territory, where he took part in battles with the indigenous natives, who erupted in fierce resistance to the cruel treatment to which they had been subjected.[24] His brother, a medical doctor named James L. Ord, served as captain of Battery C, Third U.S. Artillery, and also as commander of the U.S. Army's Fort Vancouver in Washington Territory. On May 7, 1861, Ord commanded two companies of the Third Artillery as they left Fort Vancouver for San Francisco. From there, he returned to the Atlantic coast, where he was assigned to Fort Monroe, Virginia, serving as superintendent of practical instruction.[25]

The beginning of the Civil War dramatically changed Ord's military career, as it did those of so many officers. As a native Marylander with no regard for slaves, he was initially sympathetic with the South and contemptuous of abolitionists. He was sent back to California but anxious to be assigned to the field of combat in Virginia. Nagging questions about his loyalty to the Union prompted him to display it vigorously when he arrived in that state. His first assignment there was as a brigade commander in the Pennsylvania Reserves. He participated prominently in the Battle of Dranesville in Virginia in late 1861, leading soldiers to defeat Confederates under the command of Brig. Gen. J. E. B. Stuart. It was the first Union victory in the East and brought promotions to Ord, first to a lieutenant colonelcy in the regular army and then to a major general rank in the Union Volunteers.[26] He would soon draw Lincoln's attention.[27]

William Tecumseh Sherman was yet another military figure with a California background—a fairly long and important one—who joined Lincoln's force. An Ohio native who graduated from West Point in 1840, Sherman had arrived in Monterey aboard the USS *Lexington* with Halleck and Ord and then carried out important duties under California's military governor Richard Mason. He did not have the same opportunity as Halleck to see actual military duty, but played a part in one of the most important events in California's history.

In the spring of 1848, Colonel Mason received a letter and some folded papers filled with small particles of yellow metal. They had been sent by John Sutter, the master of the sprawling land grant he had received from the Mexican authorities in the Sacramento Valley and on which he had built Sutter's Fort, one of the most notable landmarks for immigrants then coming into California. The letter explained that the particles had been discovered in the tailrace of a sawmill Sutter was building on the American River but that the land there was not part of Sutter's grant. Sutter asked Mason for a "preemption," giving him a right to occupy the land to the exclusion of others for a period of years. Sherman and Mason answered Sutter's letter, explaining that Mason had no authority to grant preemptions but that he didn't think Sutter's sawmill would cause much in the way of problems. In the meantime, Sherman and Mason subjected the yellow particles to some tests. Sherman had seen some gold on an earlier visit to northern Georgia and was quite sure that what he now saw was placer gold. A while later, Sherman and Mason went up to Sacramento and the surrounding country and found that it was crowded with men who were eagerly panning for gold. A rush was already on, with men leaving their jobs in the cities and towns and soldiers deserting their posts to make their way toward the gold country. Mason soon decided to send an official report back to Washington. He had Sherman draft it, after which he made some small corrections and sent it off by ship through Panama, where it reached President James Knox Polk on December 6, 1848, one day after he had delivered his last annual message to Congress. Polk then prepared a special message in which he announced to the nation and the world that extensive deposits of gold had been discovered in California. Years later, Sherman remembered: "Then began the wonderful development, and that great migration to California, by land and sea, of 1849 and 1850."[28]

When the Monterey convention that adopted California's first constitution came to an end in November 1849, Sherman decided to go back to his home in Ohio where his fiancée, Ellen Ewing, was living. The two were married on May 1, 1850, in Washington DC's prestigious Blair House, with a stellar list of guests, including Zachary Taylor, Daniel Webster, and Henry Clay, in attendance. The presence of these national figures signified the esteem that Ellen's father, Thomas Ewing, had earned through his service as a U.S. senator from Ohio, secretary of the treasury under presidents William Henry Harrison and John Tyler, and secretary of the interior (the first ever) under presidents Zachary Taylor and Millard Fillmore. Nine days after Sherman and his wife returned from their honeymoon, Taylor unexpectedly died, probably of gastroenteritis contracted at the groundbreaking ceremonies for the Washington Monument.

Sherman was now assigned to duty in St. Louis and then New Orleans. But military opportunities did not seem favorable in either place, so he began to look for other employment possibilities, some in his native state of Ohio, some in St. Louis, others farther away. In the spring of 1853, he accepted an offer to manage the California branch of an important St. Louis bank that would do business in San Francisco as Lucas, Turner & Co. He went to the California city with his wife and children aboard a ship that touched Panama and another that carried them north to San Francisco. As he began his management duties there, he accepted an appointment from California's governor J. Neely Johnson as a major general of the California militia. The state command presented difficult relationships with the federal officials then in California: Maj. Gen. John Wool, the commander of the U.S. Army's Department of the Pacific, and Commodore David Glasgow Farragut, then in charge of the construction of the U.S. naval shipyard at Mare Island, north of San Francisco. When severe financial troubles hit the city in 1856, Sherman was shocked, discouraged, even depressed. He had accepted deposits from some of his military friends and felt it was his duty to see that they recovered their monies.

Sherman's problems in San Francisco were confounded when a self-described Committee of Vigilance was formed in 1856. It was the second time a group of prominent businessmen had appointed themselves to bring "law and order" to the city. The first had been in 1851, when several hundred businessmen claimed that a band of immigrants from Australia, called "Sydney Ducks," were setting San Francisco buildings on fire so they could loot them while escaping justice because the regularly elected law enforcement officials were in corrupt alliance with them. The self-designated vigilantes subjected the accused criminals to kangaroo trials and summary punishment. Four were hanged, one was publicly flogged, twenty-eight were banished or deported, fifteen were handed over to the police for trials, and forty-one were released before the committee announced that its work was done and that they were disbanding.[29]

The 1856 committee was much larger. It was organized after Edward D. Baker represented the gambler Charles Cora so well that his trial ended with a hung verdict and quickly brought about the public hanging of both Cora and James Casey, who had been summarily charged with another offense.[30] Governor Johnson sought Sherman's help in putting down the vigilantes. He had no arms with which to do so, so he asked General Wool to give him some and Commodore Farragut to provide naval transportation to bring the arms to San Francisco. Wool vacillated, first promising to do so and then denying that he had ever made such a promise. Sherman despaired. He was still trying to keep his bank afloat, and the federal officials were not offering him any help to suppress the vigilantes. Frustrated, he resigned his commission. Sherman believed that the vigilantes were the equivalent of a mob and that they represented an unacceptable attack on government by law. He later condemned them, writing: "As they controlled the press, they wrote their own history, and the world generally gives them credit of having purged San Francisco of rowdies and roughs; but their success has given great stimulus to a dangerous principle, that would at any time justify the mob in seizing all the power of government; and who is to say that the Vigilance Committee may not be composed of the worst, instead of the best, elements of a community?"[31]

Business did not recover sufficiently to permit Sherman's bank to continue to make money, so in the spring of 1857 he shut it down and took his wife and his children by ship through Panama to New York. They returned for a while to their home state of Ohio, then went on to St. Louis, as Sherman was still looking for business opportunities. In 1860 the governor of Louisiana invited him to come south and establish what was denominated as the Louisiana State Seminary of Learning and Military Academy. Sherman liked the institute because of its military rule and did not particularly care about the slavery that surrounded it. He was not an abolitionist—he did not believe that the peculiar institution had to be immediately ended. He did, however, think that it had to be ameliorated, perhaps by stopping slave sales that separated family members and by allowing blacks to become educated. He firmly believed, however, that if Louisiana ever left the Union, he would leave Louisiana. When in 1861 the state seceded, he resigned his position at the seminary and headed north. Resuming his position as a U.S. Army officer, he led a brigade of volunteers at the disastrous battle of First Bull Run, but was soon transferred to Kentucky, where he worried so much about the progress of the Union war effort that he suffered a brief nervous breakdown. After his recovery, however, he became a close partner of Ulysses S. Grant, another West Point graduate who had resumed his military duties after the war broke out, rising from comparative obscurity to a role of battlefield leadership that would eventually make him into a Northern hero—and one of Lincoln's closest professional friends.

Grant did not come to California until 1852, some five years after Sherman and Halleck and ten years after Frémont. He came, however, with more actual military experience, for he had fought under Zachary Taylor and Winfield Scott in Mexico and won a promotion to brevet captain for "gallant and meritorious conduct in the battle of Chapultepec."[32] Like Sherman and Halleck, Grant was a West Point graduate but without their academic luster. While Halleck was ranked third out of twenty-one in the class of 1839 and Sherman was sixth out of forty-two in the class of 1840, Grant was a median student, graduating twenty-first out of thirty-nine in the class of 1843. He remained in the service even after the war ended, suffering much of the time from boredom and periodic bouts of excessive drinking, all the while pining for his beloved Julia Dent, whom he had married in St. Louis in August 1848. He received an assignment to the headquarters of the Fourth Infantry in Detroit, then was switched back and forth between Sackets Harbor, New York, and Detroit until May 1852, when the Fourth Infantry was ordered to California.

Grant was devoted to his wife but believed that because she was pregnant with their second child she could not endure a sea voyage by way of Panama, so he headed to California alone. His first assignment there was with the Fourth Infantry Brigade at Benicia Barracks, an army installation located midway between San Francisco and Sacramento. He was able to visit San Francisco, which impressed him with its busy crowds and thriving businesses, before reporting to a much more remote location, Columbia Barracks, soon to be renamed as Fort Vancouver, on the Columbia River in the Oregon Territory. Military action there was close to nonexistent, so Grant did some surveying, indulged in private building projects, and farmed some land, hoping he could make enough money to adequately support his growing family when they were reunited. While engaging in a surveying mission for a railroad that was to be built through the Cascade Mountains, he met George B. McClellan, then a young brevet captain. McClellan's academic record was much more distinguished than Grant's, and the two did not become friends.

In January 1854 Grant was transferred to Fort Humboldt, an infantry outpost on California's northern coast, overlooking Humboldt Bay. He found the area there heavily wooded and green. Years later, he recalled that he "left the Pacific coast very much attached to it, and with the full intention of making it my future home."[33] But he longed to be reunited with his wife and family. And he drank heavily—so heavily that he was threatened with a court-martial. So he tendered his resignation, which was formally accepted by then secretary of war Jefferson Davis on June 2, 1854.[34] Beginning his trip back home, he made a stop in San Francisco, where he quickly ran out of money. A government clerk there helped him obtain free passage on one of the steamships of Commodore Cornelius Vanderbilt's Pacific Mail Steamship line, which took him from the port of San Francisco to Nicaragua, across the peninsula, and then on to New York.

Reunited with his family, Grant managed a farm owned by his wife's family outside St. Louis, then pushed on to Galena, Illinois, where he worked in a busy leather shop owned by his father. He paid close attention to his duties in Galena and soon found himself on a surer financial footing than he had ever before known. His political views were also changing. His wife came from a slave-owning family in St. Louis, but his own views on the slavery issue were indistinct. In 1856 he voted for the Democratic presidential candidate James Buchanan against the Republican Frémont, but as the electoral season of 1860 approached he found himself inclining toward support of Stephen Douglas. He soon came to believe that Douglas really had no chance of victory, however, and that the new president would either be Breckinridge or Lincoln. This choice made it clear to him that he would support Lincoln.

The inauguration of Jefferson Davis as president of the Confederate States of America outraged Grant. After the fall of Fort Sumter and President Lincoln's order summoning seventy-five thousand state militia to come to Washington for its defense, the streets of Galena erupted into pro-Union excitement. Grant volunteered to help organize a company of volunteers who went to Springfield. Illinois, where Governor Richard Yates invited him to join the adjutant general's staff and assigned him the duty of mustering in volunteers. Frustrated at not receiving a firm position in Illinois, however, he wrote the adjutant general in Washington and asked for an appointment. In August 1861 he received an appointment from Lincoln as a brigadier general of volunteers. He was soon sent into Missouri, where he responded coolly but contemptuously to the self-posturing of Frémont. From Missouri, he was sent into Kentucky, aware of how important Lincoln considered the loyalty of that state. When Frémont was removed from Missouri, Grant continued to accept greater responsibilities. He was a general now, despite his humble background in California and in Galena, and on his way to greater responsibility under President Lincoln.

David Glasgow Farragut (born as James Glasgow Farragut) was a senior naval captain when the Civil War broke out. Born in Tennessee in 1801, the son of a Spanish immigrant father and a North Carolinian mother, he was commissioned a naval midshipman when he was only nine years old and thus enabled to serve in the War of 1812. He commanded ships that patrolled the Caribbean in the 1820s and 1830s, then, during the Mexican War, helped blockade Mexico's Gulf Coast while Zachary Taylor and Winfield Scott carried the battle into the country's interior. In 1854 he was sent to California, where he supervised construction of the Mare Island Naval Shipyard, the first U.S. naval shipyard on the Pacific coast. Located north and slightly east of San Francisco, it was well situated for observing the entry of any ships into California's economically important interior and the capital of Sacramento. After the outbreak of the Civil War, he offered his services to the navy, and his foster brother, U.S. naval commander David Dixon Porter, offered him an assignment to attack New Orleans. Farragut's Southern roots led some to doubt his loyalty to the Union, but the doubts vanished when, in early 1862, he led his ships into the Louisiana city's harbor and ordered them to begin their bombardment, which was devastating.

Men with California backgrounds had joined in Lincoln's war effort. Some he would soon find difficult to work with, while others would encourage his hopes that the conflict would soon end and the Union would survive.

The First Californian

ON SUNDAY, APRIL 21, 1861, A MEETING CONVENED IN A fashionable hotel in New York City. Nearly two hundred Californians who were visiting the mid-Atlantic state but intended to shortly return home had been drawn there by a placard that was posted on the street and emblazoned with the following words: "Californians—to Arms. California Steamers in Danger. Rally, Californians—the Federal Capital is in Danger. Californians, Oregonians, Coast men, and men who have seen service, attention. A meeting will be held at the Metropolitan Hotel at one o'clock today (Sunday), in order to form a California Regiment. None but men accustomed to work are requested to attend. Over $25,000 is on hand to equip the Regiment and sustain them."[1] At the hour named, the Californians assembled in a large room in the Metropolitan Hotel. They were called to order by J. C. Birdseye, a banker from California's Nevada County who had come east in hopes of obtaining an appointment from Lincoln as collector of the Port of San Francisco. Others in the audience included such prominent names as William Tell Coleman, the leader of the Vigilance Committees organized in San Francisco in 1851 and 1856, and Cornelius K. Garrison, a powerful steamboat owner who had been mayor of San Francisco from 1853 to 1854 and now headed up the Pacific Mail Steamship Company. Another member of the audience was Oregon's newly elected U.S. senator Edward D. Baker. Birdseye said that the object of the meeting was to enable Californians to "do their duty, equally with the men of other States, in response to the call of the Chief of the Nation," adding that "California would ever be true to the Union."

Baker was called upon to speak. He had addressed an audience estimated at a hundred thousand in Union Square the previous Sunday and had a hoarse voice, so he "could not do much talking." But he told the audience that it was "time for action," that the country "demanded fighting men," and that the only question was "how many men and how much money could be provided." For his own part, Baker said he "would do his duty." Some had said that California was not true to the Union. "If she is not," he said, "we will make her so."[2]

As far away from California as New York was, the Metropolitan Hotel meeting had some real implications for the Pacific state and for the Union, for the armed forces that came under Lincoln's command after his inauguration were vastly inadequate to the nation's looming crisis. The regular U.S. Army included only 16,367 officers and men, 1,108 of whom were commissioned officers.[3] Winfield Scott, John E. Wool, David E. Twiggs, and William S. Harney were the only general officers. The aging and corpulent Scott, then general in chief of the army, held the rank of brevet lieutenant general, while Wool, who was seventy-nine, Twiggs, who was seventy-one, and Harney, who was sixty, were brigadier generals. They were old men still in service because the military had no retirement system at the time.

California was situated in the Department of the Pacific, which was headquartered in the Presidio of San Francisco, a sprawling military installation overlooking San Francisco Bay and the Golden Gate that dated back to the days of the Spanish and Mexican occupation of the state. The Department had been created in December 1860 when the secretary of war in Washington DC, combined the two former departments of Oregon and California into one. Embracing more than five hundred thousand square miles, the new department was bounded on the east by the Rocky Mountains, on the west by the Pacific Ocean, on the north by the Canadian border, and on the south by Mexico. Within it were a variety of forts, blockhouses, and arsenals, some of which were permanent

THE FIRST CALIFORNIAN

installations and others only temporary. Fort Colville, in the far northeastern part of Washington Territory, was the most northerly, while Fort Yuma, at the confluence of the Gila and Colorado Rivers on the border between California and what was soon to become the Arizona Territory, was the most southerly. The department was manned by a total of 2,245 men who were divided into five regiments, three of which were infantry, one of cavalry, and one of artillery. Most were young men of pro-Southern sympathies, although some were strong Union supporters and even some were immigrants from foreign countries.[4]

Brevet Brig. Gen. Albert Sidney Johnston was commander of the Department of the Pacific. Born in Kentucky in 1803 and educated at West Point, he had fought for Texas in its war of independence from Mexico and, for his efforts, won appointment as the Texas Republic's secretary of war. After Texas was admitted to the Union in 1844, Johnston returned to his service in the U.S. Army, leading a regiment of soldiers during the army's invasion of Mexico and serving as commander of the army's Department of Texas from 1856 to 1858. During the last days of James Buchanan's presidential administration, Johnston was appointed to head up the newly reorganized Department of the Pacific.

Johnston arrived in San Francisco on January 15, 1861. He was nearly sixty years old but made a strong physical impression. Asbury Harpending, a young man from Kentucky with secessionist ties, described him as "a blond giant of a man with a mass of heavy yellow hair untouched by age."[5] He was a loyal officer, but he had strong sympathies with the South, most especially with Texas, and did not want to remain in command in San Francisco if Texas joined the other secessionist states. While in San Francisco, he garrisoned Fort Point, the massive fort fronting the Golden Gate entrance to San Francisco Bay that had been built under the direction of Henry Halleck, convinced that it could protect the city and the state beyond from Rebel attack. He brought ten thousand rifled muskets from the Benicia Arsenal to Alcatraz Island, a strategic location in the bay. He also rebuffed the proposals of Southern sympathizers that he join in their efforts to take California out of the Union. "If you want to fight," he told them, "go South."[6] Because others did not know of Johnston's continuing loyalty to the Union, however, rumors swirled through the Department of the Pacific and Washington that he could not be trusted. When James Nesmith, a Democrat who served alongside Edward Baker as one of Oregon's U.S. senators, told Lincoln's secretary of state William Seward that Johnston's loyalty could not be depended on, Seward passed the message on to Winfield Scott. Scott then ordered Edwin V. Sumner, who had recently been promoted to the rank of brigadier general, to proceed to San Francisco and take command from Johnston. In secret session, Lincoln and his cabinet approved the order. Tall and white-bearded, the sixty-four-year-old Sumner sailed to California via the Panama route. He arrived in San Francisco on April 24. Texas had already seceded, and Johnston had forwarded his resignation to Washington.[7]

Born in Boston in 1797, Sumner had been commissioned in 1819 as a second lieutenant in the Regular Army's Second Infantry. He became a captain of Dragoons in 1833 and, promoted to major, served under Scott during the war with Mexico. He served briefly as acting governor of the New Mexico Territory, then commanded Fort Leavenworth in Kansas and, in February 1861, accompanied president-elect Abraham Lincoln on his railroad journey from Springfield to Washington.[8]

After Johnston's resignation was accepted, he traveled south to Los Angeles, where his brother-in-law, John Strother Griffin, was a physician and ardent Southern sympathizer. He then headed eastward, following the route of the Butterfield Overland Mail through the southwestern territories and Texas. With his Union war duties over, he soon joined the Confederate military, where Jefferson Davis appointed him to the rank of full general and placed him in charge of the large Confederate Department No. 2. He was one of the Confederacy's most promising officers, but he lost his life in the terrific fighting at Shiloh, Tennessee, in April 1862.[9]

Johnston was not the only man from California who joined the Confederate forces. Horace Bell, an Indiana-born, Kentucky-educated adventurer, soldier, attorney, and newspaper publisher

THE FIRST CALIFORNIAN

who had moved to California in 1852, later wrote that Los Angeles County furnished the rebellion with "colonels, majors and captains without end, besides about two hundred and fifty of the rank and file who were . . . sent over the desert to the Confederate forces in Texas."[10] Bell knew a lot about pro- and antisecessionist sentiment in California, for he had served for a while with the disastrous pro-Southern filibustering expedition that a man named William Walker had led into Nicaragua in the mid-1850s, and had become a scout under Union army general Lew Wallace after the Civil War began. The anti-Lincoln and pro-Confederate *Los Angeles Star* confirmed much of what Bell wrote, publishing the names of more than twenty prominent men who by November 1862 had left California either to fight for secession or lend it moral support in the South.[11]

Responding to the call issued at the April 21 meeting at the Metropolitan Hotel in New York, a volunteer regiment was soon formed, and Edward D. Baker was named as its commander. Called the First California, or sometimes just "The California," it included men from various states, not just the western state.

Before very long, Baker's command of the regiment would make history, and affect Lincoln personally.

The Office Seekers

LINCOLN'S DUTY TO SELECT MILITARY AND NAVAL LEADERS who would help him win the war was not his only executive obligation. Filling civilian offices was another, and may well have been the most exhausting—and aggravating—of all. Men who were in California, who came from California, or who sought to go there were among the many hundreds who sought appointments from Lincoln. Some received them while many others did not, due not only to Lincoln's good judgment but also to circumstances that neither he nor the office seekers had any control over.

The appointment system that prevailed in Lincoln's time, known as patronage, was later subjected to heated and, in many ways, richly deserved criticism.[1] But there were some arguments in favor of it. One was that giving federal offices to loyal members of the president's political party would help unite it and benefit those who supported him. Another was that it would remind supporters that they were rewarded for their party loyalty and penalized for disloyalty. The Republican Party in 1861 was still in its infancy, with members who came from different backgrounds. Many had been Whigs. Many had been members of the Free Soil Party, or Democrats with free-soil leanings. Some were staunch abolitionists, while others had doubts about slavery's future but were willing to postpone its end until secession was put down and the Union was saved. Most were strong Union supporters. Lincoln knew the diversity in his party and understood the importance of trying to keep it together. But he also knew about the drawbacks of the patronage system and was willing to endure it, but not to love it.

When Lincoln became president, he had to replace about eleven hundred civil servants.[2] The number he had responsibility for in California is difficult to ascertain, although one historian determined that there were about a hundred fifty in the branch treasury in California, more than twenty in the Customs House in San Francisco, hundreds in the post office department scattered through the state, and others in the General Land Office, the Indian Affairs Office, and the federal courts.[3] Federal judges were not subject to removal when a new president took office, although the marshals, deputy marshals, United States district attorneys, and clerks who worked with them were. Lincoln, of course, knew that applicants for federal offices had to be honest, trustworthy, and competent to perform their duties. But he was also aware that his supporters—members of Congress, governors, and party officials—should be consulted, for their advice and counsel could be valuable, and ignoring them could be dangerous. Politicians knew how to play the game of politics; they knew how to reward their friends, their supporters, even their relatives; and they also knew how to punish their enemies, their opponents, and everybody else who wished them no good. Lincoln was a politician. He knew the rules of the game and knew he had to play by them.

As he began the process of filling offices, Lincoln tried to weed out disloyal civil servants, as well as those who were corrupt. He was not always successful in this effort, as his initial appointment of Simon Cameron of Pennsylvania as his secretary of war soon proved. Once in office, Cameron revealed himself to be as corrupt (or nearly as corrupt) as his critics claimed him to be, and in January 1862 Lincoln sent him off to St. Petersburg as the U.S. ambassador to Russia, and named Edwin M. Stanton, who served as U.S. attorney general under James Buchanan, to replace him. Stanton was a Democrat and high-powered attorney who had battled Henry Halleck in the litigation over California's New Almaden Quicksilver Mine. He soon proved that honesty was not always incompatible with ability, nor Democratic Party membership with service to the government, for he revealed himself to be honest, able, and dedicated to his job.

Lincoln was besieged in the White House, often at all times of the day, by office seekers. They approached him in the vestibule, in the anteroom to his private office, even while he was walking on the White House grounds. Many believed that they had earned their right to appointment by supporting Republicans in the election. The pay offered for most of the jobs was not impressive. The head of the Custom House in San Francisco, called the Customs Collector, received a salary of $7,900 a year, one of the highest. Under him were three deputy collectors who received $3,120 a year, and under them some seventeen other employees who received from $1,080 to $2,500.[4] These salaries would not make a man rich. If those clamoring for government posts would make the same effort to acquire other honorable jobs, one newspaper wrote that "they would die happier and wealthier men."[5] On one of his walks from the White House to the War Department, Lincoln was accosted by a man who claimed he was responsible for Lincoln's presidential nomination and, for that, he deserved to be rewarded. "So you think you made me President?" Lincoln asked him. "Yes, Mr. President, under Providence, I think I did." "Well," Lincoln replied, "it's a pretty mess you've got me into. But I forgive you."[6]

Edward Baker spent a lot of time in the White House in the early days of Lincoln's administration. He went there on official business—he was, after all, a United States senator from the state of Oregon and a loyal Republican. But as one of Lincoln's closest personal friends and a man for whom Mary Lincoln had special affection, he was also a frequent social guest. He had spent much of the 1850s in San Francisco practicing law, but also attempting to raise political support for the newly organized Republican Party in that state. He campaigned so vigorously for the new party there that he was called the "gallant champion of the Republican cause."

When Lincoln took office in Washington, California had not a single Republican representative in Congress. Its two senators,

William Gwin and James A. McDougall, were both Democrats, as were its two members of the House of Representatives. There were important Republicans in the state. The most notable was Leland Stanford, the Republican who lost the election for governor in 1859. Baker had been considered for the Republican nomination that year, but withdrew in favor of Stanford. Stanford now seemed to be the favorite candidate for governor in the election looming in September 1861.[7]

Stanford was in Washington in March 1861 when Lincoln took office. He attended the inaugural ceremonies with other Republicans and heard Baker introduce Lincoln to the assembled crowd. He also went to the White House to make recommendations for filling federal offices and attend to some of his personal business. Another Republican who was in Washington at the same time was James Simonton, a newspaper editor who had first tried to establish a Whig newspaper in San Francisco in 1849, then went back to New York and Washington to work on other newspapers. He purchased an interest in San Francisco's widely read *Bulletin* in 1859 but ran it largely from Washington. Simonton argued that Baker had no right to make recommendations for appointments in California because he was now an Oregonian and not a Californian. Simonton believed that Republicans who still called California their home had a much stronger right to give Lincoln recommendations. He also harbored suspicions about Baker's integrity—or at least claimed to. Simonton said that Baker was careless with money, sometimes even with other people's money, and that this would disqualify him from making recommendations to Lincoln.

Lincoln heard about the disagreement between Baker and Simonton and seemed to be puzzled by it. He decided that it would be wise to have a meeting in the White House where both sides of the dispute could express their views. Simonton and his followers came at about nine in the morning on March 30, 1861, and were surprised to discover that Baker was already there. He had been invited to have breakfast with the president and to meet those who had been so critical of him. Stanford also attended, but did not take an active part in the controversy. He was aware that he would be running for governor again later in the year and wanted to remain aloof from factional disputes.

The first man who spoke was Joseph A. Nunes, a Republican attorney from San Francisco. He read a paper that said that if Lincoln would appoint the men that he and his supporters recommended, it would assure that California would remain Republican. After he finished, he left the paper on the table in front of Lincoln. Simonton then began to speak in what one of the witnesses to the meeting, a man later identified as David J. Staples, called a "most violent and vituperative manner." Simonton read from a paper that said that Baker was an associate of gamblers and "all that class of persons." Baker sat at the table close to Lincoln, who listened attentively, but as the reading continued a "dark frown" began to gather on the president's face. Simonton's paper also included a list of the men he believed should be put in office and those who endorsed his position. Lincoln recognized one name on the list and turned to Baker and said, "Why, Baker, that is one of your friends." When Simonton finished speaking, he laid his paper on the table. Lincoln then asked, "Is this paper for me?" "Yes. it is for you, Mr. President," Simonton answered, "but I may want to make some emendations." "If it is for me," Lincoln replied, "let me have it now."

Lincoln then took up Nunes's paper and said, "This paper seems to be respectful in tone, and I will keep it for further reference."[8] But taking up Simonton's, he said, "This one I will burn in the presence of the man who wrote it." He then reached out his arm and thrust the paper into the nearby fireplace. Staples later remembered: "You can imagine more about that scene from what I have told you than I could undertake to sketch or state to you in detail. The president of the United States, insulted by the wanton abuse of his old-time friend—the eloquent and gallant Baker—resented it as a personal affair." Baker was sitting next to Staples and whispered, "Staples, can't you say something in reply?" Staples immediately said, "Mr. President," but Lincoln put up his hand and said, "Not a word, not a word. I don't want to hear a word. I have known Colonel Baker twenty-five years. I have known him better than any of you know him, and I don't want any defense of him from anyone." Lincoln continued, "If any of you Californians other than those who have spoken want to make any request of me, I want to hear it now." Staples recalled that no one said a word. Then, after a pause, Lincoln said, "Now I have a request to make of you. I want you to go home. You will be needed in California— far more needed there than here."[9]

Lincoln later explained why he had burned the paper that Simonton had given him. According to Noah Brooks, a California-based reporter who later became one of Lincoln's best friends, Lincoln said, "The paper was an unjust attack upon my dearest personal friend, Ned Baker, who was at that time a member of my family. The delegation did not know what they were talking about when they made him responsible, almost abusively, for what I had done, or proposed to do. They told me that that was my paper, to do with as I liked. I could not trust myself to reply in words: I was so angry. That was the whole case."[10]

Despite this angry encounter, Lincoln convened another meeting between Baker and his adversaries the same afternoon.[11] It was an entente cordiale, not completely satisfactory nor wholly objectionable to either side. Perhaps Lincoln regretted the emotion he displayed that morning, as he often did after he had showed anger.

Charles Maltby, the man Lincoln had worked so closely with in New Salem in 1831 and 1832, was one of the men who hoped to receive an appointment from the president. Maltby had been living in California since 1849, but he remembered his early experiences with Lincoln and expressed his wish to obtain an appointment. Lincoln rewarded him with two offices. One was the relatively minor post of Collector of Internal Revenue for a tax district north of San Francisco, which he appointed him to in 1862, and the other—more important—was the office of Superintendent of Indian Affairs for the entire state, which he received shortly before Lincoln's assassination in 1865.[12]

Maltby was still friendly with the president and visited him in Washington. On one of his visits, his wife, Charlotte, called on the president and obtained his signature on three copies of the Emancipation Proclamation.[13] Maltby himself testified in Congress about the official conduct of Edward Baker's son-in-law Robert J. Stevens, who had been appointed Superintendent of the San Francisco Branch Mint. Stevens had been accused of corruption, and Maltby believed that he was guilty. He hoped that he would be appointed to succeed Stevens, but when Lincoln heard the request, he demurred. "Good gracious!" he said. "Why didn't he ask to be Secretary of the Treasury and have done with it. . . . I never thought Maltby had anything more than average ability when we were young men together—now he wants to be Superintendent of the Mint!" No, he would not be Superintendent of the Mint, but after Stevens resigned and another man named Robert B. Swain was appointed to succeed him, Maltby was appointed Superintendent of Indian Affairs for California.[14]

Many Californians traveled to Washington in the hope of advising Lincoln about federal appointments. He listened to all the advice but was surprised and annoyed by the differences he heard. "Why can you not agree?" he asked the men who came to him. "Where is the difference between you in reference to your efforts to save the Union, and in the support of my administration? I see none." He continued by saying that the Republicans he had already appointed had been faithful in the discharge of their duties and would not be removed. "Future appointments," he said, "will be made from those who are capable and have been and are faithful to the Constitution and the Union, and without favor and in justice to all. Vacancies will be filled and appointments made as the public service demands."

As they retired from their meeting with the president, the men who had approached him had very different views about the significance of what he said. Years later, Maltby summarized their views. "Our mission is a failure," one man thought. "I guess the president is about right," another thought. And a third thought, "This settles the federal question."[15]

Perhaps they were all right, but didn't yet know it.

8

The Judges

LINCOLN'S RESPONSIBILITY FOR APPOINTING FEDERAL judges was much less time-consuming than his duty to fill other offices, for there were fewer judicial positions and not nearly as many applicants who sought them. It was a serious obligation, however, for the power of the federal judiciary was in some ways as great as that of Congress and the president. As specified in the Constitution, judges may hold their offices for life—or at least until they resign or are removed upon impeachment. The United States was in 1861, as it is now, divided into districts and circuits in which the federal judges perform their duties. There were judges in each of the districts, and Supreme Court justices then had the responsibility to travel through the circuits and preside over judicial proceedings, often alongside the district judges but sometimes alone. California, however, was different from the rest of the country. It was so far distant from the centers of power in the East and Middle West that Supreme Court justices could not conveniently "ride circuit" there. It took a long time, sometimes several weeks, to travel to the western state, and as much time to return, so it was deemed appropriate to have a circuit court judge in California who did not also sit on the Supreme Court.[1] He was often referred to as a "special" circuit court judge because he was the only one in the whole country who did not also belong to the nation's highest court.

There were two federal districts in California when Lincoln became president and two judges who presided over them: the

New York–born Ogden Hoffman Jr. in the Northernn District and the South Carolina–born Isaac S. K. Ogier in the southern. Hoffman had been appointed by the Whig president Millard Fillmore in 1851. Ogier had been appointed by the Democratic president Franklin Pierce in 1853 and took office in 1854. The circuit judge in California was the Georgia-born Matthew Hall McAllister, who had been appointed by President Pierce in 1855.

The federal courts in California were established in 1850. The districts were divided by an east–west line running midway between the north and the south. Northern District sessions were to be held in San Francisco, San Jose, Stockton, and Sacramento, while those of the Southern District were to be held in Monterey and Los Angeles. It was obvious from the outset that the Northern district would be busier than the Southern, so the annual salary for its judge was set at $3,500 and that of the Southern District judge at only $2,800. The duties normally exercised by circuit judges in the rest of the country were to be exercised by the district judges concurrently.[2]

Hoffman had served steadily from his appointment in 1851 until Lincoln's inauguration. Born in Goshen, New York, in 1822, he had graduated from Columbia College before going on to Harvard Law School, where he received his law degree in 1842. He came to California in 1850 and began a busy law practice in San Francisco. His appointment as district judge owed much to the eastern political connections of his father, Ogden Hoffman Sr., who was friendly with Daniel Webster and William Henry Seward. Hoffman was a skillful lawyer, a hard worker, and the principal judge called on to review land grant decisions of the U.S. Land Commission.[3]

Ogier had not served as long as Hoffman. His predecessor was James McHall Jones, a Kentucky-born attorney who had practiced law in Louisiana before coming to California in 1849, serving as a delegate to the state constitutional convention that year, and then becoming the U.S. attorney for the southern judicial district.[4] Jones's health was poor, and he died in San Jose shortly after his appointment as judge. The Southern District judgeship was apparently empty until Ogier was confirmed to fill it. A Confederate sympathizer, he left office shortly after the formation of the Confederacy and was replaced in August 1861, when Lincoln's attorney general Edward Bates recommended Fletcher Matthews Haight for the Southern District post.[5] Born in New York, Haight had been a member of the New York state legislature and mayor of the city of Rochester. After moving to Missouri, where Bates knew him, he became a successful attorney. He served in Southern California until his death in 1866. Originally a Free Soil Democrat who supported Lincoln's presidential candidacy, he later broke with him on racial issues. For twenty years after Haight died, the Southern District bench was unfilled.[6]

A significant change in California's federal court system was made in 1855 when a special circuit court was established and Matthew Hall McAllister was appointed to fill it.[7] McAlister was a Democrat and a slaveholder from Georgia who had been born in Savannah in 1800, served as U.S. attorney there, and pursued a political career that included service in the Georgia state senate, as a Superior Court judge, and several terms as mayor of Savannah. He was a candidate for governor of Georgia in 1845 but was narrowly defeated. His son Hall McAllister had come to California in 1849, established a law practice in San Francisco, and won a reputation as one of the city's most successful, and highest paid, lawyers. When he heard from his son about the success he was enjoying in California, the senior McAllister decided to move to California, arriving there in 1850 and joining his son's law practice. He went back to Georgia in 1853 to seek election as one of the state's U.S. senators, but was again unsuccessful. After a European sojourn, he returned to San Francisco, where in 1855 he received his appointment from President Pierce as judge of the newly created circuit court.[8] His jurisdiction extended over both the Northern and Southern Districts of California.[9] Judge McAllister made an impression in San Francisco, not only because he was a good lawyer but also because of the social prominence he enjoyed. He had another son besides Hall McAllister: Ward McAllister, a budding lawyer who joined his father and brother in San Francisco before going on to New York, where he became the celebrated arbiter of mid-nineteenth-century New York society. (It was Ward McAllister who coined the term "The Four Hundred" to describe the number of people in elite New York society who "really mattered.")[10] During Matthew Hall McAllister's time as judge of the U.S. Circuit Court in San Francisco, he was regarded as the most powerful judge in all of the West and his son Hall was regarded as the most admired attorney in the city.[11] McAllister continued to serve in San Francisco until 1862, when his weakening health persuaded him to ask for a leave of absence, and nine months later he resigned.[12] The circuit court position in California was now open.

Lincoln sought advice as to who he should select to succeed McAllister. He consulted his cabinet members, knowledgeable congressmen and senators, practicing lawyers, and aspirants for the position. Judge Hoffman was considered a likely candidate. He was, after all, a skillful judge, loyal to the Union, a Whig who had joined the new Republican Party, and he had worked hard for a dozen years as the district judge. Another man who was considered a qualified candidate was Stephen Johnson Field, who was then serving as chief justice of the California Supreme Court.

Born in Connecticut in 1816, Field was the sixth son of a distinguished Congregationalist minister. He moved to Massachusetts with his family while still a boy and as a teenager was sent to travel in Greece and Turkey. Returning home, he studied at Williams College, where he graduated in 1837. After reading law in Albany, New York, and practicing for a while in New York City with his older brother David Dudley Field, he left for California in 1849. Uninterested in gold mining, he practiced law in the busy mining supply town of Marysville before serving as an alcalde, winning election to the state legislature, and in 1857 being elected to the third seat on the California Supreme Court.[13] In 1859 he became chief justice when the virulently pro-Southern Chief Justice David Terry resigned to fight a duel with the Free Soil Democrat U.S. senator David C. Broderick. Field continued to serve as chief justice after Lincoln was elected in 1860, after the formation of the Confederate States in 1861, and up to the time that Matthew Hall McAllister stepped down from his circuit court seat in 1863.

Field's legal skill and judicial experience were major reasons why he was considered as a candidate to succeed McAllister. But he had other attributes. He was a scrappy man with strong views and an assertive personality. In later years, he admitted that he knew nothing of Mexican laws when he was alcalde, "but I knew that the people had elected me to act as magistrate and looked to me for the preservation of order and the settlement of disputes; and I did my best that they should not be disappointed."[14]

After he had served as alcalde for only two months, the state legislature abolished that office and created a new system of district courts. A Texan named William Turner was appointed judge of the court, and Field retired to private practice. But Turner proved to be an uneducated and hard-drinking man who ran his court like a tyrant. He engaged almost continuously in angry confrontations with Field and other lawyers, refused to listen to informed statements of the law, and imposed ridiculous fines and even sent attorneys to jail, forcing them to use court process to obtain their release. His courtroom combat continued without apparent cessation, and included an exchange of newspaper articles in which Turner's opponents wrote: "Judge Turner is a man of depraved tastes, of vulgar habits, of an ungovernable temper, reckless of truth when his passions are excited, and grossly incompetent to discharge the duties of his office." Years later, Field wrote, "Unfortunately the statement was perfectly true."[15]

Field took his pistols with him when he went to the state capital in early 1851 as assemblyman from the Marysville district. He later recalled that fully two-thirds of the members of the assembly came armed with pistols or knives, or frequently both.[16] As a member of the Judiciary Committee, he began to display his knowledge of American law. He introduced legislation creating civil and criminal codes for the state, modeled on those adopted in New York with the guidance of his brother David Dudley Field. He also introduced a bill calling for Turner's impeachment and removal from office. There was not enough time to hold a trial on the impeachment charges, however, so the assembly let the matter drop with Turner's retreat to a far Northernn District court where, as one assemblyman said, "there are only grizzly bears and Indians."[17]

While Field was in the legislature, a heavy-drinking assemblyman named Benjamin F. Moore made highly abusive statements about him on the assembly floor. A lawyer who had been a delegate to the state constitutional convention of 1849, Moore was a former Texan who had what the historian Hubert Howe Bancroft called the "bowie-knife manners of that borderland."[18] Field replied to Moore in a sober but defiant manner, calling on him to apologize "or give me the satisfaction one gentleman has the right to demand of another." Field knew that dueling was banned by the California constitution and that it barred convicted duelers from holding public office.[19] But he was not sure that the provision was self-enforcing, that is, that a duelist could be barred from office without a court conviction. He asked various members of the assembly to act as his second, which they declined to do because of the constitutional provision. Field walked into the Senate chamber one evening and encountered David Broderick, then the speaker pro tem of that body. Broderick asked him to tell him all about his dispute with Moore, then asked him to write out a note challenging Moore, which he delivered. Moore declined to engage in a duel because he was planning to run for Congress and knew that that would bar him from office. He first offered to engage in a street fight with Field but then said he would have nothing more to do with the matter. In response, Field made an assembly speech in which he called Moore a liar and a coward and renewed his challenge. This time Moore rose to offer an apology for the statements he had made. Field later said that the apology "was full, ample, and satisfactory; and of course with that the matter ended."[20]

Stephen Field had always been a Democrat, even after David Dudley Field left the party to become a Republican. David Dudley Field, like Lincoln, opposed the extension of slavery into the western territories and was one of the distinguished New Yorkers who sat on the stage of New York's Cooper Union in February 1860 when Lincoln delivered the speech that raised expectations that he might become president of the United States.[21] David Dudley Field was close to Salmon P. Chase and supported his presidential candidacy at the Republican convention in Chicago, but after it became clear that Chase was out of the race, he threw his support to Lincoln. After Chase became Lincoln's secretary of the treasury, David Dudley Field continued to act as one of Lincoln's informal advisers. All of these reasons made it clear that Lincoln would consider Stephen Field as a possible Supreme Court justice.

Stephen Field made it clear in his political campaigns that he was not an abolitionist and that he staunchly defended the right of individual states to decide whether they should have slavery; he said that federal officials had "no more right to meddle with slavery in the different States, than they have with slavery in Turkey."[22] This did not differ much from Lincoln's (and the Republican Party's) own position on that issue, for they opposed the spread of slavery into the western territories but believed that the Constitution forbade the federal government from trying to abolish it within states.[23] Field's political views on other issues were not well known in Washington. It was clear, however, that he supported the Union, for in October 1861 he declared his position on that issue in one of the first messages sent over the newly finished transcontinental telegraph. As chief justice of California, he sent the message to President Lincoln in the temporary absence of the state's governor, John G. Downey. In it he declared that the telegraph would strengthen "the attachment which binds both the East & West to the Union" and help the people "express their loyalty to that Union & their determination to stand by the Government in this its day of trial."[24]

Asked if he would be willing to replace McAllister on California's Circuit Court, Field said that he would rather retain his position as the highest state judge in California. But "if a new justice were added to the Supreme Court of the United States," he added, "I would accept the office if tendered to me."[25] Senators still pressed Lincoln to nominate him to the circuit court, and he did so, believing that a new Supreme Court seat would soon be created and that Field would be in line to fill it. Before the circuit court nomination could be confirmed, however, Congress created the tenth Supreme Court seat and a new judicial circuit that included California and Oregon.[26] The congressional delegations of both states unanimously urged Lincoln to nominate Field to the new position, as did Governor Stanford.[27]

If these recommendations were not enough to convince Lincoln that Field should be nominated, the wishes of David Dudley Field may have been the clincher. According to Henry Martyn Field, a New Yorker named John A. C. Gray, a mutual friend of David Dudley Field and Lincoln, personally called on the president to discuss the nomination. Gray found Lincoln "agreed entirely in the fitness of Judge Field," but he had one question to ask: "Does David want his brother to have it?" When Gray answered yes, the president responded, "Then he shall have it."[28] After the nomination was discussed in the president's cabinet, Lincoln's secretary of the Navy Gideon Welles wrote in his diary: "Appointments considered yesterday and to-day. Generally conceded that Field of California was the man for the Supreme Court."[29] On March 6 Lincoln sent Field's nomination to the Senate, and on March 10 it was unanimously confirmed.[30] Traveling from California to Washington, Field was able to take his seat on the Supreme Court on December 7, 1863.

On October 12, 1864, Roger Taney, the eighty-seven-year-old chief justice of the Supreme Court and author of the reviled opinion in *Dred Scott v. Sandford*, died, creating an important vacancy. Lincoln won his second election as president three weeks and six days later, on November 8. Following his victory, Lincoln was nearly deluged with letters and telegrams recommending the man to succeed Taney. Salmon P. Chase, who had served as secretary of the treasury during the early years of Lincoln's tenure and helped avert a financial catastrophe as the war roared on, was one of the best known. But there were many other suggestions. Postmaster General Montgomery Blair was recommended by senator William E. Chandler of New Hampshire. Maine's Republican U.S.

senator William P. Fessenden was recommended by vice president Hannibal Hamlin of Maine. John Jay of New York was recommended by New Hampshire's radical senator John P. Hale. Secretary of State Seward was recommended by senator Benjamin H. Brewster of Pennsylvania.[31] Lincoln waited eight weeks before announcing his choice. On December 6, the day following the opening of the Thirty-Eighth Congress, he sent a formal nomination of Chase to the Senate. The nomination was considered the same day and unanimously confirmed. Chase was now chief justice of the Supreme Court.[32]

Destiny's Land

AMONG THE MANY RESPONSIBILITIES THAT FELL TO LINCOLN
when he assumed the presidency was the proper administration,
disposition, and preservation of federal land, a large part of which
lay within the new state of California. Extending approximately
250 miles from east to west and 770 miles from north to south,
California included 163,696 square miles of land area, making it
geographically the second largest state in the Union. (Only Texas,
with an area of 268,597 square miles, was larger.)[1] Its shoreline was
1,294 miles long, with an additional 291 miles around the edges
of its offshore islands. It was a truly vast area, which became the
responsibility of the United States government to defend, protect,
and properly administer. As president, Lincoln shouldered much
of that responsibility.

The war with Mexico had been formally concluded when the
Treaty of Guadalupe Hidalgo was signed on February 2, 1848, in
the Villa de Guadalupe, a town just north of Mexico City. Devout
Mexicans considered it the most sacred spot on earth because the
Virgin Mary had appeared there in 1531 and asked that a church
be built to commemorate her visit.[2] Ratified by the U.S. Senate
on March 10 of the same year, the treaty provided for the conclusion of the war between the United States and Mexico, the des-
ignation of an international border between the two countries,
and the disposition of the vast expanses of land acquired by the
United States—land amounting to about half of the territory then
embraced by the Mexican republic.

Article VIII of the treaty provided that property belonging to Mexicans in the acquired territory would be "inviolably respected," and Article IX provided that the Mexicans would be "maintained and protected in the free enjoyment of their liberty and property." But it was not easy to "respect" and to "maintain and protect" that land. As many of the new settlers pointed out, the descriptions of Spanish and Mexican land grants were often vague, and documentary records showing how the land was acquired were often fragmentary—sometimes entirely missing. Under the Spanish and Mexican system, it was also possible for individuals to obtain more than just one grant so that when the grants were added together, individuals, or families of individuals, claimed ownership of immense land areas, sometimes amounting to hundreds of thousands of acres. Although Mexican law, derived in large part from Spanish traditions, was comfortable with such large holdings, many Americans were not. Rushing to California after the discovery of gold, they made it clear that they regarded the huge Spanish and Mexican ranchos as un-American. In the words of Stephen J. Field, the American settlers regarded them as "a monstrous wrong to which they could not be reconciled."[3] Was not the recognition of large Spanish and Mexican land grants limiting the "greatness" of Americans and checking the "fulfillment" of their "manifest destiny to overspread the continent"?[4] California had become an American state. It was "destiny's land." And many of the new arrivals believed that the land there was free for the taking.[5]

The Mexicans who claimed to be the owners of California land were typically described as "grantees," or "rancheros," because most of the land held under Mexican titles functioned as cattle ranches. Not all of the so-called grantees or rancheros were Spanish or Mexican natives, however. Many were native-born Americans who came to California before the outbreak of the war between the two countries, married into Spanish or Mexican families, acquired Mexican citizenship, and thereafter received land grants from the Mexican government. Some were from South America. Others were English, Scotch, Irish, French, or German natives. One of the most prominent was Johann August (later John) Sutter, a German

Swiss emigrant who came to California in the 1830s and received a grant to a vast expanse of land in the Sacramento Valley. A small number of the grantees, called neophytes, were native peoples who had been instructed by the mission fathers, embraced Christianity, and acquired Mexican citizenship.[6]

The holders of Mexican land grants believed, or at least hoped, that their ownership would be protected in the way that property is normally protected in law-abiding countries; that is, by the courts, who would respond to any complaints against their authenticity, examine all the evidence and applicable law, and either uphold their ownership in accordance with the Treaty of Guadalupe Hidalgo or declare it invalid, as they did with most other forms of land ownership.[7] Many Americans, however, wanted a system that would give them greater opportunities to attack the large landowners.

With the declared goal of settling the disputed land ownership claims, Congress in 1851 created a three-member Board of Land Commissioners and gave it legal authority to receive claims and decide which were valid and which were not. Decisions were to be made on the basis of the treaty, the law of nations, the laws, usages, and customs of the government from which the claim was derived (i.e., either Spain or Mexico), principles of equity, and decisions of the United States Supreme Court, so far as they were applicable. Mexicans who claimed ownership of lands were given two years within which to present their claims. If they did so, the commission considered their claims and confirmed or denied them. If they did not do so, their ownership lapsed and their lands were open to public settlement. In either case, the commission's decisions could be appealed to the United States District Court and even to the United States Supreme Court. When a final decision was made confirming a claim, a patent from the United States would issue to the successful claimant.[8]

Many of the claimants had to hire high-priced attorneys to present their cases before the Land Commission, before the U.S. District Court, and ultimately before the U.S. Supreme Court in Washington. Henry W. Halleck, the West Point–trained military officer who was to serve as Lincoln's commanding general during the Civil War, was a busy land-grant attorney in California during the 1850s. He and his firm of Halleck, Peachy, and Billings, which he headed up, represented many claimants before the commission and the District Court; and, when they did, they charged what Halleck's biographer John F. Marszalek has said were "steep" fees.[9] When land claims were appealed to the Supreme Court in Washington, an additional corps of even higher-priced lawyers was ready to represent the claimants. Reverdy Johnson, a distinguished lawyer and politician in the nation's capital, was one of the busiest. Johnson had served as a U.S. senator from Maryland from 1845–1849 and as U.S. attorney general under president Zachary Taylor from 1849 to 1850, and he would again hold a U.S. Senate seat from Maryland from 1863 to 1868. He also happened to be the attorney for the prevailing party in the controversial case of *Dred Scott v. Sandford* argued before the Supreme Court in 1857. Historian Christian G. Fritz, a careful student of legal practice in early California, has written that Johnson "enjoyed a lucrative law practice arguing appeals in California land-grant cases."[10]

Attorney fees, travel costs, and years of delay wore down the endurance of many of the holders of Spanish and Mexican land grants, forcing them to find potential buyers who would pay them a fraction of the real worth of the property they claimed. Men of prominence in both the legal profession and California's political life acquired some of the old Spanish and Mexican titles by purchase from the original grantees. Halleck himself acquired interests in California land grants. One was a portion of the sprawling Rancho Nicasio in Marin County, north of San Francisco, that included 30,848.85 acres.[11]

Because of the difficulties that many of those claiming title to the Spanish and Mexican land grants faced in proving their ownership, the Land Commission was subject to a lot of anger and criticism. Some of the unsuccessful claimants charged that the real purpose of the commission was to deprive them of the property that the Treaty of Guadalupe Hidalgo had guaranteed them. But many of those who challenged the grants held quite different opinions. They regarded the commission with respect, believing that it was preventing the Spanish and Mexican grantees from monopolizing California land and depriving new settlers of the opportunity to open it to farming or mining development.

The Land Commission began its hearings in San Francisco in 1852 and formally concluded them in 1856. During that time, a total of 813 claims were filed and 604 confirmed.[12] Many continued to be litigated during Lincoln's presidency. Lincoln himself was asked by at least one of the litigants to intervene in an appeal and was offered affidavits claiming there was fraud in the decision of the case. He declined to do so, explaining that he had no appellate or supervisory jurisdiction over the claims, especially since the United States had no interest in them. They were in the courts, and there they had to be decided.[13]

Not all of the Mexican land grants were used for cattle raising. There were also grants for pueblos, or town sites, for missions, and for presidios, or military installations. One of the most important land grants, and one that caused Lincoln the most concern during his presidency, was the one that embraced the New Almaden mine, south of San Francisco. It contained rich deposits of the red ore called cinnabar that produced quicksilver that was invaluable in the refining of gold and that a Mexican cavalry captain named Andres Castillero claimed to be the owner of. In September 1852 Castillero filed a petition for confirmation of his title before the Land Commission in San Francisco. It was the beginning of a long and bitterly contested legal struggle that would continue for a dozen years, involving not only the Land Commission but also the U.S. District Court in San Francisco, president Abraham Lincoln, and ultimately the U.S. Supreme Court.

The Land Commission initially found Castillero's grant to be valid, although problems soon arose—first, because the description of the land covered did not adequately exclude it from neighboring land, and also because competing claims to the same land were made by a man named José de los Reyes Berryessa. Needing capital to properly operate the mine, Castillero arranged with the English firm of Barron, Forbes, and Company, headquartered in

Tepic, Mexico, to form a company that would provide the capital necessary to develop the mine. While the U.S. Land Commission and the U.S. District Court in San Francisco reviewed the claims, the federal government in Washington DC became interested in the matter.

Lincoln grew concerned about New Almaden, in part because he understood the importance of California's mineral wealth and how it helped the Union maintain its fighting forces (gold was then flowing into the federal treasury), and in further part because his attorney general, Edward Bates, strongly believed that the cinnabar deposits were on public land and belonged to the federal government.[14] On May 8, 1863, Lincoln ordered the U.S. marshal in San Francisco to take possession of the New Almaden mine and put Leonard Swett in possession of it.[15] Swett was a young lawyer from Illinois who had become one of Lincoln's friends while they were both practicing law there. He had also acted as one of the convention managers who helped secure Lincoln's presidential nomination by the Republican Party in Chicago in 1860. After Lincoln was elected, Swett frequently visited him in the White House, offering advice on issues that he faced.

In the meantime, however, Swett had also become involved with a Pennsylvania-based firm called the Quicksilver Mining Company that asserted a third claim to ownership of New Almaden. When the U.S. marshal summoned troops to help him take possession of it, he was met by armed miners who refused to admit him. A conflict was close to boiling over. Frederick F. Low, the collector of the Port of San Francisco who was also the Republican candidate for California's governor, telegraphed secretary of the treasury Salmon P. Chase in Washington, advising him that the threat of using military force was "terrible," adding, "The secessionists will seize upon it as a pretext for a general uprising I fear."[16] Advised of the danger that was presented, Lincoln quickly decided to back down.[17]

Adding to the confusion, the Supreme Court was again considering the matter. In February 1864 Attorney General Bates made his first personal argument before the high court, arguing that New Almaden belonged to the United States and not to any of the private claimants. The case was so important that three former attorneys general, Zachary Taylor's Reverdy Johnson, Franklin Pierce's Caleb Cushing, and James Buchanan's Jeremiah Black, argued for other parties. On April 5, 1864, speaking for a divided court, Justice Samuel Nelson of New York issued an order that favored one of the private claimants.[18] In his diary, Bates expressed bitter opposition to the order, noting that he was "pained (sometimes shamed and disgusted)" but unable to do anything about it.[19]

Facing the grim realities of the situation, Barron, Forbes and Company sold its interest in the mine to the Quicksilver Mining Company for $1.75 million.[20] Under its new owners, New Almaden continued to operate profitably, a fact that prompted Lincoln to report to Congress in December 1864 that "numerous discoveries of gold, silver, and cinnabar mines" had been made in the Sierra Nevada, Rocky Mountains, and related regions, and that "enterprising labor, which is richly remunerative," had increased there, adding, "It is believed that the product of the mines of precious metals in that region has, during the year, reached, if not exceeded, one hundred millions in value."[21] According to Bancroft, New Almaden yielded $12 million worth of quicksilver by 1880. But the ousted British investors were still bitter. In the 1870s they filed a complaint with the British and American claims commission in Geneva, Switzerland, charging that they had been forced to sell New Almaden because they were threatened with military eviction in time of war, and the government had offered them no protection. But their claim was unanimously denied.[22]

New Almaden's cinnabar deposits continued to produce quicksilver into the 1920s, when it finally shut down and was acquired by California's Santa Clara County as a public park and museum.

SPANISH AND MEXICAN GRANTEES WERE NOT THE ONLY owners of California land. New settlers could purchase land from the grantees themselves, thus becoming owners of parts of the Spanish and Mexican grants. Their purchases were sometimes of small plots, sometimes much larger expanses of land. The grant-ees, pressed by the persistent litigation challenging their owner-ship, were often in dire need of funds, and many of the new settlers were quite able to satisfy them. Another process for distributing land allowed developers to establish towns on public land and sell parcels to people who wished to build homes or commercial establishments on them. This was done under the federal Town-site Act of May 23, 1844, which permitted settlers to formally claim three hundred twenty acres of land, lay out streets and lots, and open them to settlement. The early California towns of Crescent City, Eureka, and Red Bluff were established in the 1850s under the Townsite Act and, when the act was liberalized, even larger developments like Nevada City, Grass Valley, San Rafael, and Pla-cerville were established.[23]

Preemption was another process by which land ownership could be acquired. It authorized settlers to take possession of public land, much in the manner of squatters, and then file declarations with the U.S. Land Office, pay $1.25 per acre, and make basic improve-ments. Before March 3, 1853, the preemption process was avail-able only in eastern states. On that date, Congress extended it to California and other western states.[24]

Yet another process for distributing public land to settlers was created on May 20, 1862, when President Lincoln signed the Home-stead Act, a federal statute authorizing any person who was the head of a household and twenty-one years of age or older to acquire own-ership of a hundred sixty acres of public land by filing an application for it, settling on the land for five years, and paying a small filing fee. Applicants who wanted to obtain title after only six months of settlement could do so by paying $1.25 an acre.[25] The law had been proposed for several years by politicians who wanted to encour-age western settlement and resisted by many who didn't. Lincoln's approval of it was evidence of his further approval of the westward spread of the American population. The Free Soil Democrats had argued that all men have a natural right to a portion of the soil and that the public lands should be granted in limited quantities, free of cost, to landless settlers. The Republican Party had supported homesteads in its 1860 election campaign, while many Southern-ers opposed it, fearing that it would encourage white farmers to spread throughout the West and halt the spread of slave labor. An earlier homestead act had been defeated by only one vote in the Senate in 1858, and in 1859 President Buchanan, always anxious to please his Southern supporters, had vetoed a bill that passed both houses of Congress.

Lincoln supported the homestead proposal, telling an audience of Germans in Cincinnati in February 1861 that "the wild lands of the country should be distributed so that every man should have the means and opportunity of benefitting his condition."[26] His approval of the 1862 bill was quickly recognized as a success. Even though war was being waged with the Confederate States, by the end of 1862 some fifteen thousand homestead claims had been made in western states. More were made in 1863, prompting Lincoln to tell Congress in December of that year that 1,456,514 acres of land had been homesteaded.[27] Just a year later, he told them that 1,538,614 acres had been added to the total.[28] He was obviously pleased by the numbers. Western historian Richard W. Etulain has called the Homestead Act "pathbreaking" and suggests that it may have been "the most important piece of legislation on land policies ever enacted in the U.S. Congress."[29] California land historian W. W. Robinson writes that California settlers "made extensive use of the homestead laws." They believed that the laws were providing them with "free" land and helping to "spread the wealth," even though the final result was more complex—as most things inevitably are.[30]

Yet another law that Lincoln signed had an important impact on land throughout the United States, including California. Com-monly called the Morrill Act because it was sponsored by con-gressman (later U.S. senator) Justin Morrill of Vermont, it was also known as the Land-Grant College Act. Its purpose was to promote the development of colleges "to teach such branches of learning as are related to agriculture and the mechanic arts." Like the Homestead Act, this law had been vetoed by Buchanan but was reintroduced and passed while Lincoln was president. With the support of Ohio's influential senator Benjamin Wade and other Republicans, it passed Congress and was signed by Lincoln on July 2, 1862.[31] The law provided that every eligible state would receive thirty thousand acres of public land for each of its senators and congressmen and that the land could be sold, with the proceeds used to establish colleges. It specifically provided that "no state while in a condition of rebellion or insurrection against the government of the United States shall be entitled to the benefits of this act." In California, the funds raised under the act were used to help establish the University of California in Berkeley on March 23, 1868. The university was in time to establish branches throughout the state and earn accolades as one of the finest public universities in the country.[32]

It became clear to many visitors to California—and to a growing number of its settlers—that the state embraced some land of extraordinary beauty. There were wide valleys, broad rivers, rocky crags, and sprawling deserts adorned with cacti and other succulents. There were tall and ancient redwood trees, some that grew in the high mountains and were later identified as *Sequoia gigantea* and others that hugged the northern coastline and were identified as *Sequoia sempervirens*. There were soaring mountains, some crowned with perpetual snow, others with waterfalls that crashed down into the lower valleys during the temperate months of the year, and yet others with luxuriant forests of evergreens. As the 1850s gave way to the 1860s, pioneering photographers began to make images of the California landscape that were sold to appreciative buyers in eastern states and landscape artists who captured sweeping vistas on canvas. Yosemite Valley (often written as "Yo-Semite" in its early days) was one of the favorite subjects of the photographers and the artists. Originally the home of native peoples who called themselves Ahwahnechee, or Valley People, it began to draw white men into its midst in the early 1850s. Some built cabins there and stores and one even opened a tourist-friendly hotel. Thomas Starr King, a Unitarian minister from Boston who came to California in 1860 and helped to arouse public opinion in favor of the Union, was one of the most enthusiastic visitors to Yosemite. Soon after his arrival in San Francisco, King wrote a series of letters to the *Boston Evening Transcript*, a newspaper that had earlier published his enthusiastic descriptions of the White Mountains of New Hampshire. In one letter written in December 1860, King told his readers:

> The Yo-Semite valley is a pass about ten miles long, which, at its eastern extremity, splits into three narrower notches, each of which extends several miles, winding by the wildest paths into the heart of the Sierra Nevada chain. . . . The patches of luxuriant meadow with their dazzling green, and the grouping of the superb firs, two hundred feet high, that skirt them, and that shoot above the stout and graceful oaks and sycamores, through which the horse path winds, are delightful rests of sweetness and beauty amid the threatening theatre awfulness,—like the threads and Rashes of melody that relieve the towering masses of Beethoven's harmony. The ninth Symphony is the Yo-Semite of music.[33]

King's letters lured other visitors to the Yosemite Valley, and Yosemite's reputation grew.

On March 28, 1864, California's senator John Conness introduced a bill in Congress to provide permanent protection for the "cleft" or "gorge" in the Sierra Nevada known as the "Yo-Semite Valley," explaining that it would protect "some of the greatest wonders of the world." He was encouraged to do this by a group of naturists who knew and loved the Yosemite Valley. Lincoln had never seen Yosemite, of course, but he was impressed with what he had learned about California's natural splendors, and when the bill was passed he readily signed it.[34]

Lincoln's 1864 action was historic, for it was the first time anywhere in the United States that federal land was set aside by federal law for public use in *perpetuity*. Technically speaking, it did not make Yosemite into a "national park," for the bill that Lincoln signed did not use the word "park." When, eight years later, Congress set aside a huge tract of land around the headwaters of the Yellowstone River for permanent protection, it used the words "public park or pleasuring ground." (The bill setting aside this land was signed by president Ulysses S. Grant on March 1, 1872.)[35] Thus Yellowstone became known as the first "national park" in the United States.[36] But the only reason that Yosemite did not become a "national park" in 1864 was that the enacting legislation did not use the word "park." When in 1890 Congress set aside a huge tract of redwoods in the Sierra Nevada for public protection, it used the words "public park or pleasuring ground" in its legislation. (That bill was signed by Republican president Benjamin Harrison on September 25, 1890.) This land was quickly recognized as Sequoia National Park.[37] Less than a week later, Congress added a large tract of forest lands around the Yosemite Valley grant, while maintaining the integrity of the original grant to the state.[38] From this time forward, Yosemite, like Yellowstone and Sequoia, was generally recognized as a "national park."[39] In 1906 the federal government accepted the state's offer to return the Yosemite lands to the U.S. government and proceeded to combine both the state and federal lands into one unified Yosemite National Park.[40]

Conness's work to save Yosemite was remembered when a mountain, a creek, and a glacier in Yosemite National Park were named for him. The mountain—soaring 12,590 feet into the California sky—was one of the highest in the Sierra Nevada.[41] Many places, in California and elsewhere, although not in Yosemite, were eventually named for Lincoln.

AS PRESIDENT, LINCOLN ALSO HAD TO CONSIDER LAND grants that had been made to the Catholic church for missions that were established in California between 1769 and 1823 by the Franciscan missionaries but that were later taken away from them. The first of the missions was founded by Father Junípero Serra in 1769 and named in honor of San Diego de Alcalá. The last was established north of San Francisco Bay in 1823 by Father José Altimira and named in honor of San Francisco Solano.

There were twenty-one missions in all. During their early years, the fathers who ran the missions gathered thousands of the native peoples around them and baptized them into the Catholic faith. They taught them to build churches and adjoining buildings in the Spanish style; to plant vineyards and orchards; to raise cattle, sheep, goats, and swine; and to perform many other routine tasks, which later critics described as a kind of slave labor. But after Mexico won its independence from Spain, the government in Mexico City began a program of secularization under which the native peoples were released into private life and the mission lands were divided up among various owners. Some of the new owners were native peoples, some were descendants of the original Spanish settlers of California, some were native Mexicans, and some were newly arrived Americans. The result was a diversity of ownership, with Americans eventually owning most of the land.[42]

In 1850 Joseph Sadoc Alemany, a Dominican priest who had been born in Catalonia but later became a missionary and a citizen of the United States, was named as bishop of Monterey. In that capacity, he filed claims with the U.S. Land Commission on December 18, 1853, for the return of all the properties that had been taken from the Catholic church in California. In July of the same year, he became the first archbishop of San Francisco, a post that he held until his return to Spain in 1883. Responding to Alemany's claims, the Land Commission confirmed grants for each of the missions, although not always to the extent asked for and not always without litigation. Following the confirmations and the court approvals, the president of the United States signed patents conveying the lands to Alemany on behalf of the church.[43]

The lands covered by the patents ranged in size from 283.13 acres for Mission Santa Barbara, on the Southern California coast, to 6.48 acres for Mission San Rafael Arcángel, north of San Francisco. Beginning in May 1862 and finishing up in March 1865, Lincoln issued ten of the patents. It was possible for him to personally sign the patents, or for one of his secretaries to sign it in his name. On March 18, 1865, a little more than three weeks before his death, Lincoln personally signed three mission patents. One conveyed 44.1 acres to Alemany for Mission San Juan Capistrano in Los Angeles County; the second conveyed 283.13 acres to him for Mission Santa Barbara in Santa Barbara County; the third conveyed 53.39 acres to him for Mission San Luis Rey de Francia in San Diego County.[44] The lands conveyed to the missions by the patents were valuable gifts, treasured by the mission fathers, in part because they bore the signature of Abraham Lincoln.[45]

10

Gold, Silver, and Greenbacks

LINCOLN KNEW THAT HIS EFFORT TO END THE SOUTH'S secession would be costly, although he cannot have known at the start how long the war would last and the enormous costs that would ultimately be incurred. He knew even less where the money would come from to pay the costs, or what kind of burden the American people would have to assume to pay them. He would soon learn many things about financing the war, some of the most important of which came from California.

Lincoln was personally a thrifty man. While practicing law, he did not overcharge his clients, and when he collected a fee for his work, he split it equally with his partner, William Herndon. As Noah Brooks remembered, Lincoln was "free, generous and child-like in his money matters," and "scrupulously exact and honest" in all his dealings with public as well as private property.[1] He knew that money was important, but it was not the most important thing in life—or in the war that he was fighting with the Confederacy.[2] As president, he was determined to manage the economy as best he could, calling on the advice of men who knew more about money than he did, raising the funds through the best available means, and looking forward to a time when the nation would once again be on firm financial footing.

As the war began, the Union government had an established Treasury and a reliable source of income from the tariffs that were regularly collected. When the government spent some emergency funds in Lincoln's first year as president, he needed help, and the best source he could turn to was his Treasury secretary, Salmon P. Chase. Chase was not a financial expert, and one of the men he called on most often for financial advice was Jay Cooke, a prominent Philadelphia banker who was often accused of corrupt practices and money-lending techniques that lined his pockets as well— perhaps better than those of his customers. But he was a skillful money manager, and Chase turned to him for much of the help he needed to raise funds for the government's operation.[3]

California was one of the nation's best sources of income, even though its population was relatively small. The 1860 census showed that its population totaled 379,994 out of the nation's 31,443,321, ranking it twenty-sixth out of the nation's thirty-three states. But its gold and silver mines yielded wealth that was continuously shipped back to the eastern states. Steamships that left San Francisco bound for Central America every two weeks were laden with what the newspapers called "treasure," a combination of gold, silver, and other minerals. This was also known as "specie," or "hard money." Over the course of the war, gold worth more than one hundred million dollars left California for the East.[4] This was one-quarter of the total collected throughout the United States.[5] General Grant has been quoted as saying, "I do not know what we would do in this great national emergency if it were not for the gold sent from California."[6] There was other money, however; bank notes were issued by state-chartered banks and circulated by those who had enough confidence in the solvency of the banks to rely on the notes.

Gold and silver coins were the only money recognized under federal law. Congress was specifically authorized by the Constitution to "coin money, regulate the value thereof, and of foreign coin."[7] Traditionalists argued that the power to "coin money" did not include the power to create other kinds of money, called "fiat" money. In 1846 Congress affirmed this argument, mandating that the monetary resources of the federal government could only be gold and silver and that they had to be held in specifically designated Treasury locations.[8] Bank notes could be issued by state-chartered banks, signifying that the banks would pay the amounts specified in the notes when they were due, but these had nothing but the security of the banks to back them up; when confidence in the banks plummeted, as it did with depressing frequency, financial panics followed. When this happened—as it did in 1819, in 1837, and most recently in 1857—the value of assets plummeted, business slowed almost to a standstill, and government revenues followed suit. The Treasury then found itself in severe distress.

Recognizing the need for financing, Lincoln and Congress authorized various tax laws. On August 5, 1861, he signed a comprehensive tax bill that imposed a variety of taxes on the American people. The amount to be collected in California was specified as $254,500.38 2/3. The same act imposed an income tax of 3 percent on the annual incomes over $800 of every person living in the United States.[9] This was the first federal income tax in American history, a fact that would make it a subject of bitter controversy in the years to come.[10]

Most of the taxes imposed by the 1861 bill could not be collected until the following year, so they did not quickly replenish the beleaguered Treasury. Lincoln sought advice from his cabinet members, and on January 10, 1862, he called on the army Quartermaster General, Montgomery C. Meigs, a man he trusted. Revealing his frustration, he asked Meigs, "General, what shall I do? The people are impatient; Chase has no money and he tells me he can raise no more; the General of the Army has typhoid fever. The bottom is out of the tub. What shall I do?"[11]

Sharing Lincoln's concern, his cabinet and the financial leaders of Congress worked together on a plan they believed would address the crisis. They first passed a bill authorizing the issuance of $500 million worth of federal bonds that were authorized to be "lawful money and a legal tender in payment of all debts, public and private, within the United States," except duties and interest on federal bonds and notes. Lincoln signed this bill into law on February 25, 1862.[12] Making these bonds legal tender created a national paper currency that was popularly (often derisively) called "greenbacks" because they were printed on paper with bright-green ink on their backs.[13] Lincoln accepted the new currency, although a bitter controversy swirled about it, because he believed that it was better to issue paper money than to take the nation into perpetual debt, perhaps even losing the war as a consequence. Secretary Chase himself was at first reluctant to approve the greenbacks, for he was known as a "hard money man." But he too came around, writing: "It is true that I came with reluctance to the conclusion that legal tender . . . is a necessity, but I came to it decidedly, and I support it earnestly."[14] Chase eventually became known by some as "Old Greenbacks" for his role in creating the new paper currency.

Next, Congress enacted a law that, in the words of historian James M. McPherson, "taxed almost everything but the air northerners breathed."[15] It imposed direct taxes on a bewildering variety of sources, including alcoholic beverages, auction sales, slaughtered farm animals, soap and candles, horse dealers, stable keepers, billiard rooms, bowling alleys, yachts, business documents, playing cards, medicines, cosmetics, and many other things. It also introduced a progressive rate for the imposition of income taxes. Incomes over $600 but not over $10,000 were subject to a 3 percent annual tax, while incomes over $10,000 were taxed at the rate of 5 percent. This was yet another profound innovation in the federal tax law that would establish precedents (and controversies) for the future. The law also imposed a tax on legacies (or inheritances), with the first thousand dollars exempt and rates after that varying according to the relationship of the legatees to the deceased persons.[16] Lincoln signed this into law on July 1, 1862. Its application was in some ways confusing, but money was needed and the government was under the most severe wartime stress it had ever experienced.

Lincoln did not forget the continuing pledge of the Republican Party to tie the nation together with railroads, so on the same day he signed the tax bill, he signed another bill authorizing the construction of the transcontinental railroad and telegraph line to California, authorizing it for the use of postal, military, and other purposes.[17] Again, the nation that Lincoln led would be pointed westward.

On February 25, 1863, Lincoln signed another bill that created a national banking system that would, in the years to come, virtually eliminate the old state banking system and create a national currency.[18] Supplemented by additional legislation passed in 1864, this law authorized federal banking charters, permitted banks that obtained the charters to buy United States bonds, and authorized banks to issue bank notes. The new system was based on the realization that a uniform national currency, rather than the old state currencies that varied widely over the country, would help unify the nation's economy. Antiwar Democrats opposed the new bill, as they did almost everything that strengthened the federal government and made a successful conclusion of the Civil War more likely. On June 30, 1864, Lincoln signed a third major tax bill, increasing the income tax rates so that persons with incomes over $600 but under $5,000 would pay 5 percent, those with incomes over $5,000 but under $10,000 would pay 7.5 percent, and those with incomes over $10,000 would pay 10 percent.[19]

California contributed to the national economy in many ways. Its gold and silver production added considerably to the economy, helping many businesses expand, providing greater employment opportunities for millions of Americans, and doing much to fund the federal government's fight against secession. Approximately $185 million in gold left San Francisco bound for the East between 1861 and 1864.[20] The state paid the direct tax of $254,500.38 2/3 assessed by Congress in the tax law of August 1861, responding with a concurrent resolution of the legislature authorizing Governor Downey to promptly notify the Treasury of the payment.[21] It contributed the generous sum of $1,234,257.31 to the United States Sanitary Commission.[22] Frederick Law Olmsted, the legendary American landscape architect famous for his design of New York City's Central Park and other notable landscapes, became the general secretary of the Sanitary Commission. Olmsted was also active in California in the 1860s, serving as secretary of the nine-member Yosemite Commission that reported on the extraordinary beauty of California's Yosemite Valley and encouraged Lincoln's signature on the bill creating it as a public resource, soon to become a national park.[23] The California legislature appropriated $100,000 for increasing military defenses along the coastline. It also appropriated $100,000, and set aside another $600,000, as a separate fund for soldiers' relief. Soon after Lincoln issued his historic Emancipation Proclamation, the California legislature passed a resolution approving the proclamation and pledging to support it.[24] Governor Leland Stanford praised it, saying it would "make it memorable as the commencement of a new era in human progress."[25]

Despite all of this support, there was intense opposition in California to the federal government's creation of greenbacks. There were no banks that issued notes in the state, as business had for years been conducted exclusively with gold coins.[26] (Silver, though legally acceptable, was hardly ever used, for the market value of silver had soared above the designated monetary value, discouraging holders from putting silver coins in circulation.) The state constitution also took a decided position in favor of metallic currency, prohibiting any person, association, company, or corporation from "creating paper to circulate as money."[27] Variations in the value of greenbacks could be determined only by monitoring the price of gold on the New York exchanges, and Californians could learn these values only through the telegraph. For all these reasons, Californians generally regarded paper currency as an unstable medium that was a threat to the health of the economy. They also had serious doubts about its constitutionality.[28]

California newspapers gave ample coverage to arguments against and in support of the legal tender notes—arguments about what they called the "greenback question." In September 1862 the *Daily Alta California* reported that a cigar shop owner in San Francisco had attempted to pay his gas bill with a greenback. At first the collector refused to accept the note, but after angry words were spoken he agreed to take it but said he would cut off the cigar shop owner's access to future gas by removing his gas meter. People in the streets argued angrily, some favoring the cigar shop owner and others the gas dealer.[29] In October the *Santa Cruz Sentinel* reported that a man had tried to pay a bill with a greenback and was told that it wouldn't be accepted because it couldn't be changed into gold coin. "Well, I'm glad of that," the man reportedly said. "I've had thirty-six drinks on it in three days, and it may stand for a good deal of wear and tear yet!"[30]

In the same month, the *Marysville Daily Appeal* reported that a bitter argument had broken out between politicians who favored the circulation of greenbacks and those who opposed it. California state treasurer Delos R. Ashley had used legal tender notes to pay part of the state's federal tax obligation to the assistant U.S. treasurer in San Francisco, unleashing a furious argument. Opponents of the greenbacks reminded Ashley that California was a "specie" state and sought to create a legislative committee that would investigate his "conduct."[31] A letter writer in San Francisco commented on California's contributions to the Sanitary Commission, in which the people of the state "contributed creditably, handsomely, superbly, if you will, to the relief of the maimed, sick and wounded of our common country," but the contribution was only "two-thirds of what we are netting each month in consequence of that greenback rash in which our Atlantic friends have broken out so freely."[32] Governor Stanford responded to the arguments about Ashley's payment with a long letter in which he reminded the legislators (and voters) that California owed a debt of gratitude to the federal government for the "many favors" it had conferred on the state. He referred to the "holier and loftier dictates of loyalty and patriotism which should warm every heart in the hour of our country's need," and said they should "prevent California from imitating the example of the inimical foreign powers and capitalists, who seek to embarrass our Government and paralyze its energies by forcing upon it, for sale or redemption, the bonds and other evidences of governmental indebtedness."[33] In other words, the state's tax obligation to the federal government should be paid in coin, even though the federal government had felt obligated to create a currency that was not backed by coin.

But supporters of the legal tender law were numerous and vocal. A correspondent writing to the *Evening Bulletin* in San Francisco in July 1862 said that the legal tender notes "are certainly to become the currency of the State; and the sooner Californians accept them as such, the better it will be for themselves and the more favorable for the general government."[34]

The controversy quickly found its way into the courts, and almost as quickly was brought before the California Supreme Court, where Stephen Field, soon to be elevated to the United States Supreme Court by Lincoln, was the chief justice. In the case of *Perry v. Washburn* (1862), Field ruled that because the specific words used in the federal law did not require that state and local taxes be paid in legal tender notes, tax collectors could require that they be paid in gold.[35] And, of course, they did.

Early in 1863 the California legislature took up a new bill, commonly called the Specific Contract Law, that authorized parties to a contract calling for the payment of money to specify the kind of money the payments would have to be made in. If they chose to require that payments only be made in gold, the courts would be required to enforce it.[36] Because the statute itself did not include the words "gold" or "silver," however, historian Bernard Moses has concluded that payments could be made in anything the parties chose, even English sovereigns or Spanish doubloons.[37] State senator Thomas Shannon of Plumas County declared his opposition to the law, saying: "I believe we will have to do one of two things, either accept the national currency as money, and make it the basis of California, or secede from the Union. . . . We cannot continue to live under the present state of affairs, repudiating the Government's currency, its life blood, and pretending at the same time to be loyal so far as lip loyalty goes. I am in favor of adopting some means in this State of making legal tender notes the currency of the State, and making it a misdemeanor for anyone to refuse taking them."[38] Passed by both houses of the legislature and signed by Governor Stanford on April 27, 1863, the Specific Contract Law quickly aroused disagreements. Litigants took it into the courts where, in the summer of 1864, the California Supreme Court upheld it. Justice John Currey wrote the court's opinion in the case of *Carpentier v. Atherton*, declaring that the law did not conflict with the federal law making United States notes lawful money. It only added to the rights created by that law and by the common law. It was thus legal and enforceable.[39]

In the 1864 session of the legislature, some members sent a message to Secretary of the Treasury Chase, asking, "Is California's gold law against national policy?" Two days later, on February 8, 1864, Chase answered, "I am clearly of the opinion that the California gold law is against national policy and shall be much gratified to see California declare herself in favor of one currency for the whole people, by its repeal."[40] Chase was a valuable member of President Lincoln's cabinet. Through his counseling and the contacts he made with leading investors, he was able to help Lincoln finance the war effort. Lincoln admired Chase, as he did almost every member of his cabinet, although he grew wary of him as the war progressed. Lincoln was always ready with anecdotes to ease tensions, and he liked to tell jokes. Chase did not, commenting to a friend, "The truth is that I have never been able to make a joke out of this war."[41] Chase could see faults in others but none in himself. As his Ohio political rival, senator Benjamin Wade, commented, "Chase is a good man, but his theology is unsound. He thinks there is a fourth Person in the Trinity, S. P. C. [Salmon P. Chase]."[42] If Chase lacked modesty, Lincoln did not.

When Chase visited Lincoln in Springfield soon after he won the presidential election, a local man named John Bunn passed Chase on the stairway leading down from Lincoln's office. When Bunn entered the office, he told the president-elect: "You don't want to put that man in your cabinet."

"Why?" Lincoln asked.

"Because he thinks he is a great deal bigger than you are," Bunn answered.

"Well," Lincoln continued, "do you know of any other men who think they are bigger than I am? . . . Because I want to put them all in my cabinet."[43]

GOLD, SILVER, AND GREENBACKS

FIG 1. Abraham Lincoln on January 8, 1864. Photograph by Alexander Gardner. Courtesy Library of Congress, LC-DIG-ppmsca-19211.

FIG 2. California's original Bear Flag. Painted on a piece of
unbleached cotton in Sonoma in 1846 by Mary Todd Lincoln's
cousin William L. Todd. Wikimedia Commons.

FIG 3. Stephen J. Field, the California-based lawyer and judge who was Lincoln's first appointment to the United States Supreme Court. Wikimedia Commons.

FIG 4. Edward D. Baker, the dynamic lawyer, political leader, and military officer whom Lincoln called his "dearest personal friend." He came to California in 1852 to practice law and politics, then went on to Oregon in 1860, where he was elected to the U.S. Senate. Author's collection.

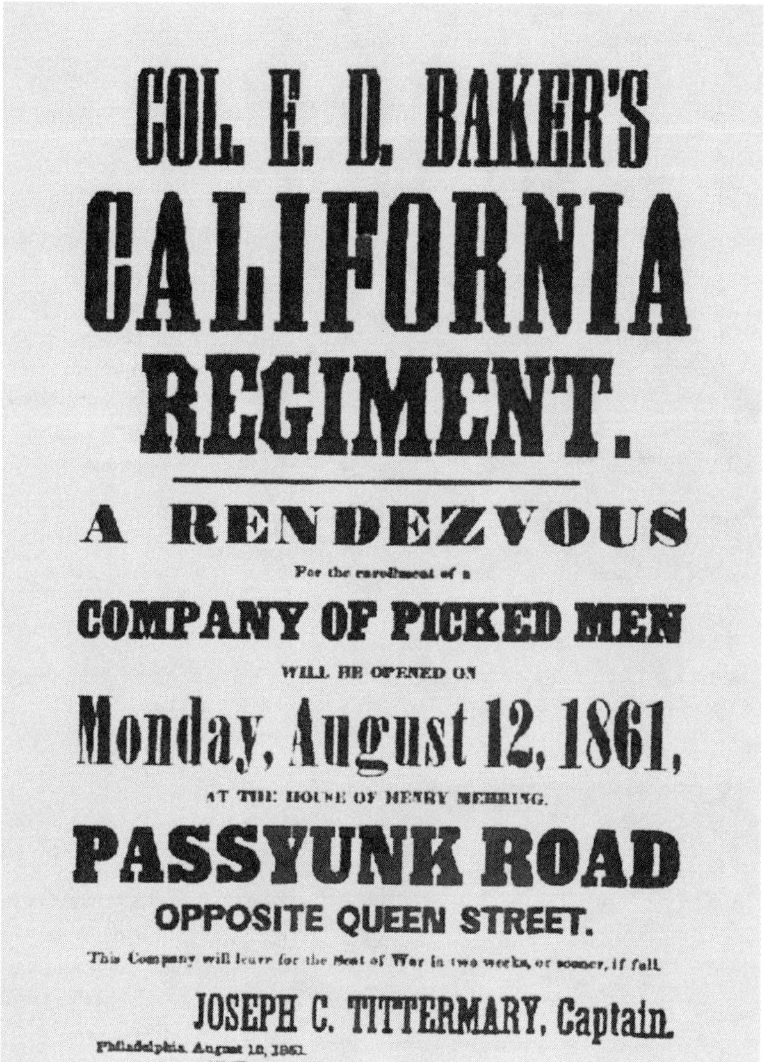

FIG 5. Edward D. Baker's California Regiment
recruiting poster. Author's collection.

FIG 6. David C. Broderick, the California-based U.S. senator whose gold-plated cane was, after his death in a duel, presented to Lincoln in the White House. Photograph by Julian Vannerson. Courtesy Library of Congress, LC-DIG-ppmsca-26838.

FIG 7. California's majestic Yosemite Valley. On June 30, 1864, Lincoln signed a law requiring that it be inalienably preserved "for public use, resort, or reservation," making it, in effect if not in actual words, the nation's first national park. California Historical Society.

FIG 8. John Conness. Irish-born politician who represented California in
the U.S. Senate from 1863 through 1869, helping to raise the funds necessary
to finance the Union forces in the Civil War, sponsoring congressional
legislation making Yosemite the first natural park set aside under federal
law for the permanent benefit of the public, and presenting David C.
Broderick's gold-plated cane to Lincoln in the White House. Courtesy
Library of Congress, Brady Handy Collection, LC-DIG-cwpbh-01372.

FIG 9. Thomas Starr King. Eloquent Unitarian minister from Boston who came to San Francisco in 1860 and traveled widely through California, arguing that it should remain in the Union, thus earning a place representing California in the U.S. Capitol's Statuary Hall in Washington DC. Wikimedia Commons.

FIG 10. Cornelius Cole. California-based journalist and lawyer who met with Lincoln in the White House on the last day of the president's life and heard him speak of his wish to visit California and perhaps make a home for himself and his family. Cole served California in the U.S. Senate from 1867 to 1873 but did not die until 1924, thus becoming the oldest living U.S. senator in American history. Frontispiece to Cole's *Memoirs of Cornelius Cole* (1908).

FIG 11. Edwin M. Stanton. Pennsylvania-based lawyer who participated in important land cases in California before Lincoln appointed him to the position of secretary of war in 1862. Courtesy Library of Congress, Civil War Collection, LC-DIG-cwpb-06437.

FIG 12. John G. Downey. Irish-born merchant, land developer, and Democratic politician who supported the Union while he served as California's governor from January 1860 to January 1862. Wikimedia Commons.

FIG 13. Leland Stanford. New York–born lawyer, merchant, and politician who became governor of California in late 1861. A member of Lincoln's Republican Party, he firmly supported the Union and became one of the founders of the western branch of the transcontinental railroad that Lincoln ardently supported. Thereafter he and his wife, Jane Lathrop Stanford, founded Stanford University. Wikimedia Commons.

FIG 14. John C. Frémont. Legendary western explorer and U.S. senator representing California whom Lincoln campaigned for when he ran for president in 1856. After the outbreak of the Civil War, Lincoln appointed Frémont as Union military commander in Missouri but soon removed him because of his impulsive and disruptive conduct. Wikimedia Commons.

FIG 15. Albert Sidney Johnston. Kentucky-born army officer who was commander of the Department of the Pacific in San Francisco when the Civil War began but quickly resigned his position to join the Confederate forces and met his death in April 1862 at the Battle of Shiloh. Courtesy Library of Congress, LC-DIG-pga-04023.

FIG 16. Edwin V. Sumner. Boston-born general who became commander of the Department of the Pacific in San Francisco in early 1861. He later fought in the Civil War Peninsula campaign and at the battles of Antietam and Fredericksburg. Courtesy Library of Congress, Civil War Collection, LC-DIG-cwpb-04626.

FIG 17. Winfield Scott Hancock. Pennsylvania-born army officer
who was the U.S. Army quartermaster in Los Angeles at the onset
of the Civil War, but after returning east commanded the Union
Army's II Corps at Gettysburg in 1863. In 1880 he was the Democratic
candidate for president, narrowly losing to Republican James A.
Garfield. U.S. National Archives and Records Administration.

FIG 18. Joseph Hooker. Massachusetts-born army officer who spent nine years operating a farm in California before accepting Lincoln's appointment to lead the Army of the Potomac in 1863. Courtesy Library of Congress, Civil War Collection, LC-DIG-ppmsca-19396.

FIG 19. William Tecumseh Sherman. Ohio-born army officer who spent important time living and operating a bank in California before achieving real fame leading Union soldiers through Georgia, burning Atlanta, and helping Lincoln achieve victory over the Confederate rebels. Photograph by Matthew Brady. U.S. National Archives and Records Administration.

FIG 20. Henry W. Halleck. New York–born army officer who came to California during the Mexican War, remained to help organize the infant state's new government, and became one of the Gold Rush era's most powerful lawyers, before returning east to accept Lincoln's appointment as commander in chief of all the Union armies. Photograph by John A. Scholten. Courtesy Library of Congress, Civil War Collection, LC-DIG-cwpb-06956.

FIG 21. Edward Otho Cresap Ord. Maryland-born army officer who performed important services in California before returning east where, as a Union major general, he helped destroy Robert E. Lee's Army of Northern Virginia and witnessed Lee's surrender at Appomattox Courthouse. Wikimedia Commons.

FIG 22. Ulysses S. Grant. Ohio-born army officer who spent important time in California before becoming Lincoln's Union commander during the Civil War and leading his forces to the surrender of the Confederate general Robert E. Lee in 1865. Courtesy Library of Congress, Civil War Collection, LC-DIG-cwpb-06947.

FIG 23. David Glasgow Farragut. Tennessee-born naval officer who spent important time in California before commanding naval forces during the Civil War and becoming the first full admiral in the U.S. Navy. Courtesy Library of Congress, Civil War Collection, LC-DIG-cwpb-05211.

FIG 24. James Henry Carleton. Maine-born U.S. Army officer who in 1862 led the First California Infantry Regiment (soon dubbed the California Column) eastward from California, driving the Confederates out of New Mexico and permitting Lincoln to sign the law creating the new territory of Arizona. Wikimedia Commons.

FIG 25. A crowd of San Franciscans gathered to honor the assassinated President Lincoln in 1865. Courtesy Library of Congress, Civil War Collection, LC-DIG-stereo-1s04307.

FIG 26. Lone Mountain. A prominent eminence west of San Francisco with clear views over the Golden Gate and the Pacific Ocean, where both David C. Broderick and Edward D. Baker are buried. Lincoln hoped one day to climb its summit, set his eyes on the Pacific Ocean, and assess his desire to make his home in California after he left the White House. Engraving from *Old Mexico and Her Lost Provinces: A Journey in Mexico, Southern California, and Arizona by Way of Cuba* (1883) by William Henry Bishop.

LONE MOUNTAIN CEMETERY,

FIG 27. Lone Mountain Cemetery. Prominent heroes are buried here on an eminence west of San Francisco and where Lincoln hoped one day he could stand and look out over the Pacific Ocean. Lithograph by the Gold Rush firm of Kuchel and Dresel, San Francisco. Author's collection.

FIG 28. Noah Brooks. Maine-born journalist who first became acquainted with Lincoln in Illinois. After moving to California in 1859 and from there being sent to Washington to cover news for the *Sacramento Daily Union*, Brooks became one of the president's best friends and confidants, sending 258 news-filled letters back to California under the pen name "Castine." Wikimedia Commons.

FIG 29. Statue of Abraham Lincoln by sculptor Pietro Mezzara that was erected in front of the Abraham Lincoln School in San Francisco on April 14, 1866, the first anniversary of Lincoln's death. It remained standing until the earthquake and fire of 1906 forced it down. Courtesy Library of Congress, LC-USZ-62–102558.

FIG 30. Abraham Lincoln by California-based sculptor Haig
Patigian, installed in front of the San Francisco city hall in
1926, where it is still located. Wikimedia Commons.

FIG 31. *Lincoln the Lawyer*, a bust by California-based sculptor
Julia Bracken Wendt installed in Lincoln Park in Los Angeles on
July 4, 1926. It remains there today. Author's collection.

FIG 32. Western terminus of the Lincoln Highway, located in San Francisco's Lincoln Park, overlooking the Golden Gate and the entrance to the Pacific Ocean. Lincoln Highway Association.

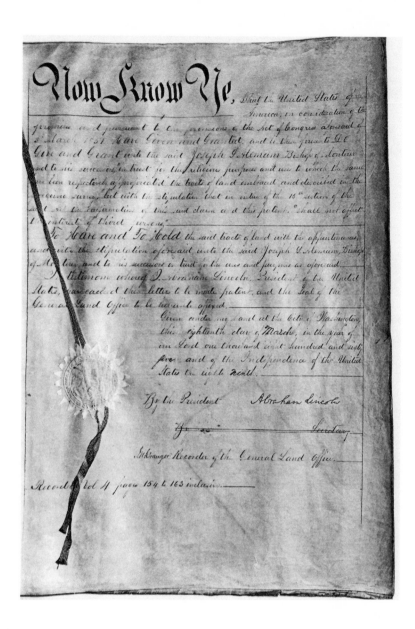

FIG 33. "Now Know Ye." Patent signed on March 18, 1865, by President Lincoln returning ownership of 44.1 acres of land to California's Spanish Mission San Juan Capistrano, located south of Los Angeles. Mission San Juan Capistrano Collection

FIG 34. Mission San Juan Capistrano. An arched passageway of one of the Spanish missions Lincoln returned to California's Catholic Church by a signed patent. Courtesy Library of Congress, Carol M. Highsmith Archive Collection, LC-DIG-highsm-21188.

FIG 35. The Lincoln Memorial Shrine in Redlands, California, sixty-three miles
east of Los Angeles. Opened in 1932, it remains the only museum and library
dedicated to Lincoln's memory west of the Mississippi. Author's collection.

11

The Native Peoples

A REVIEW OF LINCOLN'S RELATIONS WITH CALIFORNIA'S
Native Americans, traditionally called Indians, is not pleasant.[1] It
is, however, one that an honest history of Lincoln's dealings with
California cannot ignore. The fate experienced by the state's native
peoples during Lincoln's presidency was dark and depressing. But
the history of the native peoples for centuries before that time was
similarly dark and depressing, and for years after it continued to be
so.[2] Lincoln historian Mark E. Neely Jr. has made a statement that
helps at least in part to understand why Lincoln's relations with
the native peoples have been so poorly understood. "It remains
difficult to describe Lincoln's Indian policy," Neely has written,
"because he made so few statements on the problem and because
he took little direct action in Indian affairs."[3]

Lincoln knew little about what was happening to the native peoples of California while he was in the White House. Like native
peoples in much of the rest of the United States, California's Native
Americans were suffering from denial of the most basic human
rights and from the fear that they might ultimately face extinction.
There were white Americans who sympathized with their plight—
some deeply—but many who cared little about it. If Lincoln had
addressed their suffering directly, he would probably have tried
to ameliorate it. He was at heart a man who believed in fairness
and justice, at least so far as he was able to understand it. He did
not do so, in part because he knew little about the problems of
the Native Americans and in part because he believed that bet-

tering human rights was a gradual process. He did not urge an immediate end to the enslavement of African Americans, but he was confident that that result would be obtained gradually. The same result, perhaps, would meet the Native Americans' plight.

It has often been estimated that California was first populated by Native Americans about twelve thousand years before Europeans first arrived, although some archaeologists have suggested that they may have arrived as long as a hundred thirty thousand years ago.[4] Spanish invaders made tentative approaches to California, some by land and some by sea, in the sixteenth century, and Spanish priests and soldiers came in 1769, led by the Franciscan missionary Junípero Serra and the Catalonian nobleman Gaspar de Portolá. In addition to the twenty-one missions, four presidios (forts) and four pueblos (civic towns) were established by the Spanish. Sir Francis Drake, an English navigator and pirate, briefly touched on the coast in 1579, claiming the land for Her Britannic Majesty Queen Elizabeth I, and Russian fur-trappers and traders under the leadership of Ivan Alexander Kuskov came down from Alaska in 1812 to establish a colony called Fort Ross north of San Francisco Bay, which they left in 1841. North and east of the Spanish and Russian settlements, controlled after 1821 by Mexicans who had won their independence from Spain, the land was still populated by native peoples. The stated goal of the Spanish missionaries was to baptize the natives and thus save them from eternal damnation. But it was also to put them to work building mission churches and surrounding structures, raising crops that fed the padres and the native peoples, and helping defend the territory from foreign encroachment—by the British or the Russians, particularly.

The native peoples suffered from the hard labor they were subjected to and from the contagious diseases that the Europeans brought to America. The Europeans had over many centuries acquired resistance to viruses and bacteria that the Native Americans had never encountered. During the 1830s and 1840s alone, more than sixty thousand of California's native peoples fell victim to the newly arrived European diseases.[5] Violence was also a source of suffering for the native peoples. Many of the Europeans regarded battle as a solution to life's problems, and when they came to America they brought the solution with them. It was, like the infectious diseases they brought, a source of suffering for the native peoples, although on a much smaller scale.[6]

The racial divide between the Spanish invaders and the native peoples was not as sharp as the divide between slave masters and chattel slaves in the American South. Under Spanish and Mexican law, native peoples could own land and even sell it; they could marry across racial lines; they could become priests; they could worship with Europeans in their churches, receive forgiveness for their sins, and aspire to eternal salvation. As the pioneer demographer Sherburne F. Cook has noted, the Spanish incorporated the native peoples into their social structure while the newly arriving Americans rigidly excluded them from theirs.[7] One of the most notable Native Americans in the Spanish and Mexican period was Pablo Tac, who was born at Mission San Luis Rey de Francia in 1820 and taken to Rome in 1834 by the Franciscan Father Antonio Peyri. There he and another native boy named Agapito Amamix studied for the priesthood. Tac became a scholar of his native language, called Luiseño, because his people lived around the mission. He studied both Spanish and Latin and, for the benefit of the Catholic linguist cardinal Giuseppe Mezzofanti, wrote a grammar of the Luiseño language, composed a dictionary of it, and wrote a history of the Luiseño people. Amamix died in Rome in 1837. Tac died there in 1842, but his works were preserved in the archives of Cardinal Mezzofanti.[8]

Many Spanish settlers in California carried Native American blood in their veins; some also had African Americans ancestors. Such men were entitled to vote and to hold important official positions. One prominent Californian who had African American, Native American, and Spanish ancestors was a man named Pío Pico, who was born near Los Angeles in 1801, served two terms as governor of the Mexican province of California in the 1830s and 1840s, and was remembered in California's history as one of its most prominent Hispanic citizens.[9] Another was a man named

Manuel Dominguez who, despite his Native American ancestry, owned one of the largest ranchos in Southern California, served as a member of the *cabildo* (council) and as alcalde of the pueblo of Los Angeles, was elected to membership in the provincial legislature, and became prefect of the Southern District of Alta California. In 1849 he was elected as a delegate to the state constitutional convention that met in Monterey. During the convention debates, some American delegates made a proposal to limit the right to vote to white males, thus excluding both blacks and Native Americans. Henry Halleck, then a delegate from Monterey, said that if the proposal passed, "several of the most worthy citizens of California would be excluded from exercising the right of franchise" and one of those citizens "was a member of this very Convention." The member Halleck referred to was Manuel Dominguez.[10] Halleck's observation made little difference, however, for the convention went on to limit voting rights to white male citizens while, as a kind of concession to those who believed in broader rights, it authorized the state legislature to extend voting beyond the racist limit by two-thirds votes "in such special cases as such a proportion of the legislative body may deem just and proper."[11] Delegate Dominguez thus left the convention as a citizen without the rights enjoyed by whites. Eight years later, he was also prevented from giving testimony in a San Francisco court because he was not a white.[12]

Military violence continued after the Americans took control of California—by the "wicked war" described by Ulysses S. Grant—and they expected to keep it by resorting to violence.[13] The California constitution had barred slavery from the new state—a move that many thought helped its admission to the Union—but it had not prohibited the passage of a host of bitterly racist laws that were directed against any African Americans (free or slave) who might make their way into the state, and also against the Chinese and Native Americans. The Native Americans suffered again, as they had under previous occupations. Now, however, their suffering spread beyond the coastal region occupied by the Spanish and Mexican padres and rancheros and into California's vast

THE NATIVE PEOPLES

interior—the great Central Valley, the soaring Sierra Nevada that loomed over the state's eastern border, the parched desert that bordered the Colorado River in the southeast, and the wooded reaches extending along the northern coastline and into Oregon.

The Native American population of California when the United States took possession has been estimated at about a hundred fifty thousand—a dramatic drop from the number first encountered by the Spanish settlers.[14] California's admission to the Union as the thirty-first state gave rise to a state government that had authority to deal with the native peoples, while federal authorities in Washington viewed the native population with interest, some of it to protect its welfare but much of it in the conviction that conflict between the white and the native populations was inevitable. U.S. Army commanders lost little time sending troops into the Native American country. When the federal forces did not achieve the results desired by white settlers, the state government organized volunteer militias and authorized them to pursue the natives, believing that the federal government would pay them because it had the constitutional responsibility to protect every state against "domestic violence."[15] One of the militia units authorized to deal with the native peoples in the foothills of the Sierra Nevada was the Mariposa Battalion, which conducted its operations in 1851 and 1852 at the eastern edge of the San Joaquin Valley. It was led by a former Illinoisan named James Savage, who had come to California with the overland party of former Missouri governor Lilburn W. Boggs in 1846. Savage operated a trading post where he dealt with the natives and, by some reports, took several of them as wives. In one of Savage's campaigns against the natives, he and his battalion entered the Yosemite Valley.[16] The campaigns of the Mariposa Battalion ultimately took the lives of at least seventy-three natives. Lincoln, of course, had no knowledge of this, or probably of any of the other campaigns conducted against California's native peoples. He was then practicing law in central Illinois, helping to solve legal problems for the white people who lived there and making an honest living for his family.[17]

In 1852 Congress authorized the U.S. Indian Affairs commissioner, Andavan S. Loughery, to appoint three men to meet with California's native peoples and try to reach agreements under which the whites and the native peoples could live together without conflict. They were Redick McKee of Virginia, George W. Barbour of Kentucky, and Oliver M. Wozencraft of Louisiana. Separating the state into three large areas so they could meet with as many natives as possible, McKee, Barbour, and Wozencraft negotiated with more than four hundred tribal leaders and obtained agreements to eighteen treaties under which the native peoples relinquished their claims to all California territory except 11,700 square miles, or about 7.5 percent of the total.[18] These exceptions were to be legally recognized as reservations. The California negotiators believed that the native peoples had made tremendous sacrifices to obtain these reservations, as did president Millard Fillmore. The California legislature, however, disagreed sharply, and urged the U.S. Senate to reject the treaties, which it did on July 8, 1852.

Without any land legally recognized by the United States, California's Native Americans were now subject to a growing number of attacks from whites who claimed all of the land. At Fillmore's urging, Congress in March 1853 authorized five "military reservations" not to exceed twenty-five thousand acres each.[19] Because these areas were not authorized by treaty, however, they were not legally protected from white invasions, and the native peoples who occupied them continued to endure kidnapping raids, thefts of animals and farm products, sexual assaults, and a depressing number of murders. Without any land they could call their own, without protection in the courts (where they were forbidden by California law to give testimony against whites), and with the inability to defend themselves against growing attacks by whites, the native peoples were as desperate—perhaps more so than they had been before.

In 1853 Congress created a new office called the Superintendent of Indian Affairs for California. Fillmore appointed Edward F. Beale, who had been a naval officer at the time of the California conquest, to fill the office. In August 1853 Beale established a reserve for the native peoples within U.S. Army land in a mountainous region of Southern California called Fort Tejon. Beale was succeeded in 1855 by Thomas J. Henley, a former U.S. congressman from Indiana who had come to California in 1849 and served in the California state legislature from 1851 to 1853. Henley established similar reserves for native peoples far to the north. These reserves lacked water, game, and suitable agricultural lands, however; they were soon overrun by whites who occupied the land, hunted the native peoples, and introduced starvation and diseases. In 1858 the state militia established a fort in the far northern Hoopa Valley to make war on the two local groups of natives, adding further to their suffering.

By 1861 the population of California's Native Americans had become even smaller than it had been when the United States took control—probably not more than thirty thousand in all. President Lincoln was now the man who could help them—or perhaps not. The native peoples really had no way of knowing what their future held.

Lincoln's background had provided him with little personal contact with native peoples. His primary recollection of them was a story that his father, Thomas Lincoln, his uncle, Mordecai Lincoln, and other members of the Lincoln family constantly reminded him of. It was that, in 1786, while his grandfather (also named Abraham Lincoln) and three of his sons were planting a cornfield on their property in frontier Kentucky, "Indians" had killed his grandfather in an ambush and attempted to make off with his father. The story was repeated so often, and in so many versions, that Lincoln later said it was "the legend more strongly than all others imprinted upon my mind and memory."[20] There is no doubt that he believed the story and that it affected his opinions of the native peoples, although it was something he had heard about rather than experienced firsthand.[21]

Lincoln's next significant contact with natives occurred in 1832, when he volunteered for service in the short-lived Black Hawk War. He saw no fighting in the conflict, although he and the men who served with him discovered some terrible evidence of cruelty committed by their native opponents: the bodies of dead whites who had been scalped, decapitated, and mutilated.[22] While the fighting went on, he and his fellow militiamen also had some friendly encounters with Cherokees from Iowa who had come into Illinois under peace terms. They talked with the Cherokees, watched them dance, and engaged in friendly sporting competitions.[23] On one occasion, militiamen brought an old native named Jack into Lincoln's camp. They claimed that he was a spy, even though he was bearing a letter of introduction from the then secretary of war Lewis Cass. When they said that they had the right to shoot him on the spot and seemed ready to do so, Lincoln strongly objected. As one of his neighbors later recalled, he intervened between Jack and his would-be executioners and said: "Men, this must not be done—he must not be shot and killed by us."[24] Years after his Black Hawk service ended, he joked that during his time with the militia he had had "a good many bloody struggles with the musquetoes [*sic*]; and, although I never fainted from loss of blood, I can truly say I was often very hungry."[25] He was willing to joke about his Black Hawk War experience, but he did not dismiss it as unimportant. His political ambitions were already being felt, and he undoubtedly realized that his militia service would persuade voters that he was a brave man. More importantly, perhaps, his experience taught him that natives could be aggressive, combative, and cruel. Lincoln did not forget these lessons he took from the Black Hawk War as he went on with his life as a lawyer and politician.

The beginning of military conflict between the Confederacy and the Union government headed by Lincoln added a new dimension to the plight of the Native Americans. Those who lived in California were still regarded by both sides as enemies, and federal funding for campaigns against them continued. U.S. Army major Gabriel Rains, commander at Fort Humboldt, sought to negotiate with the natives to ease tensions between them and the whites in the area, but his successor, Capt. Charles S. Lovell, chose instead to send troops into conflict with them. Brevet Brig. Gen. Albert Sidney Johnston, who was soon to leave his post as commander of all the U.S. Army forces in California and join the Confederacy, ordered Lovell to hunt down the native peoples. As a consequence, dozens of natives in the far northwestern corner of the state were summarily killed, with the assistance of California state militiamen.[26] Reporting this news, the *San Francisco Herald* told its readers in June 1861 that the troops were not engaged in "fighting the Indians, but in slaughtering them."[27]

In March 1861 Lincoln appointed an Illinoisan named William P. Dole as his Indian Affairs commissioner. Dole had not yet been to California, but he received reports of the plight that the natives there were suffering, and in November 1861 he condemned the conflict in the northwestern part of the state, saying that the natives were "hunted like wild and dangerous beats of prey." He said the parents were murdered and their children were kidnapped. Private hunters were authorized by state law to capture some natives and subject them to forced labor, while others were simply shot down.[28] Some native peoples were enlisted to help whites lead raids against other native peoples.[29] Killing was not an exclusively white activity, although it was encouraged by many whites.

In July 1861 Col. Francis Lippitt took command at Fort Humboldt and reinstated the diplomatic approach to the natives instituted by Major Rains. Lippitt prohibited making war on the natives except in self-defense or pursuant to superior orders and sought to locate them on permanent reservations. But Brig. Gen. George Wright adopted a different policy, ordering Lippitt to make a "clean sweep" of the natives in his district and declaring: "Every Indian you may capture, and who has been engaged in hostilities present or past, shall be hung on the spot. Spare the women and children." Following Wright's orders, Lippitt's troops engaged in widespread killing. By September 1862 Lippitt's men held nearly nine hundred prisoners at Fort Humboldt.[30] From the northern to southern reaches of the state, natives were now captured and put to work, sometimes with the approval of legal authorities and sometimes without. On November 26, 1862, Dole reported that California's native peoples were "not even unmolested upon the scanty reservations set aside for their use." Reservations were established, including one on Northern California's Smith River. But food was so scarce there as to cause widespread starvation, and sleeping quarters were often only available on water-soaked ground. One native voiced his and his fellow people's frustration, asking: "When Captain Lincoln, *big chief*, send Indian blankets?" The *Mendocino Herald* reported that a leader named Lassik and his followers had surrendered near Fort Seward and soon "took cold and died." The *Herald* added, "We suspect the cold they died with was mainly cold lead."[31]

While the turbulence continued in the northern and southern parts of the state, vigilantes crossed over the Sierra Nevada and invaded the homeland of the Paiute-Shoshone and the Mojave peoples. California cavalrymen and Nevada dragoons soon arrived to reinforce the vigilantes. In December 1862 the Southern Californian Indian agent John P. H. Wentworth negotiated a treaty providing these natives a two-thousand-acre reservation plus food, blankets, and other supplies. But when Wentworth's request for $30,000 to carry out the terms of the treaty reached Washington, Congress failed to pass it, and when the natives responded with attacks on white travelers and soldiers, the army unleashed yet another killing campaign. U.S. Army cavalry captain Moses A. McLaughlin led an expedition against the fleeing natives in April 1863. In June 1863 the *Sacramento Daily Union* told its readers that the Owens River war was "over" and that McLaughlin's men had "not only destroyed the Indians' provisions, but discovered and guarded all the springs so closely that they actually died of thirst."[32] Killing also continued in the northwestern part of the state, where U.S. Army colonel Henry Black led a furious campaign against the local natives that was so successful that by June 1864 General Wright was able to report that the hostilities in the northwest were now "virtually closed."

During Lincoln's early days in the White House, he was besieged by men from California and elsewhere who sought positions in the Indian Affairs Commission. He asked for recommendations and heard personal pleas before making his choices. With William P. Dole named to head the federal commission, George Hanson was chosen as Superintendent of Indian Affairs for California's Northernn District and John P. H. Wentworth as Superintendent of Indian Affairs for its Southern District. In 1865 Lincoln appointed his old

Illinois friend Charles Maltby as Superintendent of Indian Affairs for the whole state of California.[33] Maltby took his job seriously, touring the native reservations and making thoughtful proposals for the betterment of the native peoples' conditions.[34]

Lincoln was busy all the time with military affairs, naming generals to lead his armies, evaluating their skills and determination, and agonizing when bad news reached him in Washington. The news he received from Minnesota added to his concern. In August 1862 that state's governor, Alexander Ramsey, had informed secretary of war Edwin Stanton that Sioux people who lived along the state's western border were waging war against whites. "A most frightful insurrection of Indians has broken out along our whole frontier," Ramsey reported. "Men, women and children are indiscriminately murdered, evidently the result of a deep-laid plan, the attacks being simultaneous along our whole border."[35] There was some worry in Washington that the Sioux attacks were coordinated with the Southern secession, for Confederates had already made alliances with the native peoples in the so-called Indian Territory (later to become Oklahoma). There was even a suspicion that the English might be joining the Confederates and mounting an attack from Canada. Governor Ramsey wanted Federal troops, so the Third Minnesota Volunteer Regiment, which had seen action in Tennessee, was ordered to return to Minnesota.[36]

Dole was in Minnesota, watching the action and approving the request for further reinforcements. Lincoln was agonized by continuing news reports, and by the beginning of September he created a new Military Department of the Northwest and sent Maj. Gen. John C. Pope to command it. The loyalist governor of Missouri, Samuel J. Kirkwood, sent word that native peoples to the west of his state were joining with those in Minnesota to threaten the entire western border. When Pope arrived in Minnesota, he acted vigorously, saying, "It is my purpose utterly to exterminate the Sioux if I have the power to do so, and even if it requires a campaign lasting the whole of next year." Pope's campaign did not take a whole year, and by October 9 he was able to inform General Halleck: "The Sioux war may be considered at an end."

It had been a short but bloody war. Estimates of white deaths ran from around five hundred even to as high as one thousand. The number of native casualties was not determined, but the number of native men captured and condemned to death was precise. After short and sometimes cursory trials before a five-man military commission, 303 native men were sentenced to be hanged. Pope sent the list of condemned men to Lincoln, warning the president that if not all the guilty were executed, further native violence could be expected.

Lincoln was legally obligated to review the convictions. He wanted to avoid the awful duty, and General Pope at one point suggested that he turn the whole matter over to the state government. Lincoln did not accept the suggestion, however, but asked assistants to review each case and then set about the arduous task of deciding what fate should await the convicts. It was clear that the people and government of Minnesota were hungry for blood and vengeance, but as Lincoln continued his review it became clear to him that not all the men who had been sentenced to death deserved their sentences. This conviction was reinforced by Henry B. Whipple, the Episcopal Bishop of Minnesota, who happened to be a cousin of General Halleck, and who was urging mercy. Whipple made his position clear to the military authorities, and even visited Lincoln in Washington to explain it. Lincoln was not a member of any organized church, but he was willing to listen to the call for mercy and seriously consider it. He knew, of course, that the decisions he was called on to make had political and military consequences. If he was harsh and vindictive, as the Minnesotans wanted him to be, he would be seen as strong and determined, not just by the people in that state but also by the Confederates. If he was overly merciful, he would be seen as weak and unwilling to meet Rebels with strength and determination.

On December 6 Lincoln ordered that 39 native men be hanged, not the original list of 303. One additional name was removed from the list by a reprieve, so that on December 26, 38 natives were hanged in the public square in Mankato, Minnesota. The number of men he had spared from execution by this single action—

264—was the largest in American history. But the number he had sent to mass execution—38—was also the largest single execution in American history.[37]

The U.S. Senate passed a resolution on December 5 requesting that Lincoln "furnish the Senate with all information in his possession touching the late Indian barbarities in the State of Minnesota, and also the evidence in his possession upon which some of the principal actors and head men were tried and condemned to death." On December 11 he complied with the Senate request, stating in part: "Anxious to not act with so much clemency as to encourage another outbreak on the one hand, nor with so much severity as to be real cruelty on the other, I caused a careful examination of the records of trials to be made, in view of first ordering the execution of such as had been proven guilty of violating females. Contrary to my expectations, only two of this class were found. I then directed a further examination, and a classification of all who were proven to have participated in *massacres*, as distinguished from participation in *battles*."[38]

In his annual messages to Congress, Lincoln detailed some of the depredations committed by Native American peoples. He also expressed the hope that Congress would engage in a system of reform—or as he called it "remodeling"—of the government's so-called Indian Affairs system. On December 1, 1862, he told Congress that "many wise and good men have impressed me with the belief that this can be profitably done." On December 8, 1863, he told Congress that "subsequent events have satisfied me of its necessity."[39]

As the Civil War ground to its conclusion, the killing of native peoples in California wound down. The state's Native American population had been reduced to less than thirty thousand and the number of federally supported soldiers was suddenly diminished. Lack of support from both Washington and Sacramento reduced the ability of whites to hunt and kill native peoples, though the desire of many of them to do so was still strong. Lincoln's last days in the White House included not only his supervision of the end of the military struggle with the Confederacy but also his effort to affect an amendment to the U.S. Constitution putting a final end to African American slavery. Lincoln tried with all his might to persuade Congress and the individual states to support such an amendment. The U.S. House of Representatives and Senate passed one in 1864, and it received its last needed ratification in December 1865, thus becoming the Thirteenth Amendment to the Constitution. It weakened Native American servitude in California, but it did not end legal peonage or kidnapping. The state legislature's adoption in 1872 of revised civil and penal codes that, among other things, permitted native peoples to give legal testimony in courts, helped strengthen native justice. The codes became effective in 1873.[40]

California joined in the prompt ratification of the Thirteenth Amendment, adding its formal approval on December 20, 1865.[41] Sadly, however, it did not join in the ratification of the Fourteenth Amendment, prohibiting the denial of life, liberty, or property without due process of law, until May 6, 1959, and it did not join in the ratification of the Fifteenth Amendment, banning the denial of the right to vote on the basis of race, color, or previous condition of servitude, until April 4, 1962. Its full assent to these basic constitutional protections of basic rights thus had to wait almost a century.

Lincoln received letters from an English-born reformer named John Beeson, who had first attempted to persuade him of the need for Native American reform around the time of the Sioux executions. He met with Beeson some time in 1864, listening to his continuing pleas and considering them carefully. "My Friend," he said to Beeson, "I have heard your arguments again and again. I have said little but thought much, and you may rest assured that as soon as the pressing matter of the war is settled the Indians shall have my first care and I will not rest until Justice [sic] is done to their and your Sattisfaction [sic]."[42]

As he continued his earnest efforts to defeat the Confederate states and save the Union from destruction, Lincoln thought seriously about the government's troubled relations with the native peoples. Bishop Whipple visited him in the White House, conveying his passionate thoughts about the native peoples' plight in Minne-

THE NATIVE PEOPLES

sota. He also told Lincoln about the ineffectiveness and corruption in the Indian Affairs offices in Washington and other states.

Historians have carefully analyzed Lincoln's relations with the native peoples.[43] They have not found them terribly bad, but they have not found them terribly good either. He did not know enough about the native peoples to fully understand their plight, or what he could—or should—do to improve their relations with other people in the United States. He did not understand how much the Civil War was affecting relations between white Americans and native peoples. He did not understand, as historian Elliott West has written, how the acquisition of western territories—California, Oregon, Idaho, Nevada, and Arizona among them—encouraged more virulent attacks against the native peoples and how it exacerbated racism against not only native peoples but also the Chinese. The history of the nation and the history of the American West mutually influenced one another. They were not separate, but parts powerfully influencing the great whole.[44]

Not long after meeting Whipple, Lincoln met a friend from Illinois and told him about his meeting with the bishop. "He came here the other day," Lincoln said, "and talked with me about the rascality of this Indian business until I felt it down to my boots. If we get through this war, and I live, *this Indian system shall be reformed!*"[45] The "ifs" in this statement had pronounced effects on the future of both Lincoln and the Native Americans.[46]

12

The War Continues

LINCOLN'S CONCERN ABOUT MILITARY AFFAIRS, THE WINNERS and losers of battles between the North and the South, continued. The men he had chosen to lead Northern armies played a key part in those affairs, and he paid close—sometimes agonizing— attention to them.

After Gen. Edwin V. Sumner arrived in San Francisco on April 24, 1861, to take command of the Department of the Pacific, he sent a dispatch to the War Department in Washington, informing them of what he had learned about California. He reported that military conditions there were generally favorable, although anti-Union sentiment was growing in Southern California. That part of the state was "becoming dangerous," he added, and it was "indispensably necessary to throw reinforcements" into the area.

Sumner reported that supporters of secession had told the people there that they would be "ruined" by taxes that had been imposed "to maintain the war."[1] Henry Hamilton, pro-Southern editor of the *Los Angeles Star*, confirmed Sumner's allegation, telling readers that new taxes had been imposed "to enable the Administration to carry on a wholesale butchery of the people of the Southern States, who have the temerity to ask to be let alone, and allowed to govern themselves." "Was ever such a law devised?" he asked. "Woe to you who do not support 'Uncle Abe,' for he is invested with greater power than ever Caesar possessed over the Romans. . . . His Imperial Majesty, Abraham the Second (in direct succession from the illustrious Founder of the Kings of the Earth), Emperor of the United sovereignties [*sic*] of America, has been graciously pleased to order that a tax of 15 cents a pound be levied upon all the tea, coffee and sugar consumed by his subjects—for the purpose of subduing his enemies."[2]

Sumner took action by creating a new Military District of Southern California and sending Brig. Gen. George Wright to take command of it. He removed all officers whose loyalty to the Union was doubtful and armed the ocean steamers that regularly carried gold from California to Panama for transfer to other ships that would carry them on to New York and Washington. He ordered army regulars to withdraw from their duty patrolling native peoples in the West and dispatched them to California's Fort Mojave and Fort Tejon, where they quickly established Federal authority.[3] He continued to advise Lincoln's War Department that he had "no doubt but there is some deep scheming to draw California into the secession movement; in the first place as the 'Republic of the Pacific,' expecting afterwards to induce her to join the Southern Confederacy. . . . The troops now here will hold their positions and all the Government property, but if there should be a general uprising of the people, they could not, of course, put it down." Sumner assured his superior that "the course of events at the East will control events here. So long as the General Government is sustained, and holds the capital the Secessionists cannot carry this State out of the Union."[4]

The military orders of Sumner were received by the army quartermaster posted in Los Angeles, Capt. Winfield Scott Hancock. Born in 1824 in Montgomery County, Pennsylvania, Hancock had attended West Point, graduating eighteenth in a class of twenty-five in 1844. When the war with Mexico erupted, he became a staff officer under Maj. Gen. Winfield Scott, the man for whom he was named, and saw action in the Battle of Churubusco, Mexico, on August 20, 1847. After the war, he was given assignments in Florida, Kansas, and Utah before being sent in 1858 to California, and stationed in Los Angeles.

The intensely pro-Southern and pro-secessionist sentiments that prevailed in Southern California forced Hancock to be vigilant in protecting the arms he was pledged to guard. When he received news of the fall of Fort Sumter, he sent letters to General Scott asking that he be returned eastward.[5] Finally, in the summer of 1861, he received the orders he asked for, and headed back to the war zone, beginning a combat career that led him to the Battle of Gettysburg, where he was successful in thwarting flanking movements by Robert E. Lee. He was seriously wounded in the battle, however, and had to spend six months in recuperation. He was much admired by General Grant, who called him the "most conspicuous" of all the Union commanders who had never exercised independent command.[6]

Sumner was called away from San Francisco in October 1861 and replaced by Brig. Gen. George Wright, who served until he was succeeded by the Ohio-born Maj. Gen. Irvin McDowell, commander of the poorly prepared Union forces at the Battle of First Bull Run. Only forty-two years old, McDowell arrived in San Francisco on June 30, 1864.[7]

Lincoln's initial call for seventy-five thousand militia volunteers following the fall of Fort Sumter was followed by additional calls. On July 24, 1861, then secretary of war Simon Cameron sent California governor John G. Downey a call for one regiment of infantry and five companies of cavalry to guard the overland mail route from the Carson Valley in the Nevada Territory to Salt Lake City in Utah and Fort Laramie in Wyoming. Under that call, one full regiment of ten companies of infantry was raised, which became the First California Infantry, and five companies of cavalry, which became the First Battalion of the First California Cavalry. A second call was made to Downey on August 14, this time for four regiments of infantry and one of cavalry to be placed at the disposal of General Sumner. Native Californians volunteered, with encouragement from President Lincoln and his military subordinates.[8]

The ranks of the native Californians included many prominent Hispanic names, among them Andrés Pico, brother of Pío Pico, two-time governor of Mexican California; Salvador Vallejo, brother of Mariano Guadalupe Vallejo, former commanding general of the army in Mexican California; José Ramon Pico, a prominent native Californian from the northern part of the state; and Antonio Maria de la Guerra, a member of the most prominent Spanish Californian family in Santa Barbara.[9]

Public sentiment in California on the best way to meet the Confederate secession varied widely. On May 11, 1861, the streets of San Francisco were crowded with pro-Union supporters who marched to the beat of bands, waved flags, and listened to fervent pro-Unionist speeches. One of the most enthusiastic speeches was delivered by the previously fence-straddling Democratic senator Milton Latham, who had decided that supporting the Union and opposing the Confederacy was a much better path to follow. The *Daily Alta California* told its readers that the city had not been so crowded at any time in its history and that not less than a hundred thousand people had come to participate.[10]

Pro-Union sentiment was not as enthusiastic in other places. Responding to the San Francisco demonstration, which he did not participate in, Governor Downey wrote a public letter saying that he did not believe "that an aggressive war should be waged upon any section of the Confederacy, nor do I believe that this Union can be preserved by a coercive policy." A self-described "Union Man" responded in the pages of the *Sacramento Daily Union*, asking what Downey meant "by such language. Does he believe that it is improper to use the powers of the Government to put down the arm of rebellion which has been raised for the purpose of putting down the Government? Would he call putting down a rebellion which has disgraced us as a nation, an aggressive war? Is this what he means by 'coercion policy'?"[11] Another newspaper in the mining area of the Sierra foothills examined Downey's letter, explaining to its readers that it had formerly supported him for another term as governor but could no longer do so. It described his letter as "the language, emphatically, of equivocation."[12]

Sentiment in Southern California was strongly pro-Confederate. Angry crowds gathered in the Bella Union Hotel and the Montgomery Saloon in Los Angeles to shout their praise of Jefferson Davis and sing angry songs such as "We'll Hang Abe Lincoln to a Tree" and "We'll Drive the Bloody Tyrant from Our Dear Native Soil."

A few days after news of the surrender of Fort Sumter reached Los Angeles, a huge portrait of Confederate general P. G. T. Beauregard was hung in the Bella Union's saloon and welcomed with cheers. Henry Hamilton of the *Los Angeles Star* was the journalistic voice of the city's anti-Unionist feelings. He condemned President Lincoln as a tyrant, writing that "instead of a Federal Government composed of a Legislature, Judicial and an Executive Department, we find the whole power of government seized by one man, and exercised as irresponsibly as by the Czar of Russia."[13]

Los Angeles–based attorney Joseph Lancaster Brent was one of the most active Confederate sympathizers in Southern California. Born in 1826 in Maryland, he became an attorney in Louisiana and came to California in 1851, settling in Los Angeles. In his law practice, he served as Los Angeles city attorney and represented many of the men whose titles to land grants they had received from the Spanish and Mexican authorities were being challenged.[14] His political life was also active. He served as a Los Angeles city councilman, as superintendent of schools, and was twice elected to the California legislature, all the while helping to manage the Los Angeles affairs of Senator Gwin. In 1852 he joined a convention that sought to divide the largely agricultural southern half of the state from the mining and business-oriented northern half, but without success.[15] In early 1861 he joined a group of other prominent Southern Californians, including Governor Downey, who signed a petition to form the Los Angeles Mounted Rifles, an eighty-member militia whose stated purpose was the preservation of order in the southern part of the state.[16] After news of the fall of Fort Sumter reached California, however, the Los Angeles Mounted Rifles left for Texas to join the secessionists there. Brent left Los Angeles in November 1861 for San Francisco, where he boarded the steamer *Orizaba* on the first leg of a voyage that would take him to Panama and, after crossing the isthmus, permit him to go on to New York and then the Confederate states. Gwin, now a former senator, and Calhoun Benham, a prominent San Francisco-based attorney who had served as second to Judge David S. Terry in the duel in which he killed Senator Broderick, were aboard the same ship. All three were avid Confederate supporters, but in different ways. Gwin would remain a politician, but Benham and Brent were anxious to put on uniforms and fight. They happened to find some of General Sumner's officers aboard the *Orizaba* and tried to persuade them to join their journey to join the Confederacy. But when the stoutly Unionist Sumner, who had just surrendered his San Francisco command to General Wright, himself appeared on the ship, he ordered the arrest of Brent, Gwin, and Benham on treason charges. Sumner made the mistake, however, of allowing the arrested men to remain in their cabins, and there were whispers that they gathered all evidence against them and quickly dumped it overboard. When they got to New York, Sumner demanded that the men pledge to take no action against the Union in return for parole, but negotiations went on, finally reaching Lincoln, who allowed them to go on their way, perhaps believing that it was useless to extract meaningless promises. Brent and Benham reached the Confederates, where they joined the armed forces. Brent eventually became the chief of ordinance under Confederate general John B. Magruder and was sent for a while to Vicksburg and Port Hudson before returning to Magruder.[17] San Francisco's *Daily Alta California* prematurely reported him dead in October 1863, but he continued to fight.[18]

One of the most unusual supporters of the Confederate cause in Southern California was an African American named Peter Biggs. Born into slavery in Virginia in about 1820, he was owned by several different whites before he came to California in 1846 as the servant of a member of the so-called Mormon Battalion, a group of about five hundred Latter-day Saints who joined the American military during the war with Mexico. Biggs was in Los Angeles in 1850 and listed in the U.S. Census as one of only twelve blacks then living in the town. He lived a life as a free man (whether formally manumitted by his owner or just left alone after his owner left the state), married a young Hispanic woman, and operated a barber shop that catered to the needs of the local pro-Southern population. He found it necessary to curry favor with the local residents by proclaiming his support for Jefferson Davis and the secessionist states and celebrating news of the assassination of Abraham Lincoln after it reached California. Whether he personally shared these views or just adopted them to curry favor with the local pro-Southern population is not clear. After celebrating Lincoln's assassination, he was arrested by the local military and, with other whites who joined in the celebration, taken to the nearby military installation called Drum Barracks. He was held there until July, when he was released, but only after taking an oath of loyalty to the Union and obedience to its laws.[19]

Pro-secessionist fervor was strong in the town of Visalia, located in California's Central Valley. Southern supporters there regularly rode through the town, cheering Jefferson Davis and Stonewall Jackson. After a small federal garrison was established just north of the town, the secessionists ridiculed the Union soldiers as "Lincoln hirelings" and challenged them to fight. One fight resulted in the death of a Union soldier and the wounding of two Visalia secessionists. One Union officer stationed in the nearby garrison informed his superior that there were "more secessionists in this and the adjoining counties than there are in proportion to the population in any part of the United States this side of Dixie, or the so-called Confederate Government; and not only that they are in great numbers, but that they are organized and armed, ready at a moment's warning to take up their arms against the Government of the United States."[20] In October 1862 the *Visalia Equal Rights Expositor* characterized Lincoln as "a narrow-minded bigot, an unprincipled demagogue, and driveling, idiotic, imbecile creature." In December 1863 the same newspaper denounced Lincoln and his cabinet as "the most tyrannical and corrupt crew that ever polluted the earth with their presence."[21]

One of the most prominent Confederate sympathizers in the entire state was Benjamin Franklin Washington. He had been born on a Virginia plantation in 1820, the great-grandson of Samuel Washington, president George Washington's brother. He became a lawyer in his native state before crossing the plains to California in 1849, where he tried his hand at mining and then started a political and journalistic career that quickly made him a favorite

THE WAR CONTINUES

of the "Chivalry" (or "Chiv") faction of the Democratic Party.[22] (Their party rivals, led mainly by David Broderick, were sometimes called the "Shovelry," to distinguish them from Gwin's followers and emphasize their working-class roots.) He held some local offices in Sacramento before president James Buchanan, on the recommendation of Senator Gwin, appointed him to the financially coveted post of Collector of the Port of San Francisco. At the same time, he explored the possibility of becoming the state's governor or one of its U.S. senators, frequently announcing his intention to run but never achieving either office. He also achieved prominence in the newspaper industry, working as coeditor of the *Sacramento Daily State Journal*, then as editor of the *Democratic Press* in San Francisco, and in 1865 as editor of the *San Francisco Examiner*—all pro-Southern papers. All the while he was an energetic spokesman for Confederate ideology; and, after the Civil War ended, he helped launch the myth of the "Lost Cause," portraying the "Old South" as a land of pastoral simplicity simply seeking to exercise its constitutional rights when it was trampled upon by an oppressive and undemocratic North.[23]

California was never attacked by Confederate forces, although the realization that they might attempt to do so never completely disappeared. In the fall of 1861, a minor skirmish between rebel sympathizers and loyal troops took place in San Diego County. The most prominent sympathizer there was Daniel Showalter, a member of the state legislature representing John C. Frémont's home county of Mariposa. When the legislative resolution affirming California's loyalty to the Constitution and Union came up for a vote in May of that year, Showalter refused to vote for it. Challenged by Charles Piercy, a legislator from San Bernardino County who favored it, Showalter and Piercy met in Marin County for a duel, in which Showalter shot Piercy through the mouth and killed him. Since dueling was illegal in California, Showalter now headed south as a fugitive. In November he was apprehended in San Diego County by a patrol of the First Volunteer Cavalry and taken as a prisoner to Fort Yuma, where he spent several months in custody. He and his fellow rebels were finally released after giving their word of honor that they would not take up arms against the Union. They quickly violated the pledge and headed south into Texas. Showalter joined the Confederate army but was ultimately relieved of his command in May 1865. He then fled into Mexico, where he managed a hotel in the coastal town of Mazatlán.[24]

A much more menacing danger arose when Confederate troops from Texas invaded New Mexico. Jefferson Davis had long had an interest in New Mexico, and in Arizona, which was still a part of the New Mexico Territory when the war began. He believed that the southwestern territory had warm weather that could possibly support cotton plantations and the expansion of slavery. All planters knew that cotton depletes the soil and cannot be grown in the same fields year after year without replacing it with other crops that will replenish the soil, or simply moving on to new plantings in undeveloped land.[25] The southwestern territory was also a good place for the construction of a transcontinental railroad, which Lincoln fervently favored, and that Davis believed could connect the Southern states with the Pacific coast somewhere near San Diego. Davis sensed that it would open up vast sea lanes that led to Asia—a route that some proslavery Southerners liked to call "the great slavery road."[26] And he also believed that it was a land filled with gold and silver, which, if captured by the Confederacy, could help sustain the secessionist government.

Some of the rebels in Texas were anxious to extend Confederate rule over New Mexico. One was Lt. Col. John R. Baylor of the Second Texas Mounted Rifles, who led about three hundred men into New Mexico in July 1861. He proclaimed the southern half of New Mexico as the territory of Arizona, captured the town of Mesilla, and then started to march up the Rio Grande toward the most populous parts of the territory.[27] Another was Henry Hopkins Sibley, a West Point graduate and veteran army officer who quickly resigned his U.S. Army commission and hurried to Richmond, Virginia, to present a plan for the conquest of the Southwest to Confederate president Jefferson Davis.

Davis met with Sibley early in July and talked with him about the Texan's plans for the military conquest of New Mexico. After the war, Sibley's artillery commander, a Texan named Trevanion T. Teel, claimed that Sibley had shared grandiose plans with the Confederate president. According to Teel, after conquering New Mexico, Sibley said he would reinforce his army with New Mexicans, supply himself with U.S. Army military stores stashed in the territory, and march toward Colorado, Utah, and California, gathering supporters along the way. The mining regions of California and the fabulously rich deposits of silver in Nevada's Comstock lode would come under Confederate control. "The objective aim and design of the campaign was the conquest of California," Teel said. "'On to San Francisco' would be the watch word." Sibley would also open negotiations with the governors of the Mexican states of Chihuahua and Sonora and the territory of Baja California, and make them part of the Confederacy. Benito Juárez, president of the Republic of Mexico, who was then attempting to force the invading French army out of Mexico, would be unable to do anything about a pact between the northern governors and the Confederates and could not stop it.[28] Whatever Sibley might actually have said, Davis listened to him and conferred a brigadier general's commission on him. He also gave him orders to return to Texas and raise troops for his invasion of New Mexico.

Sibley arrived in Mesilla in December 1861, then advanced northward to capture Albuquerque, Santa Fe, and other key locations in New Mexico. When news reports of Sibley's movements reached General Sumner in San Francisco, he ordered Col. James Carleton of the First California Infantry Regiment to leave San Francisco for Southern California.

Carleton was a colorful army officer, originally from Maine, who had participated in a war with Native Americans in 1838 and joined the regular army in 1839. He traveled to California with Brig. Gen. Stephen W. Kearny in 1846, then fought in the Mexican War, where he was breveted for gallantry in the Battle of Buena Vista. Just promoted to the rank of colonel, and soon to be breveted as a brigadier general, Kearny was ready to follow General Sumner's orders. He first went to Southern California, where he oversaw the construction of the military establishment that became known as Drum Barracks.[29] He quickly dispatched a cavalry company to guard the road to Fort Yuma to prevent Confederate incursions, while he drilled his troops for a more extensive expedition.

News meanwhile arrived that Sibley's army had defeated Union troops under Col. Edward Richard Sprigg Canby at a place called Valverde on the Rio Grande, and from there had marched westward to capture Tucson. Carleton now gathered his troops together: the Fifth California Infantry, one company from the Second California Cavalry, and Company A of the Third U.S. Light Artillery. With a force numbering two thousand men and two hundred supply wagons, Carleton left his position on the Southern California coast in early April and headed toward Fort Yuma, where he arrived in May 1862. Reporting to his superiors on his expedition's movements in Arizona, including many skirmishes with the Native Americans, he named the expedition the "Column from California." It would later be remembered as the "California Column."[30]

In the meantime, Union Maj. John M. Chivington of the First Colorado Volunteers received orders to march toward Santa Fe. In a mountain pass called La Glorieta, about twenty miles southeast of Santa Fe, he encountered a force of close to three hundred Texans under Maj. Charles L. Pyron. The pass was a mountain defile through which the old Santa Fe Trail led American travelers into New Mexico, some to trade with the residents there and many others on their way to settle in California. Chivington's troops battled with Pyron's Confederates on March 26 and 27, 1862, soundly defeating them. The battle losses were substantial, with thirty-six Confederates killed, sixty wounded, and seventeen taken as prisoners. The Union loss was one officer and twenty-eight men killed, two officers and forty men wounded, and fifteen prisoners taken.[31] This engagement is typically remembered as "The Battle of Glorieta Pass." Some historians have dubbed it the "Gettysburg of the West."[32]

Leaving Yuma, Carleton now marched westward toward Tucson. Arriving there on May 8, he found that the Confederates had evacuated the town forty-eight hours earlier. He designated himself military governor of the Arizona Territory and rested there

THE WAR CONTINUES

for a month, before continuing his march toward the Rio Grande. Occupying forts along the way, he proceeded to Santa Fe, where he took command of the newly established Army Department of New Mexico, replacing Canby. The Confederates under Sibley had in the meantime abandoned New Mexico and retreated to San Antonio in Texas. Their dream of capturing the southwestern territories was over.

The Confederate forces' withdrawal into Texas now encouraged men who were more friendly to the Union to seek an eastern-western division of the New Mexico Territory. The eastern half, to retain the name of New Mexico, would, of course, adjoin the Texas border, and the western half, called Arizona Territory, would adjoin California. Many Unionists believed that this division would discourage any further Confederate incursions. A newspaper publisher, land developer, and businessman named Charles Poston, later remembered as "The Father of Arizona," happened to be in Washington, where he was well acquainted with Samuel Heintzelman, a West Point graduate and U.S. Army officer who had formerly been commander at Fort Yuma. Poston lobbied both Congress and President Lincoln for a bill that would achieve the desired east-west division. A bill was introduced in the House of Representatives in March 1862 to accomplish this, but it did not pass.

In 1863 the bill received the approval of both houses and went to Lincoln, who signed it into law on February 24, 1863. It created the east-west division that Poston asked for. Anticipating similar language that would become part of the Fifth Amendment to the Constitution when it was ratified at the end of 1865, the bill provided that "neither slavery nor involuntarily servitude" would be permitted in the territory, "otherwise than in the punishment of crimes, whereof the parties shall have been duly convicted."[33]

Poston, who became Arizona's first delegate to the U.S. House of Representatives, commissioned Tiffany & Co. to make a massive inkstand of pure Arizona silver. He then presented it to Lincoln, not just to thank him for his signature on the territorial bill but also to remind him that Arizona was a source of great mineral wealth. Later, Carleton had samples of pure gold from the area around Prescott, Arizona, sent to Lincoln's secretary of the treasury, Salmon P. Chase, with a request that he present them to Lincoln as further evidence of Arizona's mineral wealth.[34]

In the annual message he delivered to Congress on December 8, 1863, Lincoln noted events that had taken place in the southwestern territories. "The condition of the several organized Territories is generally satisfactory," he told Congress, "although Indian disturbances in New Mexico have not been entirely suppressed. The mineral resources of Colorado, Nevada, Idaho, New Mexico, and Arizona are proving far richer than has been heretofore understood."[35]

The California Column remained in the Southwest, reopening mail routes that had been shut off when the Confederates invaded, regarrisoning Union army forts, protecting supply roads from attacks, and providing defenses against attacks by the Apaches, who had not yet accepted American rule of a country they regarded as their own. They also made use of the corps of camels that Jefferson Davis had established when he was James Buchanan's secretary of war. Davis believed that camels would thrive in the southwestern deserts, as they did in those of Africa and the Middle East. In September 1862 Carleton turned his command over to Col. Joseph R. West.

Many young volunteers from California were anxious to go east and enter the army, but because of the defensive needs of the western state they were kept close to the Pacific coast. A group of volunteers then sought permission to go to Massachusetts and help that state fulfill its militia quotas. Californians made donations to raise the funds necessary to equip them and send them east. Before they left, they were cheered in public meetings. Thomas Starr King, the Unitarian minister who would soon journey to California and become one of the most eloquent defenders of the state's Union loyalty, regaled them in his church and went to visit them in their armory. Called the "California Battalion," these volunteers formed part of the Third Massachusetts Cavalry and took part in more than fifty encounters with the Confederates in the Virginia theater.[36]

As the war progressed, some secessionists formed groups that made efforts to further their cause in California. In early 1864 the Knights of the Golden Circle held up two stagecoaches near the mining town of Placerville. The Knights had been formed in the 1850s to advance the cause of slavery by filibustering into southern countries like Mexico and Central America, hoping to form a "golden circle" of slave states that would extend as far south as the tip of South America.[37] Their California leader was a former Missourian named Rufus Henry Ingraham, who headed up a group known as Captain Ingraham's Partisan Rangers. Another group of bandits was led by a rancher and former alcalde from Stockton named George Gordon Belt. He organized a group of partisan rangers that included men named John Mason and Jim Henry and sent them out to pillage the property of Union supporters in the countryside. For two years, the so-called Mason Henry Gang committed robberies, thefts, and murders along the central California coast and in the Central Valley. According to the best available evidence, they were unable to send any gold to the Confederacy.

The military authorities remained vigilant. In August 1862 Lincoln's secretary of war Edwin M. Stanton authorized local law enforcement officials to arrest persons who were discouraging army enlistments or giving aid and comfort to the enemy. When General Wright received Stanton's orders, he had a three-man commission oversee the proceedings and ordered the erection of a prison on Alcatraz Island to confirm the convicts.[38]

There was little naval activity off the Pacific coast, although the danger that an attack might be mounted, if not on one of the coastal fortifications, then on ships steaming in and out of California harbors, was never forgotten. Lincoln had imposed a blockade on the Confederate coastline, and its enforcement occupied almost all of the Union's naval power. One ship was always kept on station on the Pacific, however, to protect the valuable gold shipments that were regularly sent to the Atlantic states and to guard the important Pacific Mail from interruption. Orders that passed back and forth between Union army authorities and California almost always passed through Panama. The naval shipyard at Mare Island, north of San Francisco, was the permanent base of the U.S. government's Pacific Squadron.

Efforts were made to mount naval attacks. One—a clumsy but deadly serious attempt made in 1863—was the primary work of Asbury Harpending, who had joined forces with California secessionists. According to his own memoirs, Harpending had gone to Richmond, Virginia, and obtained a letter of marque from Jefferson Davis.[39] Letters of marque had been used in former American wars, but Lincoln considered their employment in the Civil War as sheer piracy, since the Confederacy was not a legitimate government but an aggregation of traitors.[40] With his Confederate letter, Harpending hoped to capture a ship in San Francisco Bay that was carrying gold and silver, seize the precious metals, and transport them to the Confederacy. His effort was discovered before it could be carried out and stopped by the sloop of war USS *Cyane.* He and his principal cohorts, Ridgley Greathouse, a Kentucky-born San Franciscan, and Alfred Rubery, a young Englishman who had visited the South before the war and admired its wealthy agricultural society, were arrested and tried before judges Stephen Field and Ogden Hoffman.

Although Field had just been appointed to the U.S. Supreme Court by Lincoln, he was still exercising his trial duties in the U.S. Circuit Court. With Field and Hoffman presiding, all three defendants were convicted. Sentencing Harpending, Field said, "The offense of which you have been convicted is treason—the highest offense known to the law. . . . Asbury Harpending, the judgment of the Court against you is that you be imprisoned for the period of ten years and that you pay a fine to the United States of $10,000; that your imprisonment be in the County Jail of the county of San Francisco until Congress provides some other place for your imprisonment."[41]

Harpending and Greathouse were transferred to the prison on Alcatraz Island.[42] Their imprisonment was shortened, however, when Lincoln issued a "Proclamation of Amnesty and Reconstruction" on December 8, 1863, granting pardons to "all persons who have, directly or by implication, participated in the existing rebellion." The pardon was, however, subject to exceptions, one of the most important of which provided that no pardoned person's slaves would be returned. Slavery was, in Lincoln's mind, clearly and forever ended—even though the Constitution had yet to be amended to achieve that end.[43]

Rubery did not receive the same relief as Harpending and Greathouse because Field determined that Lincoln's proclamation applied only to Americans, not to foreigners, and Rubery was from England.[44] But Lincoln, responding to entreaties from John Bright, a prominent member of the British Parliament who opposed slavery and favored the preservation of the Union, extended his forgiveness to Rubery with a special pardon that he issued less than a week later.[45]

The military authorities in California were generally restrained, but when they encountered supporters of secession they believed were dangerous to the preservation of the Union, they acted boldly. One such man was Charles Weller, a brother of former governor John Weller, an avid supporter of John Breckinridge's effort to win the presidency in 1860, and chairman of California's Democratic State Central Committee. In July 1864 Weller had told a crowd of mostly Irish immigrants that the Democrats would not be able to go to the polls the following November and therefore had to arm themselves. McDowell's order confining Weller on Alcatraz continued until his release on August 18.[46]

ON SEPTEMBER 17, 1862, UNION TROOPS UNDER MCCLEL-lan met Confederate troops under Lee in a furious battle along Antietam Creek near Sharpsburg, Maryland, forcing Lee to retreat. McClellan was so slow and almost hesitant in pursuing Lee that Lincoln believed he might never capture him. So on November 5 he notified McClellan of his removal and, a few days later, named Ambrose Burnside as his replacement. Burnside was an affable officer from Rhode Island, well-liked by other officers, but almost as hesitant as McClellan, so when he attacked Lee at Fredericksburg, Virginia, in December, he suffered more than twelve thousand casualties and was forced to retreat. Recognizing Burnside's weakness, Lincoln called Joseph Hooker, one of the generals who had spent a long time in California, to the White House and offered him the Union command.

Born in Massachusetts in 1814, Hooker had graduated twentieth in a class of fifty at West Point in 1837, and then gone on to fight bravely in the Seminole and Mexican Wars.[47] In Mexico he served as chief of staff for both Zachary Taylor and Winfield Scott, but earned the enmity of Scott when he testified against him in the court-martial of another general. He was sent to California in 1849 as adjutant to Brig. Gen. Persifor F. Smith, commander of the Pacific Division of the U.S. Army, but on February 21, 1853, he resigned his commission and took up the life of a farmer in the Sonoma Valley, north of San Francisco. He remained there until the outbreak of the Civil War, when he went to Washington and approached Lincoln directly, asking for a combat position. Lincoln knew that Hooker's reputation was mixed. He was considered a determined battler—his nickname was "Fighting Joe"—but he also had a reputation as a heavy drinker, a gambler, and a womanizer. He was nevertheless given command of a division that participated in the Peninsula campaign of March through August of 1862 and the battles of Seven Pines, White Oak Swamp, Malvern Hill, Second Bull Run (Manassas), and Bristoe Station. On January 26, 1863, Lincoln wrote Hooker a personal letter:

Major General Hooker:

General.

I have placed you at the head of the Army of the Potomac. Of course I have done this upon what appear to me to be sufficient reasons. And yet I think it best for you to know that there are some things in regard to which, I am not quite satisfied with you. I believe you to be a brave and a skilful [sic] soldier, which, of course, I like. I also believe you do not mix politics with your profession, in which you are right. You have confidence in yourself, which is a valuable, if not an indispensable quality. You are ambitious, which, within reasonable bounds, does good rather than harm. But I think that during Gen. Burnside's command of the Army, you have taken counsel of your ambition, and thwarted him as much as you could, in which you did a great wrong to the country, and to a most meritorious and honorable brother officer. I have heard, in such way as to believe it, of your recently saying that both the Army and the Government needed a Dictator. Of course it was not *for* this, but in spite of it, that I have given you the command. . . .

Beware of rashness, but with energy, and sleepless vigilance, go forward, and give us victories.

Yours very truly

A. Lincoln.[48]

Hooker reorganized the Army of the Potomac, improved its intelligence gathering abilities, and boosted the confidence of his troops. He devised a plan he believed would secretly flank Lee's forces on the south side of Virginia's Rappahannock River. When he met Lee at the Battle of Chancellorsville in May 1863, however, Lee outflanked his troops, inflicting heavy losses. Hooker's reputation was badly damaged, and his own confidence to lead his troops was crippled when General Halleck refused his request for additional troops. So on June 28, 1863, three days before the battle of Gettysburg, he surrendered his command to Maj. Gen. George Gordon Meade. Meade continued to serve as U. S. Grant's status and reputation grew. On March 4, 1864, Lincoln signed a certificate making Grant a lieutenant general, a rank previously held only by George Washington.

Discussion about the upcoming presidential election began in 1863, if not sooner. Lincoln's supporters were concerned about whether he would be nominated for a second term—or would even seek a second nomination. No president since the Democrats' Andrew Jackson had served more than one term, and the persistence of the military conflict with the Confederate states added to the uncertainty that surrounded Lincoln's status. In October 1863 Illinois congressman Elihu B. Washburne wrote Lincoln about various matters, including that his brother Maj. Gen. Cadwallader

C. Washburn [*sic*] was seeking a leave of absence to enable him to attend to important personal business.[49] Congressman Washburne also informed Lincoln that Thomas Campbell, a member of the California state legislature from San Francisco, had written him that if Lincoln sought the nomination he would clearly support him, but "the whole patronage of the Government in California" would be against him. Lincoln replied to Washburne in a letter dated October 26, 1863, stating, "A second term would be a great honor and a great labor, which together, perhaps, I would not decline, if tendered."[50]

In November 1863 California senator John Conness came to the White House with a group of supporters, most who were citizens of Pennsylvania, to present Lincoln with a gold cane that had belonged to California's deceased senator David C. Broderick. According to the *Cincinnati Gazette*, Lincoln accepted the cane "and, with much emotion, replied that he never personally knew the Senator's friend, Mr. Broderick, but he had always heard him spoken of as one sincerely devoted to the cause of human rights." The cane was "of that class of things, the highest honor that could be conferred upon him. If, in the position he had been placed, he had done anything that entitled him to the honor the Senator had assigned him, it was a proud reflection that his acts were of such a character as to merit the affiliation of the friend of a man like David C. Broderick."[51]

Despite his willingness to accept the upcoming nomination, Lincoln was not optimistic that he would be reelected. His Republican Party had joined with pro-Union Democrats and others to form what they called the National Union Party, hoping to give non-Republicans the chance to support him without seeming disloyal to their own party. But Lincoln was not confident that the voters would give him a second term as their national leader. No president since Andrew Jackson had been elected to two terms in office. Lincoln's erstwhile secretary of the treasury, Salmon P. Chase, had furtively sought to replace him as the Republican Party nominee, although he had soon withdrawn from the competition, still leaving some opposition to Lincoln's candidacy. Further, there was a growing sense of unrest about the continuation of the war and Lincoln's seeming inability to bring it to a close. The Democrats boldly proclaimed the Civil War a failure, demanded the immediate end of hostilities, and called for a national convention to restore the Union by negotiating with the Confederates.

On August 23 Lincoln recorded his feelings on paper, writing: "This morning, as for some days past, it seems exceedingly probable that this Administration will not be re-elected. Then it will be my duty to so co-operate with the President-elect as to save the Union between the election and the inauguration; as he will have secured his election on such ground that he can not [*sic*] possibly save it afterwards."[52] Lincoln folded the paper and securely sealed it before asking the members of his cabinet to sign its back without reading it. He had been nominated at the National Union Convention in Baltimore on June 7, with Andrew Johnson of Tennessee as his vice-presidential running mate. Johnson had been chosen because his strong Unionist sentiments seemed to outweigh his other pro-Southern opinions. The National Union platform called for the preservation of the Union and the abolition of slavery. The Democratic Party held its convention in Chicago on August 29 and nominated Lincoln's former commanding general George B. McClellan for president and George H. Pendleton of Ohio for vice president. At the same time, a small group of Republicans formed a "Radical Democracy" party and, meeting in Cleveland on May 31, nominated the California pioneer John C. Frémont as their candidate, but Frémont withdrew before the election.

As the election drew nearer, Lincoln's prospects seemed to improve. Maj. Gen. Sherman had successfully captured Atlanta in early September, and Union major general Philip H. Sheridan had achieved major victories in the Shenandoah Valley in the autumn. People who supported Lincoln's reelection as president marched through the streets of Northern California cities waving flags and playing march music. Those who opposed Lincoln were also active, parading through the streets to bands playing tunes like "Dixie Land" and "Johnny Comes Marching Home."[53]

The election was held on November 8, 1864. California's preliminary voting totals, which came over the telegraph lines, were mostly good for Lincoln. As the numbers for him grew, a column of some four thousand men marched through San Francisco's streets, singing "The Battle Cry of Freedom," while women crowded balconies laughing, crying joyously, and waving handkerchiefs and flags.[54] The final totals were very good. In California, Lincoln received 62,053 popular votes, or 58.6 percent of the total, while McClellan received 43,837 votes, or 41.4 percent of the total. Nationally, Lincoln received 2,218,388 popular votes to McClellan's 1,812,807, a total of more than 55 percent of the electoral votes to McClellan's slightly less than 45 percent.

On December 6, 1864, Lincoln delivered his final message to Congress on the state of the Union. It was, of course, generally favorable, and in many ways hopeful. It included, among other things, a statement repeating his ardent support of the construction of the transcontinental railroad connecting California and its mineral riches to the rest of the nation:

> The great enterprise of connecting the Atlantic with the Pacific States by railways and telegraph lines has been entered upon with a vigor that gives assurance of success, notwithstanding the embarrassments arising from the prevailing high prices of materials and labor. The route of the main line of the road has been definitely located for 100 miles westward from the initial point at Omaha City, Nebr., and a preliminary location of the Pacific Railroad of California has been made from Sacramento eastward to the great bend of the Truckee River in Nevada. . . . It is believed that the product of the mines of precious metals in that region has during the year reached, if not exceeded, one hundred millions [sic] in value.[55]

On March 4, 1865, Lincoln delivered his second inaugural address on the east front of the Capitol. It was one of the most thoughtful speeches he had ever given, one that sensed the coming victory in the war against secession and slavery but also expressed his hopes for the future. It has been remembered by many as Lincoln's "greatest speech."[56] Excerpts from it are most memorable:

THE WAR CONTINUES

Fondly do we hope, fervently do we pray, that this mighty scourge of war may speedily pass away. Yet, if God wills that it continue until all the wealth piled by the bondsman's two hundred and fifty years of unrequited toil shall be sunk, and until every drop of blood drawn with the lash shall be paid by another drawn with the sword, as was said three thousand years ago, so still it must be said "the judgments of the Lord are true and righteous altogether."

With malice toward none, with charity for all, with firmness in the right as God gives us to see the right, let us strive on to finish the work we are in, to bind up the nation's wounds, to care for him who shall have borne the battle and for his widow and his orphan, to do all which may achieve and cherish a just and lasting peace among ourselves and with all nations.[57]

Once in command of the Union armies, General Grant undertook a relentless and bloody campaign against Lee's Army of Northern Virginia. On April 12, 1865, he accepted Lee's surrender at Appomattox Courthouse, Virginia.

When news of Lee's surrender reached California, the *Daily Alta California* rejoiced:

> In the lands of royalty, on the death of a King and the accession of his successor to the throne, the proclamation is made, "The King is dead—long live the King." We can paraphrase the same by exclaiming today, "Rebellion is extinguished—long live President Lincoln." The Chief General of the rebels, Lee, has laid his arms down and surrendered to Lieut.–Gen. Grant, upon terms proposed by the latter. The precise terms, we are uninformed of, but presume they are characteristic of our commanding General, the example of which he made at Vicksburg. We have cause to rejoice—the whole civilized world has cause to join with us, and all civilization will reecho the sentiment.[58]

The war was not yet over—peripheral battles had yet to be fought in the hinterlands—and one of the most important of all the arms had not yet been laid down. It was a pistol in the hands of an actor who invaded a box in Ford's Theatre in Washington DC on April 14, 1865. The bullet shot from the actor's pistol would reverberate far beyond the national capital, far beyond California even, and throughout the world. In California, however, it would be greeted by astonishment.

13

Letters from Washington

FROM THE END OF 1862 UNTIL AUGUST OF 1865, READERS OF one of California's most important newspapers received frequent and informative reports from Lincoln's White House. They were the work of a young newspaper reporter named Noah Brooks, who became one of the president's best friends in the capital city. Published in the *Sacramento Daily Union*, the reports—called "Letters from Washington"—were signed with the reporter's pen name, "Castine."

Noah Brooks was one of the most interesting figures in the history of mid-nineteenth-century American journalism. Born in the village of Castine on the coast of Maine in 1830, he became an orphan when he was only seven and was raised by his older sisters. He left Castine for Boston when he was seventeen and there began to study art and journalism. He eventually became more productive as a writer than as an artist, although he spent much of his time painting landscapes, and even furniture, houses, and boats, to earn money. He moved to Illinois in 1854, where he first became acquainted with Lincoln, but moved on to California five years later and began to work on newspapers.

While living in the Illinois town of Dixon, Brooks tried to earn money by painting houses and operating a paint store, but he soon began to write for newspapers. Covering the political campaign of 1856, he heard Lincoln give a long speech in support of the presidential candidacy of John C. Frémont. At a rally in the Illinois town of Oregon, he heard Lincoln give another pro-Frémont speech. There he and Lincoln met personally, talking together for an hour or more about the campaign and the future of the Republican Party. Both had been Whigs but had converted to the new party in the conviction that it would address the nation's problems, notably the spread of slavery, more effectively. Frémont's campaign was, as Lincoln anticipated, a failure.[1]

Brooks homesteaded a tract of land in Kansas in 1857, hoping to make a home there for himself and his wife, Caroline, while at the same time helping to keep slavery from spreading into the territory. But when the crops he planted there failed, he returned to Illinois, where he again met Lincoln, this time during the Lincoln-Douglas debates of 1858. His efforts to earn a living in Illinois were also poor, so in 1859 he headed west, joining a party of men headed for the Pike's Peak area of what would later become Colorado, where gold had been discovered in 1857. When they reached Fort Laramie, they learned that enthusiasm for the gold fields around Pike's Peak was rapidly coming to an end, so they decided to push even farther west, this time heading for California. It was a long and demanding trip, taking them through the Mormon settlement at Salt Lake City, through the Humboldt Sink, and over the soaring Sierra Nevada into the Golden State, where they arrived in late summer, tired but pleased to see beautiful country all around them.

They reached the town of Marysville in October. It then ranked as the third most populous California city, behind San Francisco and Sacramento, and Brooks soon found work there—first as a painter but, more importantly, as a journalist. He wrote newsletters for the San Francisco *Evening Mirror* and, in the fall of 1860, became a part owner of the *Marysville Daily Appeal*. As the only daily newspaper outside San Francisco that supported Lincoln's presidential candidacy, the *Appeal* led a majority of Marysville's voters into Lincoln's 1860 electoral column. Brooks's recollections of his acquaintance with Lincoln surely helped:

> Several years ago it was our good fortune to come frequently in contact with the man who is now the distinguished banner—

bearer of the Republican party, and who, soon, in all human probability, will be called by the voice of the people to take the Presidential chair. In 1856, among the other eloquent men who canvassed the State of Illinois for Fremont [sic], was Lincoln, who spent the months of September and October in attending the numerous meetings which were held all over the State, speaking everywhere to crowds who always turned out to hear the "Henry Clay of Illinois," as he was then for the first time denominated. During the latter part of September, he first spoke in the town in which we then resided, and we shall never forget the profound impression which his speech created upon the minds of all who heard him. There was an irresistible force of logic, a clinching power of argument, and a manly disregard of everything like sophistry or claptrap, which could not fail to arrest the attention and favorably impress the most prejudiced mind. . . . Democrats who had withstood the arguments and truths of scores of able men were forced to confess that their reason was led captive while they listened to the plain, straight-forward and sledge-hammer logic of the speaker.[2]

When the votes were counted in the county surrounding Marysville, Lincoln received more votes than any of his three opponents: Stephen Douglas, John Breckinridge, and John Bell. He outpolled Douglas and Bell in Marysville itself, although Breckinridge actually received twelve more votes than he did.[3]

Mrs. Brooks joined her husband in Marysville, where the two lived happily until her unexpected death, in May 1862, from the complications of childbirth. Brooks was shattered by this loss but determined to continue his work. He soon got a position as a "special correspondent" for the *Sacramento Daily Union*, which called for him to go to Washington and send back reports on events and people in the war-torn city. He sailed out of San Francisco on November 1, 1862, on the steamship *Golden Age*, which took him to Panama. From there he found passage on another ship that took him to New York, where he arrived on November 24. From there it was a short trip to Washington, where he began his work.[4]

Brooks was not on intimate terms with Lincoln when he first arrived in Washington, but as he covered Congress and some military events, he also heard the president speak in public. He soon received a message from Lincoln, saying that he had heard that Brooks was in town and wanted to see him "for old times' sake." Years later, Brooks remembered their first White House meeting. "Do you suppose I ever forget an old acquaintance?" Lincoln said. "I reckon not."[5] Of course, Brooks was delighted to have access to the chief executive, who would become one of his most valuable news sources. But he also became a friend, for Lincoln seemed to enjoy Brooks's visits and the times they spent together as much as Brooks did.

Years after the president's death, Brooks was frequently credited as having become one of Lincoln's closest friends in Washington. Not all historians agree with that assessment, however. The respected California-based historian Don Fehrenbacher has doubts about the oft-reported intimacy between the two men.[6] Lincoln scholar Harold Holzer expresses some skepticism about many of the statements Brooks wrote about Lincoln—describing them as "claims."[7] But Lincoln biographer and historian Michael Burlingame, who closely studied Brooks's Washington writing career, writes that the stories of the friendship between the two men were probably accurate. "During the Civil War," Burlingame writes in an edition of Brooks's work published in 1998, "few people seem to have been closer to Lincoln" than Brooks.[8] Whether Brooks was in fact one of Lincoln's closest friends in the White House, his reports about what went on in the nation's capital during the war, and particularly what President Lincoln did and said, reached large reading audiences in California. They were in a way a direct channel between the nation's capital and the far distant Pacific coast state.

Brooks's first "Letter from Washington" bore the date of December 4, 1862, but was not published in Sacramento until December 20. It was more than four thousand words long and gave readers a lot of details about what was happening in the capital and how it was affecting Lincoln. It had not been sent over the telegraph, for the telegraph company charged high fees for long messages, so letters like Brooks's were transmitted to California by ship or by the Overland Mail, which ran stagecoaches.

Brooks told his readers that the trial of Fitz John Porter, for charges brought against him by Inspector General Brig. Gen. Benjamin S. Roberts, was underway. He included a letter that Maj. Gen. John Pope had sent to Maj. Gen. Henry W. Halleck reporting on unfortunate military events in Tennessee. He explained that Congress was in session but that it had "not manifested much of a disposition to go to work." He reported that the Senate would soon receive a list of new brigadier generals, totaling "some fifty in number," from President Lincoln. He described the policy of the "anti-administration party" in Congress, headed up by senator Garrett Davis of Kentucky. He described a new "Monitor" that was being built in New Jersey, with iron deck beams and bomb-proof plating, for transportation to the California coast, to meet any attacks that might arise there. And he concluded with a report of "how the president looks," describing him and his wife, Mary, as they attended Dr. Phineas D. Gurley's Presbyterian Church, "where they habitually attend." He wrote:

The building was crowded, as usual, with dignitaries of various grades, besides sinners of lesser note and rank. Conspicuous among them all, as the crowd poured out of the aisles, was the tall form of the Father of the Faithful, who is instantly recognized by his likeness to the variety of his published likenesses. . . . Whatever may be said of Abraham Lincoln by friend or foe, no one can ever question the pure patriotism and the unblenching honesty of the man. He inspires that feeling by his personal presence as much as by his acts; and as he moves down the church aisle, recognizing, with a cheerful nod, his friends on either side, his homely face lighted with a smile, there is an involuntary expression of respect on every face, and men, who would scorn to "toady" to any President, look with commiserating admiration on that tall, mourning figure which embodies Abraham Lincoln, whom may God bless.[9]

Brooks found Washington to be dominated everywhere by long lines of army wagons and artillery that continuously rumbled through the streets. He had come from the shores of what he called "the Peaceful Sea" (the Pacific Ocean), so he was troubled by what he later recalled was "the clatter of galloping squads of cavalry," "the clank of sabers," and "the measured beat of marching infantry," which were "ever present to the ear." Soldiers in blue uniforms could be seen everywhere on the sidewalks. Army regulations forbade them from drinking while on duty, so most bar rooms had signs posted saying, "Nothing sold to soldiers." To soften this warning, Brooks said that some of the drinking places displayed "artistically painted signs showing the three arms of the military service over which were printed the words 'No liquors sold to.'"[10]

The reports that Brooks sent back to California were filled with interesting descriptions of places and people and analyses of important events. In his "Letter from Washington" dated December 12, 1862, he told his readers about the admission to the Union of the new state of West Virginia, saying it was "of doubtful expediency and of disputed constitutionality" and that it was motivated more by the desire of Congress to release the people of the new state from "the bogus government at Richmond than to acquire any greater strength in the legal States." He described an appearance General McClellan made before a court of inquiry presided over by Maj. Gen. Irvin McDowell, saying: "The General [McClellan] is small, quite small—rather dapper and trimly built; not slight, but with round, full outlines, the face being Smooth and almost boyish, though not very fair, but indicative of good living. McDowell, who sits opposite, with his square, full face, and commanding figure, twice the General in looks that McClellan is."

He told readers about the creation of the new Bureau of Internal Revenue, "a novel exercise of Federal resource" that "demands a new set of national energies to meet the constantly recurring emergencies." He told readers that the Overland Mail from California was now arriving with greater regularity in the capital city; and returns from the Federal assessor in California, a prominent Republican named Caleb T. Fay who had hopes for election as governor, indicated a revenue of $97,785.15. He commented: "The worthy gentleman who made these returns to the Commissioner of Internal Revenue will probably be gratified to know that as the Chief Clerk looked over the beautifully written pages of the schedules, he said, 'These are the best gotten up returns which have ever been made to this office from any State.'"

In the same issue, Brooks told readers that extensive preparations were underway "to furnish a bountiful Christmas dinner to all of the inmates of the military hospitals in the city and vicinity." The movement had been started by the wife of secretary of the interior Caleb Blood Smith. Mary Lincoln joined in the effort, sending an order to Pennsylvania "for over five hundred chickens and turkeys for her share of the feast."[11]

On December 26 he addressed complaints made by some Californians that the news sent there by telegraph was being censored. He assured his readers that if they weren't getting news, people in the rest of the country weren't getting it either, "for if anything concerning battles or consummated military movements is made public here, you in California get it; and there is no censorship of the telegraph except so far as relates to the movements of armies not yet consummated, and which it is necessary should be kept out of the public prints until they are accomplished."[12]

On January 3, 1863, Brooks penned a letter that dealt with one of the great events of the war—and of American history—Lincoln's Emancipation Proclamation, which he called the president's "freedom proclamation." None doubted that it would be issued, for Lincoln had earlier drafted a preliminary proclamation dealing with the same subject, "yet it did take everybody by surprise," Brooks wrote, "for notwithstanding all of the pooh-poohing of the opposition, this long-looked-for document comes fraught with momentous consequences." He continued:

In this age of marvels and of mighty events nothing seems greatly marvelous [*sic*], and we rush on to the next sensation heedless of the last. But the proclamation has proclaimed liberty and freedom, broad and unconditional, to all of that dark dominion of rebeldom which our arms are now to bring back to the sway of the sovereign rule. This is the new era, and is but the beginning of the end. Whatever may be the consequences, the act and the theory of the proclamation are sublime.

He told his readers that when the proclamation made its appearance in the Washington papers, it "was received with great sensation," and when it made its appearance in the last edition of the city's *Evening Star*, "there was a grand rush for it." He noted that the proclamation included some improvements over the wording of the preliminary proclamation and that the popular verdict was that it was "a dignified, able and statesmanlike paper." He said that even those who doubted whether the measure would actually achieve the results desired—saving the Union—could not help but admire its "calm, judicious phraseology."[13]

Brooks attended sessions of the Senate and the House of Representatives and reported on speeches made there that affected California. Early in February he told his readers that California senator James McDougall had given a speech excoriating the French invasion of Mexico and warning that it could have far-reaching effects, some going as far as California. The French claimed that they were only trying to collect debts properly due to them, but they were really trying to establish a dynasty and acquire cotton lands that would extend their political and economic control far into North America. Brooks reported that Massachusetts senator Charles Sumner answered McDougall by saying that the only way to oppose European influence in Mexico and other Latin American countries was by the suppression of the rebellion in the United States. Once that was accomplished, the other dangers from European powers would vanish.[14]

The letters from "Castine" covered most everything of importance that was taking place in Washington. He wrote about the gloomy morale felt in the city after the Union defeat at Fredericksburg. After the near disaster at Chancellorsville, Brooks wrote:

The wildest conceivable rumors were at once set on foot, and if one believed half that he heard he would go to bed that night with the full consciousness that Hooker was under arrest, that the President had gone down to put Halleck in command, that Stanton had resigned, that Lee had cut Hooker to pieces and was approaching Washington via Dumfries, that McClellan was coming on a special train from New York, also Sigel, likewise Butler, ditto Frémont and several other shelved generals.[15]

He recorded his observations of prominent officials, writing that Secretary of State Seward was "small in stature, big as to nose, light as to hair and eyes, averse to all attempts upon his portrait, and very republican in his dress and manner of living." Secretary of War Stanton was "stout, bespectacled, black as to hair and eyes, and Hebraic as to nose and complexion." Secretary of the Treasury Chase was a "large, fine-looking" man whose "well-flattered picture may be found on the left—had end of any one-dollar greenback, looking ten years handsomer than the light-haired secretary."[16]

Most interesting of all of the images Brooks described for his California readers were those of the man who lived in the White House. In later years, he remembered that Lincoln's face was "colorless and drawn" in 1862, and that his "newly grown whiskers added to the agedness of his appearance."[17] Lincoln was agitated after news came from Chancellorsville. "I shall never forget that picture of despair," Brooks wrote. "He held a telegram in his hand, and as he closed the door and came toward us I mechanically noticed that his face, usually sallow, was ashen in hue. The paper on the wall behind him was of the tint known as 'French gray,' and even in that moment of sorrow and dread expected I vaguely took in the thought that the complexion of the anguished President's visage was almost exactly like that of the wall." Lincoln gave the telegram to Brooks and said, "Read it—news from the Army."[18]

Brooks traveled out of Washington. He attended the political conventions in 1864. He went to Illinois and New England, and he visited Federal enclaves in Florida and South Carolina. Armed with a pass from Lincoln, he visited General Meade's headquarters at Williamsport, Maryland. When General Grant trapped Robert E. Lee in the Richmond-Petersburg fortifications in 1864, he took a steamship to the front to observe the tense confrontation where, dodging bullets, he saw the spires and windows of what he called "the doomed city" of Richmond.

About the same time, Brooks reported on the popular vote in Maryland that adopted a new state constitution abolishing slavery. The blacks in Washington had celebrated the event with a "jubilation" and a torchlight procession that marched to the White House where loud and repeated cheers brought out the president. Responding to the summons, Lincoln began by saying, "I have to guess, my friends, the object of this call, which has taken me quite by surprise this evening." A chief spokesman for the crowd shouted, "The emancipation of Maryland, sah." To which Lincoln replied:

> It is no secret that I have wished, and still do wish, mankind everywhere to be free. And in the State of Maryland how great an advance has been made in this direction. It is difficult to realize that in that State, where human slavery has existed for ages; ever since a period long before any here were born—by the action of her own citizens—the soil is made forever free. I have no feeling of triumph over those who were opposed to this measure and who voted against it, but I do believe that it will result in good to the white race as well as to those who have been made free by this act of emancipation, and I hope that the time will soon come when all will see that the perpetuation of freedom for all in Maryland is best for the interests of all, though some may thereby be made to suffer temporary pecuniary loss. And I hope that you, colored people, who have been emancipated, will use this great boon which has been given you to improve yourselves, both morally and intellectually; and now, good night.[19]

Enthusiastic cheers greeted the president's speech as he delivered it.

After Lincoln was reelected to a second term in November, events moved rapidly. In January 1865 he told Brooks that he was thinking of naming him to some official position, perhaps naval officer or surveyor of the Port of San Francisco, but after reflection decided that he would be more useful close at hand. Friends and advisers had been urging him to relieve his private secretaries, John G. Nicolay and John Hay, of their duties in the White House. Lincoln thought that Brooks would be an ideal man to take Hay's place, and if he did he could continue to write his Sacramento news reports. Brooks was happy to work for the president but realized that he could not continue to send his reports to Sacramento and discharge the secretary's duties in the White House at the same time. When Lincoln named Nicolay as consul and Hay as secretary of the American Legation in Paris, Brooks agreed to leave his newspaper work for a chance to serve "a man so dear to me."[20]

On April 1 Brooks reported that there was evidence in Washington that a "collapse of rebeldom" was drawing near. "Without any reference to the military movements which have begun within the past week, it is tolerably certain, from the accumulating testimony of rebels and of Unionists best situated for the purpose of obtaining information, that the so-called Southern Confederacy is 'done gone.' . . . The rebel army is demoralized beyond any hope of recovery."[21] On April 6 he reported that the Rebel capital of Richmond had been evacuated and that Lee's army had been "swept back from its base." "We have calmly and resignedly borne many great disasters and afflictions," he wrote, "and it is well the nation now has its greatest joy in the reflection that this is not a mere victory of brute force, but it is a crowning triumph to the principles of American liberty and American nationality; we are nearer now to the final proof that Americans can govern themselves, and that we are not a shipwrecked nation."[22]

On the evening of April 11, Lincoln appeared at a window above the semicircular avenue in front of the White House with the rolled manuscript of a speech in his hand. Standing behind him, concealed by drapery, Brooks held a candle over the manuscript as Lincoln read, dropping each page to the floor as it was finished. "The night was misty," Brooks wrote, "and the exhibition was a splendid one. The reflection of the illuminated dome of the Capitol on the moist air above was remarked as being especially fine; it was seen many miles away. Arlington House, across the river, the old home of Lee, was brilliantly lighted, and rockets and colored lights blazed on the lawn, where ex-slaves by the thousands sang 'The Year of Jubilee.'"[23]

Brooks reported on the event for his California readers, saying that there was "something terrible about the enthusiasm with which the beloved Chief Magistrate was received—cheers upon cheers, wave after wave of applause rolled up, the President modestly standing quiet until it was over. The speech was longer and of a different character from what most people had expected, but it was well received, and it showed that the President had shared in, and had considered, the same anxieties which the people have had, as this struggle had drawn to a close."[24] Brooks later remembered that the speech began with the words: "We meet this evening, not in sorrow, but in gladness of heart. The evacuation of Petersburg and Richmond, and the surrender of the principal insurgent army, give hope of a righteous and speedy peace, whose joyous expression cannot be restrained." Brooks told his readers that he himself was "near the front, and had the high pleasure of transmitting much of the good news to you, but no part of the honor or plan or execution is mine. To General Grant, his skillful officers and brave men, all belongs. The gallant navy stood ready, but was not in reach to take active part."[25]

The speech dealt mainly with the policy the government would follow in the reconstruction of the Southern states. It was "not the sort of speech which the multitude had expected," Brooks remembered. "In the hour of his triumph as the patriotic chief magistrate of a great people, Lincoln appeared to think only of the great problem then pressing upon the Government, a problem which would demand the highest statesmanship, the greatest wisdom, and the firmest generosity."[26]

When Brooks called again at the White House on April 14, Lincoln told him that he "had had a notion" of sending for him to go to the theater that evening with him and Mrs. Lincoln but that she had already made up a party to take the place of General and Mrs. Grant, who had unexpectedly left the city for New Jersey. On the way back home, Brooks met Schuyler Colfax, who was about to leave for a trip to California. They chatted for a while on the sidewalk, talking about the trip and the people Brooks knew in San Francisco and Sacramento. Brooks told Colfax that he and Lincoln had often talked about the possibility of the president taking up residence in California after he left the White House. Back home, Brooks played cards with his roommate. They soon heard a clatter on the outside streets. Brooks joked that it might be caused by cavalry units trying to capture the fugitive Confederate general Wade Hampton, and then went to bed. The next morning, his landlord awakened him by banging on his door and shouting, "Wake, wake, Mr. Brooks! I have dreadful news."[27]

The war was over, Lincoln's presidency was over, and by the end of June Noah Brooks's time in Washington was also over.

Andrew Johnson, Lincoln's successor as president, did not choose Brooks to be his private secretary, but he did appoint him as naval officer of the Port of San Francisco.[28] Brooks was content, for he longed to return to California. On July 1 he boarded the steamship *Ocean Queen* in New York and headed out to sea. Sailing with Thomas Shannon, a former Republican congressman who had been appointed as surveyor of the Port of San Francisco, Brooks reached Panama ten days later, then crossed the isthmus by train and boarded the steamship *Constitution*, which, with a short stop in Acapulco, took him and Shannon north to San Francisco, where they arrived on July 25.[29]

Brooks carried out his duties in the Port of San Francisco for a year before resuming his occupation as a journalist. He became the editor of the San Francisco *Daily Times* in 1866 and in 1867 became the managing editor of the *Daily Alta California*. Mark Twain knew him when he was with the *Alta* and later remembered him there as "a man of sterling character and equipped with a right heart."[30] In 1868 Brooks became one of the associate editors of the *Overland Monthly*, a monthly journal published in San Francisco where it was widely considered to be the western rival of the prestigious *Atlantic Monthly.* He traveled to New York in 1871, where he became night editor of Horace Greely's powerful *New York Tribune.* Three years later, he became an editorial writer for the *New York Times.* Then, in 1884, he assumed the duties of editor in chief of the Newark, New Jersey, *Daily Advertiser.*[31]

Brooks wrote many popular short stories, articles, and books in the years that followed.

He returned briefly to his birthplace on the coast of Maine coast in 1894, but in 1897 he came back to California for a visit. The *San Francisco Call* described him as "a newspaper man of National celebrity and a gifted contributor to recent literature of Abraham Lincoln" and said that he was "profoundly interesting when speaking of Lincoln."[32] Brooks went back home after a visit of two or three weeks, but moved back to California early in 1903. He was only sixty-seven years old, but his health was failing, and he died in Pasadena on August 17, 1903.[33]

He left no children. He did, however, leave a legacy in the form of the 258 "Letters from Washington" that had spanned the continent during the Civil War, tying Lincoln to California, and ultimately helping historians learn more than they would otherwise have known about the president and the western state.[34]

14

The View from Lone Mountain

ONE OF THE EARLIER EVENTS OF THE WAR HAD A PROFOUND effect on Lincoln. It was close to sunset on October 21, 1861, when he crossed Lafayette Park to visit the headquarters of General McClellan and receive the latest military news. He regularly made that walk, for the general's office had a telegraph receiver and the White House did not.

Two days earlier, anticipating possible Confederate incursions across the Potomac, McClellan had ordered a general reconnaissance of the upper Potomac Valley, and his subordinate, Brig. Gen. Charles P. Stone, had responded by leading Union forces across the river at Ball's Bluff, near the Virginia town of Leesburg. But Stone's foray was brief and only tentative, and he soon came back with his men. Under Stone's command, Col. Edward D. Baker led his regiment of volunteers, the First California, on October 22, 1861. Lincoln knew that Baker had taken his men up the river. He did not know, however, what the results of their march would be.

As the president entered the telegraph office, the keys were clicking, but the news was not good. Baker had led his men up the bluff above Edwards Ferry, where they met fierce Confederate fire, and Baker had been killed. Two journalists were waiting in McClellan's anteroom and saw the president as he emerged from the telegraph room, "unattended, with bowed head, and tears rolling down his furrowed cheeks." He almost fell as he stepped into the street. The journalists quickly rose from their seats to help him, but he did not need help. As the president disappeared down the street,

McClellan came out to see the journalists. "I have not much news to give you," he said tersely. "There has been a movement of troops across the Potomac at Edwards Ferry, under General Stone, and Colonel Baker is reported killed. That is about all I can give you."[1]

It was "about all" to McClellan, but not to Lincoln. The number of Federal troops lost in the encounter was relatively small—49 men killed, 158 wounded, and 714 reported missing—compared with the losses at the First Battle of Bull Run (Manassas), where 460 Federal soldiers had been killed, 1,124 wounded, and 1,312 were reported as missing.[2] For Lincoln, however, Ball's Bluff was a tragedy of major proportions. When he returned to the White House, he told Mary that Baker had been killed, and the following day he discussed the consequences of the encounter at Ball's Bluff with his cabinet. They shared the president's displeasure with the event, if not his bitter sorrow.

After Baker's death, Lincoln told William L. Stoddard, his personal secretary, that he loved Baker "like a brother, and mourned his untimely death bitterly."[3] He told Noah Brooks that Baker's death "smote upon him like a whirlwind from a desert."[4] Lincoln's affection for Baker had much to do with the years of political and legal activity they shared when they were young men in Illinois, but it was also attributable at least in part to the years Baker spent in California during the 1850s. Those years nourished Lincoln's growing interest in the western state and his oft-expressed wish to visit it, perhaps even to make his home in it, after he left the White House.

Baker's friendship with California's Democratic senator David C. Broderick, who shared his opposition to slavery, had encouraged him to act as Broderick's second in the duel with David S. Terry that resulted in Broderick's death. It also enabled him to address the mourners who assembled on Lone Mountain, a prominent eminence west of the city rising some 421 feet above sea level, when Broderick's body was brought there to be buried. Lone Mountain had clear views to the north across San Francisco Bay and to the west toward the Pacific Ocean. Baker told the mourners that Broderick died "having written his name in the history of the great struggle for the rights of the people against the despotism of organization and the corruption of power."[5]

Baker made his way back to Washington DC after Lincoln's victory in the presidential contest of 1860 and his own victory in the Oregon senatorial election that year, where he was united with his old friend and took up his Senate duties. News of his tragic death leading a regiment of troops at Ball's Bluff shocked not only Lincoln but also his followers in California and Oregon. His body was initially interred in the Congressional Cemetery in Washington, but was soon readied for transport back to San Francisco.

Oregonians wanted Baker to be buried in their state. Instead, his body was taken to San Francisco's Lone Mountain and the same burial ground in which Broderick had been interred just over two years earlier. Now, Thomas Starr King delivered the eulogy over Baker's body. One California newspaper reported that Baker's grave was near Broderick's, "and on the highest point of land in the Lone Mountain Cemetery," adding, "In sight of the place, and near, is the Ocean, the Golden Gate and the Bay. Further, the vision is almost unlimited, and the boundaries of the State eastward may nearly be traced."[6] King later said that Baker's death was "a great loss to this coast." Historian Glenna Matthews has written that the death of Baker, "with all its emotional coloration, with funeral services on each coast, can stand as a symbol of California's increasing integration into the national fabric."[7]

Soon after Baker's death, Lincoln's third son, the ten-year-old William Wallace Lincoln (called "Willie"), put pen to paper and drafted a poem that was printed in the *National Republican* on November 4 and later reprinted all over the country. It began with words that obviously indicated the affection the ten-year-old boy felt for the fallen Baker:

There was no patriot like Baker,
So noble and so true;
He fell as a soldier on the field,
His face to the sky of blue.[8]

Recollections of Lincoln indicate that he thought a lot about his departed friend Edward Baker and the place where his body was laid to rest. One evening in the summer of 1863, when he was living in the Soldier's Home on the heights north of the White House, a visitor spoke to him about Baker's burial place in the cemetery on Lone Mountain. Isaac N. Arnold, a Chicago newspaper editor, later wrote that "the name seemed to kindle his imagination and touch his heart. He spoke of this 'Lone Mountain' on the shore of the Pacific, as a place of repose, and seemed almost to envy Baker his place of rest. Lincoln then gave a warm and glowing sketch of Baker's eloquence, full of generous admiration, and showing how he had loved this old friend."[9]

Francis B. Carpenter, a portrait artist who spent considerable time with Lincoln, left a similar recollection of an unnamed lady from California who also visited Lincoln in the Soldier's Home. She had been present when Baker's body was laid to rest in San Francisco. She had heard Thomas Starr King's eulogy and was moved by it. As Carpenter recalled, she thought "the bare mention of Lone Mountain filled the minds of those who heard it with a solemn sense of awe and sorrow." She was not surprised when Lincoln seemed to allude to it in this way, "and gave, in a few deep-toned words, a eulogy on one of its most honored dead, Colonel Baker."[10]

Lincoln scholar Milton Shutes later told his readers that Lincoln in fact wanted to visit Lone Mountain and that he had often talked with Noah Brooks and Cornelius Cole about California, "the new country with the great future." There seems little doubt that he did talk about it; that he did remember much about Baker; that he did want to visit Lone Mountain one day and see "the new country with the great future," after the great Civil War was over.[11] History knows that he never made it there.

15

What Was Remembered

THE FIRST NEWS OF LINCOLN'S DEATH CAME TO CALIFORNIA by telegraph on Saturday morning, April 15, 1865. It was initially received with what the *Daily Alta California* called "doubt and hesitation," for there were "few who could bring themselves to believe that a crime so unspeakably atrocious could have been committed."[1] But proof soon began to accumulate. In San Francisco, newspaper extras furnished details that destroyed hope that some mistake had been made in the reporting. Shops everywhere were closed and business suspended. Bells atop the city hall, churches, and fire houses tolled, and guns were fired from the military station on Alcatraz Island.

Anger soon began to replace disbelief, and furious men began to march through the streets. A crowd of about one hundred and fifty gathered in front of the office of San Francisco's pro-Confederate *Daily Democratic Press*, forming a semicircle, while three or four of them entered, climbed a stairway, and began to throw type, cases, desks, stands and other implements out a second-story window. As each article reached the street, it was greeted with cheers. An immense throng formed to watch the violence, encouraging the men to proceed to the office of the *News Letter*, which was invaded in the same way. They then went on to the office of the Catholic newspaper *The Monitor* and then the French-language *Echo du Pacifique*, which occupied the same building as the *Alta California*. About the time these scenes were being enacted, Gen. Irvin McDowell, then commander of the Department of the Pacific, appeared on the street with chief of police Martin Burke. McDowell was asked to address the crowd, which he did. He said that he understood the anger that some of the men felt, but he could not countenance their resort to violence. "Law and order must prevail," he said. "Your assemblage here in this compact body, with these violent proceedings, gives rise to the gravest apprehensions on the part of many good people. Trust me in the matter of this Press. I am here to protect this country from all its enemies, both domestic and foreign, and I shall do it."[2] Violence dissipated, but not the anger—nor the brooding sorrow.

In Sacramento, a large meeting of citizens convened in the state capitol, where governor Frederick F. Low addressed them. Referring to the recent conclusion of the Civil War fighting, the governor said:

> Our rejoicings have in one short day been turned into lamentations; our houses of gladness have been turned into mourning, and our hearts that were overflowing with joy are now bowed down with sorrow. The thousands of flags that yesterday were given to the breeze, blazing with light and glory in honor of recent victories, now droop at half-mast; and the eye of the patriot, which beamed with joy at the prospect of honorable and lasting peace, is now suffused with tears, weeping over the loss of him to whom we looked, with unshakeable confidence, as the one appointed of God to carry this nation through our difficulties and re-establish it on a firm and sure foundation.[3]

On Wednesday, April 19, a huge funeral procession assembled in San Francisco's Washington Square to honor the deceased president. It included military men headed up by General McDowell, judges, lawyers, diplomatic representatives from foreign countries who had offices in the city, church men, and federal, state, and local officials. There was also an assemblage of almost three hundred black citizens and a much smaller group of Chinese citizens. A hearse similar to the one used when Edward Baker's body was transported to Lone Mountain joined the procession. It carried a coffin marked with gold letters spelling LINCOLN and the further words FIRM, FAITHFUL, and TRUE. The procession marched through the city to the Mechanics' Pavilion, a large exhibition hall, where a professor named Ebenezer Knowlton read the complete words of Lincoln's second inaugural address and a group of singers called Uncle Abe's Choir sang "The Battle Hymn of the Republic." The *Alta* estimated the total participants in the event at fourteen to fifteen thousand and called it "the greatest demonstration ever made on the Pacific Coast."[4]

In Sacramento, a throng filled the city's pavilion to hear Governor Low speak and Judge Robert C. Clark read Lincoln's second inaugural address.[5] Marysville mourned for the fallen president on the same day, as its *Daily Appeal* reported that the "people truly mourned the loss of a great and good man—and the ceremonies partook more of the canonization of a martyred Saint than the funeral rites and obsequies of a man."[6]

Reaction to the news of Lincoln's death in Los Angeles was mixed. Much of the secessionist sympathy that prevailed there during the war remained. Cavalry troops from Drum Barracks came into town and, in response to orders from their headquarters, made several arrests. Four men, one an American, another "an English son of Israel," a third a Prussian, and a fourth a Frenchman, were all arrested for having expressed gratification for Lincoln's murder.[7] Other people in the city were genuinely sorrowful. The common council declared April 19 a day of mourning. The stores were closed, as they had been in Northern cities, and businesses were not in operation, as a funeral procession wended its way through the center of the city. It culminated at the city hall, where an Episcopal clergyman preached a sermon. Two weeks later, when a city election was held, Unionist candidates won.[8] It was the first time that Los Angeles had seen such an election result. Sentiment was changing, even in the "City of the Angels."[9]

In the northern part of the state, sorrow over Lincoln's death continued. A heroic statue of him was dedicated in San Francisco a year after his death. Nine feet tall, it stood on a pedestal ten feet tall and was described as "majestic and commanding." The left arm was extended with the hand holding a scroll, presumed to be the Emancipation Proclamation. The statue had an unusual story that inspired San Franciscans and others who came to see it. It was created by a sculptor and cameo cutter named Pietro Mezzara while Lincoln was still living and displayed in San Francisco's very popular Mechanics Fair just after his death. Mezzara was of Italian ancestry but was born in France and spent many of his most productive years in San Francisco. The San Francisco School Board had already begun the construction of a school for boys that bore the president's name, but it was not completed until after he died. Mezzara offered the statue to the school, and it was erected there on April 14, 1866, the first anniversary of Lincoln's assassination. Governor Low dedicated it with other dignitaries gathered around him. Because it had been cast in plaster, the statue suffered some damage in later years, but in 1888 it was duplicated in a white metal known as French bronze. It survived in that form until it was brought down in the fire that accompanied the momentous earthquake that struck San Francisco on April 18, 1906. The statue has been acclaimed as the first heroic bronze statue of Lincoln ever erected.[10]

Statues of the martyred president also appeared in Southern California. A bronze bust titled "Lincoln the Lawyer" was unveiled in Lincoln Park in Los Angeles on July 4, 1926. It was the work of Julia Bracken Wendt, who had been born in Illinois in 1870 and studied sculpture in Chicago under the famous midwestern sculptor Lorado Taft. It was based on a life mask by Leonard Volk and photographs taken at the time of Lincoln's first inauguration. The sculptor had married the landscape painter William Wendt in 1906 and gone with him to California, where both had long and successful careers. Eight thousand people attended the unveiling of "Lincoln the Lawyer" while a band played and a distinguished western journalist named Charles Fletcher Lummis spoke to the crowd. Explaining her work, Wendt said that she "tried to express quiet repose, rather than the dramatic or picturesque." The pedestal below the bust is inscribed with the words of the Gettysburg Address. Julia Bracken Wendt died in Laguna Beach, California, in 1942, but her reputation as one of the most distinguished women sculptors in America lived on after her death. Her "Lincoln the Lawyer" remains in Lincoln Park today.[11]

On February 12, 1927, a bust of Lincoln was unveiled in the southern San Joaquin Valley town of Bakersfield. It was the work of David Edstrom, a sculptor who was then living and working in Los Angeles. Edstrom had been born in Sweden in 1873 (his birth name was Pehr David Emanuel Edström) but crossed the Atlantic with his family to the United States in 1880. They made their home in the town of Ottumwa, Iowa, where Edstrom's father became a preacher with the Swedish Mission Church. In 1894 Edstrom decided that he had artistic ambitions and left Ottumwa on a freight train, traveling as a hobo to the Atlantic coast, then finding a ship on which he could work as a stoker that would take him to Sweden. In Stockholm he became a student at the Royal Institute of Technology and the Royal Swedish Academy of Arts, working to support himself as a gardener and a teacher who helped working men learn English before they migrated to the United States. He soon acquired a reputation as an accomplished sculptor and an enthusiastic circle of friends and supporters. He married the sister of one of Sweden's most celebrated writers, Oscar Levertin, and became a friend of Sweden's Crown Prince Gustaf Adolf, for whom he did portrait busts of the prince and his wife, Crown Princess Margaret. Critics began to compare his work to that of such noted European sculptors as Auguste Rodin, Constantin Meunier, and Medardo Rosso. Edstrom traveled widely in Europe, doing work and giving exhibitions in Florence, Venice, Paris, Berlin, Amsterdam, and London. He returned to the United States in 1915 and eventually made his home in Los Angeles, where his sister Hannah Skorgerson lived. The *Los Angeles Herald* noted his arrival in the city, dubbing him the "American Rodin" and "a second Michael Angelo [*sic*]." He worked on the Bakersfield bust, titled "The Monumental Lincoln," for four years before it was unveiled before an enthusiastic crowd. Fifty copies were widely exhibited, one of which was in city of Riverside and another in the Lincoln Memorial Shrine in the city of Redlands. He died in 1938.[12]

Another statue of Lincoln was unveiled in San Francisco in February 1928. A seated figure mounted above a high granite pedestal installed in front of the San Francisco city hall, it was financed by public subscriptions made by the Lincoln Monument Association and an association representing the city's Lincoln School, where the statute of Lincoln had stood before it was brought down by the earthquake and fire of 1906. The sculptor was Haig Patigian, who had been born in Van, Armenia (now part of Turkey), in 1876. He came to the United States in 1891, first taking up residence in Fresno, the Central Valley town that was the center of a grape-growing district and home to many Armenians who fled their persecution in the Ottoman Empire. Patigian worked for a while as a grape picker and sign painter, then moved to San Francisco in 1899, where he took art instruction at the prestigious Mark Hopkins Institute of Art and began his career as a sculptor.

One of Patigian's first notable works was a statue of the recently assassinated president William McKinley, which was erected in the northern coastal town of Arcata in 1909. Another was a massive bust of Lincoln that was completed in his San Francisco studio in September 1909 and that he planned to send to Philadelphia's Pennsylvania Academy of Fine Arts, where some of his other work had been exhibited.[13] Patigian made two trips to Paris, exhibiting work at the Paris Salon and receiving encouraging praise from Auguste Rodin before returning to California and continuing his work. Over the years, he did many portrait busts, monumental figures, and architectural sculptures. One of the best known was a statue of Thomas Starr King. It became one of the two figures representing California in the U.S. Capitol's National Statuary Hall; the other was of Junípero Serra and was replaced only when a statue of president Ronald Reagan took its place in 2008. Patigian's Lincoln sculpture in front of San Francisco's city hall was dedicated on February 13, 1928, as part of the city's celebration of Lincoln's birthday, with some five thousand military veterans in attendance and an address delivered by California's former U.S. senator James D. Phelan. It remained one of his most notable works, inspiring countless observers with the city's admiration for the Civil War president. Patigian continued to live in San Francisco until his death in 1950.[14]

One of the most impressive busts of Abraham Lincoln in California was installed on the campus of the University of California in Berkeley in January 1921. It was a bronze cast of a bust that Gutzon Borglum, the sculptor of Mount Rushmore in South Dakota, had carved out of marble in 1908 and installed in the U.S. Capitol in 1911. The cast was presented to the university in 1909 by Eugene Meyer Jr., a graduate of the class of 1896. It was intended to be installed in the University's Doe Memorial Library, then under construction, but was ultimately mounted atop a pedestal designed by the famed university architect John Galen Howard that stood on the south side of the university's soaring Sather Tower, popularly called "The Campanile." The bust was unveiled by the university president David P. Barrows on February 12, 1921, the hundred twelfth anniversary of Lincoln's birth. It commemorated Lincoln's role in signing the Morrill Act of 1861, the federal law that led to the establishment of agricultural and engineering colleges across the nation, and to the creation of the University of California in 1867.[15] A copy of the Borglum bust was also installed outside the Lincoln Tomb in Springfield, Illinois, when it was reconstructed in 1930–31.

An impressive building called the Lincoln Memorial Shrine was opened on February 12, 1932, in the Southern California city of Redlands, about sixty-three miles east of Los Angeles. It was built by an English-born American businessman, labor activist, and philanthropist named Robert Watchorn. Born into a coal miner's family in Alfreton, Derbyshire, England, in 1858, Watchorn had immigrated to the United States in 1880 and begun his working life as a poorly paid coal miner in Pennsylvania. He and his wife, Alma, had two sons, one also named Robert who died in infancy and another named Emory Ewart Watchorn—always called Ewart—who served as a bomber pilot in the U.S. Army Air Service in World War I but died of an attack of blood poisoning in 1921. Robert Watchorn was an early officer of the United Mine Workers Union and, by appointment of president Theodore Roosevelt, commissioner of immigration at Ellis Island in New York. He joined the Union Oil Company early in the twentieth century and went on to form his own Watchorn Oil and Gas Company, headquartered in Oklahoma City. Before Ewart's death, he and his father had become fascinated with the story of Lincoln's rise from poverty to a position of influence and promise; they had come to believe that if the English had a better understanding of Lincoln, they might come to love America. So the money Robert had accumulated in his business career enabled him to build the Lincoln Shrine to honor both the president and his son Ewart.

Originally an octagonal rotunda built of reinforced concrete faced with Indiana limestone, the shrine was adorned with a Lincoln bust cut out of Carrara marble by the American-born, French-trained sculptor George Grey Barnard, who was noted for many sculptures, most notably a grand statue of Lincoln erected in Lytle Park, Cincinnati, in 1917. The interior walls of the rotunda were decorated with murals done by the American painter Dean Cornwell, and the outside walls were carved with quotations from Lincoln. The shrine was enlarged in later years with two wings that adjoined the rotunda and were filled with a research library and museum exhibits. Robert Watchorn donated the shrine to the city of Redlands, to be managed by the nearby A. K. Smiley Public Library, which still manages it. He made frequent visits over the years to his hometown of Alfreton and, in 1938, built an impressive Abraham Lincoln Library there. Used by the British government to care for wounded soldiers during World War II, it became the Alfreton Masonic Hall in 1970, while still retaining its outside inscription as the Abraham Lincoln Library. Watchorn died in Redlands in 1944. The Lincoln Memorial Shrine in Redlands remains the only museum and research center dedicated to Lincoln's memory west of the Mississippi.[16]

On March 14, 1941, an eight-foot-tall limestone statute of Lincoln was installed in the newly completed United States Courthouse in Los Angeles. It was the work of a twenty-three-year-old Fresno-born art student named James Lee Hansen. It attracted a lot of attention because Hansen had won a prize of $7,200 for creating it but also because it depicted Lincoln as a bare-chested young man who was tugging at the waistband of his pants. Many found it immodest. Others, pointing out that Lincoln's right hand was tugging at his pants but his left hand held a book, defended it as refreshingly original. They also reminded critics that partially (or even completely) nude statutes of famous Greek and Roman heroes, real and mythical, such as Poseidon, Hermes, Apollo, and Julius Caesar, biblical heroes such as Michelangelo's David, and even American heroes such as George Washington, had been seen and admired for thousands of years. Hansen told the newspapers that he had modeled Lincoln's physique on his own.[17]

ABRAHAM LINCOLN'S BIRTHDAY WAS WIDELY HONORED IN California in the years following his death, with commemoration ceremonies and locally declared holidays closing schools, banks, and other facilities. His birthday was not a state holiday until February 12, 1909, the hundredth anniversary of his birth. The legislature passed two laws that year, one making the hundredth birthday a legal holiday and another prescribing that it would also be honored in future years. The first law provided for half-day sessions of the public schools to allow "the customary exercises in memory of the martyred president." The second provided that if in future years February 12 fell on a Sunday, the holiday would be observed on the following Monday, and if it fell on a Saturday it would be observed the previous Friday.[18] Lincoln's birthday was never recognized as a federal holiday, although George Washington's was by a law first passed in 1879 that was applicable only to government workers in the District of Columbia, and another passed in 1885 that applied to government workers throughout the country.[19]

California's Lincoln holiday was widely honored, for his memory there was supported by many of the people of the state. But the holiday received a stimulus when a political movement was born bearing his name and explicitly dedicated to renewing his political philosophy. It started in 1907 when Chester H. Rowell, founder and editor of the *Fresno Morning Republican*, and Edward Augustus Dickson, political editor of the *Los Angeles Express*, established what they called the Lincoln League for the purpose of curbing what they regarded as the corrupt political power of the Southern Pacific Railroad. Because Theodore Roosevelt, a reformist Republican, was then the president in Washington, they soon adopted the name of the "Lincoln-Roosevelt Republican League," and then simply the "Lincoln-Roosevelt League." Their use of Lincoln's name was prompted by their respect for the Civil War president's memory and their recollection of the words he had used in his Gettysburg Address: "That government of the people, by the people, for the people, shall not perish from the earth."[20] The stated goal of the League was to curb the domination of the state government by the Southern Pacific Railroad, which they believed had strangled it by opposing free elections, hand-picking candidates for important offices, and directing office-holders to follow their directions. Reform movements had been attempted in previous years, and they had experienced limited success, but the members of the Lincoln-Roosevelt League believed a more fundamental reform was needed. Newspapers in many parts of the state announced their support for its principles, encouraging candidates. The most notable candidate was a skilled lawyer named Hiram Johnson, who had been active in the prosecution of a corrupt politician in San Francisco named Abe Ruef.[21] When the Lincoln-Roosevelt League promoted Johnson's candidacy for governor, he won the Republican nomination and the general election in 1910. As Earl Warren, one of Johnson's successors in the governor's chair, noted, Johnson's election led to "an administration of reform measures never equaled in California or probably any other state before or since."[22] Johnson was a powerful speaker and a determined personality, and he was successful in winning the nomination as Theodore Roosevelt's vice-presidential candidate on the Progressive (or "Bull Moose") ticket in 1912. He helped Roosevelt win the state's votes that year, but not the general election, which went to a Democratic newcomer, Woodrow Wilson. But Johnson won big margins in California when he ran for reelection as a Progressive in 1914 and for the United States Senate in 1916. He sought the nomination of the Republican Party for president in 1920 and 1924 but was passed over both times. He continued to hold his Senate seat until his death in 1945, gradually becoming more conservative but continuing to remind Californians of the success of the Lincoln-Roosevelt League.[23] Reforms advocated by members of the League were achieved, including such things as direct primary elections, initiative, referendum, and recall, the regulation of public utilities, forest conservation, and outlawing child labor and prostitution.

As the Lincoln-Roosevelt League was making its influence felt, Earl Warren was also beginning to make his mark. Born in Los Angeles in 1891, he had grown up in the San Joaquin Valley town of Bakersfield and attended college in Berkeley. After graduating from the University of California's law school in 1914, he went on to an unusually successful legal and political career, first serving as district attorney of Alameda County, then as attorney general of California, then as the only man elected three times to the state's governorship, and in 1953 as chief justice of the United States. He was widely admired by reform-minded Americans but reviled by men and women who hated reform, particularly his opposition to racial segregation. He was inspired in part by Abraham Lincoln's legacy. Of course, politicians typically spoke with reverence and awe of the great Civil War president. Warren did much of that too. In 1952, when he was running for the Republican presidential nomination for a second time (his first time was in 1948), he was invited to address a political club in Boston with their annual Lincoln Day Address. He told his audience that it was often difficult to judge the great figures of history according to the standards of later times, but added:

> Not so with Lincoln. His greatness lies in the fact that he was able to live by fundamental principles and to maintain a spirit applicable to all times and under all circumstances. His clear understanding of democracy and its application to mankind in his or any other day has never been better expressed than when he said: "As I would not be a slave, so I would not be a

master. This expresses my idea of democracy. Whatever differs from this, to the extent of the difference is not democracy."[24]

Warren's admiration for Lincoln was real. He kept a portrait of the Civil War president in his office for much of his political career and, according to his aides, silently stared at it when he had difficult problems to solve.[25]

Warren was criticized, like Lincoln, for offenses, some real and some imagined by his opponents. And he made some serious mistakes. His support, even advocacy, for the removal and relocation of Japanese American citizens during World War II was one of the most serious, and one that he later acknowledged was wrong. In his memoirs, published after his death, he wrote: "I have since deeply regretted the removal order and my own testimony advocating it, because it was not in keeping with our American concept of freedom and the rights of citizens. Whenever I thought of the little children who were torn from home, school friends, and congenial surroundings, I was conscience-stricken."[26]

But Warren did many things that most Americans could admire and that strengthened the enforcement of constitutional rights. He was one of the leaders in the crusade to end racial segregation in America; he helped pave the way for fair and just legal representation for accused criminals; and he helped establish rules for equal voting rights for all Americans. Carrying out these principles, he was the author of the Supreme Court opinions in the famous (and often bitterly controversial) cases of *Brown v. Board of Education of Topeka* (1954), declaring racial segregation in public schools unconstitutional; *Reynolds v. Sims* (1964), holding that the Constitution requires states to apportion both houses of their legislatures to approximately equal voting population; and *Miranda v. Arizona* (1966), holding that the Constitution requires that all persons arrested be advised of their right to have an attorney present before they can be questioned.[27] Lincoln would very likely have supported these decisions, as they were in harmony with his own views, particularly those regarding racial equality, which were growing in scope and vision as he went through life. *Brown v. Board of Education of Topeka* was, if nothing else, a complete refutation of the opinion that chief justice Roger Taney had written in 1857 in the *Dred Scott* case, a decision that Lincoln campaigned against and that was, at least in part, responsible for his nomination as the winning presidential candidate of the Republican Party in 1860.

While California's Lincoln-Roosevelt League was making its influence felt throughout the nation, a historic road was opening the way for automobile traffic across the country from New York to California. It was called the Lincoln Highway and was dedicated to Abraham Lincoln by its founders, two important men in the development of automobile traffic in the United States: Carl G. Fisher, a business leader from Indiana who was also the founder of the Indianapolis Motor Speedway, and Henry B. Joy, president of the Packard Motor Car Company.[28] Fisher and Joy believed that a hard-surfaced highway could be built from the Atlantic to the Pacific and that automobiles could use it to travel from coast to coast. Joy proposed that such a highway be built to honor Abraham Lincoln, who had been one of the pioneers in the development of transportation routes that would facilitate the movement of people, farm products, and industrial products—and, as history would soon reveal, military troops, equipment, and supplies.[29] As early as 1832, the twenty-three-year-old Lincoln had extoled the virtues of such improvements, saying: "Time and experience have verified to a demonstration, the public utility of internal improvements. That the poorest and most thinly populated countries would be greatly benefitted by the opening of good roads, and in the clearing of navigable streams within their limits, is what no person will deny."[30] Lincoln had been an important force in the authorization of the transcontinental railroad that brought train passengers and freight to California after the conclusion of the Civil War; he had worked to promote railroads while he was in Illinois and signed important legislation that the Republican Party supported, making the railroad possible while he was president.[31] He was, in his own words, "a western free state man," and a man who looked to

California, grateful for its help in preserving the Union and longingly feeling, and often stating, that he hoped to visit there and perhaps even make a home there for himself and his family. His name was an appropriate one to be conferred on the new road.

In September 1912 Fisher called for the highway to be completed in 1915, when the Panama-Pacific International Exposition was scheduled to open in San Francisco, and in 1913 a Lincoln Highway Association was established, with Henry Joy as its president. The cost was estimated to be $10 million, but when Congress refused to appropriate the money, private contributors began to contribute the necessary funds. They included Theodore Roosevelt, Henry Ford, and Thomas Edison. Statues of Lincoln were commissioned to show where the highway led and whom it honored. Concrete markers were eventually located at one-mile intervals to provide more detailed directions. The highway followed a diverse path through thirteen states: New York, New Jersey, Pennsylvania, West Virginia, Ohio, Indiana, Illinois, Iowa, Nebraska, Wyoming, Utah, Nevada, and California.[32] It was a total distance of some 3,384 miles from start to end. In some places it passed over city streets. In others it skirted the edges of farms, and in yet others it led along trails cleared through forests, down into valleys and steep defiles, and up through high mountain passes. The road was unpaved at first, but work continued to make the surface hard. When it reached California, it passed through the Sierra Nevada mountain passes and divided itself into two branches—one that passed along the north shore north of Lake Tahoe and another that skirted the south shore—but both uniting at Sacramento and then continuing on to San Francisco. There it ended in the city's Lincoln Park, situated atop beautiful grounds overlooking the Golden Gate and the entrance to San Francisco Bay. The location there was similar to Lone Mountain, the nearby prominence that Lincoln had hoped to visit after the death of Edward D. Baker, but it had even better views of the Pacific Ocean that Lincoln had hoped one day to see.[33]

The Lincoln Highway was not the only way in which Californians remembered the Civil War. As there were many in the state who revered the memory of the Great Emancipator and Savior of the Union, there were also many who cherished the memory of the man who sought to divide the Union and protect slavery, Jefferson Davis, and Robert E. Lee, the Confederate general who led armies in an effort to achieve the same result. Thousands of migrants from the former Confederate states flocked westward in the aftermath of the war, helping to perpetuate popular support for the myth of the "Lost Cause." Prodded by California branches of the United Daughters of the Confederacy and politicians who shared their views, mountain peaks and massive redwoods were named for Davis, for Lee, and for other Confederates, such as generals Robert S. Garnett and George E. Pickett. Monuments honoring Davis and Lee were erected in the northern and southern parts of the state. One was put up in Horton Plaza in the center of downtown San Diego, across the street from the U.S. Grant Hotel, built to remember the leader of the victorious Union armies. One of the most extensive memorials to Confederates was the Jefferson Davis Highway. Unlike the Lincoln Highway, which was built to facilitate motorized travel across the country, the Jefferson Davis Highway was begun in 1913 as a rival to the Lincoln Highway by renaming automobile trails and roads that extended across the country from Virginia to California. Remembering the fervor of slave owners to build a railroad that would extend slavery to the Pacific coast, critics called it the "great slavery road," but supporters exalted it as a monument to the man who led the Confederacy and its effort to divide the Union. The pro-Southern names and monuments continued into the twenty-first century, when revulsion against racism and prejudice began and Americans reexamined all memories of their history, good and bad.[34]

Promotion of the Lincoln Highway ended in 1928. By that time, state governments were taking the responsibility for highway building and attaching numbers to them. In the 1950s president Dwight D. Eisenhower became a champion of a proposed interstate highway system, in part because he had traveled over the Lincoln Highway when he was a young army officer and in part because his experience in war-torn Germany had demonstrated that highways could be used for the transport of troops and military equipment. The Interstate System was authorized by Congress in 1956 and built over a period of some thirty years. As it was put into use, some parts of the original Lincoln Highway were abandoned while others were still used by curious travelers, history lovers, or just sightseers. It was a reminder of President Lincoln and of the prominence of his legacy, all of which led to California, the state he had hoped one day to visit—perhaps even to live in—but never made it to.

Popular sentiment about the way in which Americans should remember Lincoln and other historic figures entered into a period of turbulence in 2018, a year in which news reports of the tragic deaths of African Americans at the hands of police and anger about racial injustice swept across the country. Widespread animosity against such figures as Christopher Columbus, Junípero Serra, George Washington, Thomas Jefferson, Francis Scott Key, Andrew Jackson, and Ulysses S. Grant grew in force and volume. In many cities and states, the popular sentiment resulted in the removal of statues and monuments, the vandalization of others, and a growing demand for the removal of yet others. Lincoln was not immune from the popular storm. In Chicago, threats were made for the removal of statues of him, including one of the greatest ever produced in the United States—the towering figure of Lincoln begun by the acclaimed sculptor Augustus Saint-Gaudens in 1884 and unveiled in the city's Lincoln Park in 1887. In San Francisco the statue of Lincoln by Haig Patigian erected in front of the city hall was doused with red paint, and the San Francisco School Board threatened to remove the names of Abraham Lincoln and more than forty other historic figures from the city's schools. Lincoln's name had long been born by one of San Francisco's most respected high schools. The school board's decision was, according to statements released by three of its members, based on disapproval of Lincoln's action in permitting thirty-eight Sioux natives to be hanged following the bloody uprising they engaged in in 1862. Those board members did not mention—and most likely did not know—that after personal review of the sentences, Lincoln pre-

WHAT WAS REMEMBERED

vented the execution of 264 of the Sioux.[35] The school board soon relented, apparently hearing the criticism leveled against their lack of historical knowledge of what Lincoln had done not just for the Sioux but also for African Americans. And the Lincoln statue by Haig Patigian was cleansed of the red paint and left standing in front of the city hall. Lincoln scholars reviewed these actions and commented on them. California-based biographer and historian Ronald C. White said that he was "taken aback by the moral superiority exhibited by many of today's critics of Lincoln, Washington, Jefferson and other leaders of earlier centuries."[36] Acclaimed Lincoln scholars Sidney Blumenthal and Harold Holzer wrote in an article published in the *Chicago Tribune* that the hysteria directed against Lincoln was "painful and absurd" and an example of "iconoclasm gone mad."[37] Their voices were heard, and the school board members responsible for the threats to rename the schools were soon removed from office.[38]

Lincoln's city hall statue was not taken down. His name was not removed from the San Francisco high school. His memory endured—not as a perfect man, but as one who saved the Union of the United States from destruction, who inspired millions of people around the world with hopes for justice and fairness and equality, and whose hope that he might one day make California his home was prevented by one of the great tragedies of history.

Chronology

1809   **February 12** Lincoln is born in Hardin (now LaRue) County in the then-western state of Kentucky.

1811   **February 24** Edward D. Baker is born in London.

1816   **December** The Lincoln family moves farther westward to southern Indiana.

1830   **March** The Lincoln family again moves westward to Perry (later part of Spencer) County in Indiana.

1831   **July** Now twenty-one years old, Lincoln begins his life as a single man in New Salem, Illinois.

1832   **April 21** Lincoln volunteers for military service in the Black Hawk War.

1834   **August 4** Lincoln is elected to the Illinois General Assembly.

1836   **September 9** Lincoln receives license to practice law.

1837   **April 15** Lincoln arrives in Springfield, Illinois.

        June 30 Joseph Hooker graduates from West Point.

1842   **November 4** Lincoln marries Mary Todd.

1843   **August 1** First Lincoln son, Robert Todd Lincoln, is born.

1846   **March 10** Second Lincoln son, Edward Baker Lincoln, is born.

        May 11 Congress declares war against Mexico.

1847   **January 26** Henry W. Halleck, William T. Sherman, and Edward Otho Cresap Ord arrive in Monterey, California, aboard the Sloop of War USS *Lexington*.

December 6 Lincoln takes his seat in the U.S. House of Representatives.

December 22 Lincoln offers eight resolutions in the House of Representatives disputing President Polk's version of how the war with Mexico began.

1848   **Spring** California's military governor Col. Richard B. Mason receives some particles of yellow metal from John Sutter. He and William T. Sherman test them and identify them as gold.

July 25 Ord joins Sherman to produce a map of Sacramento.

November 7 Zachary Taylor is elected president.

1849   **June 4** Joseph Hooker arrives in San Francisco aboard a coastal steamer.

July–August Ord and William Rich Hutton map the Pueblo of Los Angeles.

1850   **February 1** Lincoln's son Edward Baker Lincoln dies.

July 9 President Zachary Taylor dies.

December 21 Third Lincoln son, William Wallace Lincoln, is born.

September 9 California is admitted to the Union.

1852   **August** U.S. Army lieutenant Ulysses S. Grant arrives in California, visits San Francisco, and is stationed for a month at Benicia Barracks.

September 14 Grant leaves for new home at Columbia Barracks on the Columbia River.

1853   **February 21** Joseph Hooker resigns his army commission and takes up the life of a farmer in California's Sonoma Valley.

December 21 Lincoln's fourth son, Thomas (Tad) Lincoln, is born.

1854 **January** Ulysses S. Grant is transferred to Fort Humboldt, an infantry outpost on California's northern coast. He is so impressed with California that he has visions of making his home there with his family.

June 1 Grant leaves San Francisco aboard a passenger ship bound for Nicaragua.

June 2 Secretary of war Jefferson Davis accepts U. S. Grant's resignation from the army.

September 16 David Glasgow Farragut arrives in California, where he supervises the construction of the Mare Island Naval Shipyard.

1855 **February 8** Lincoln loses effort to win election to the U.S. Senate.

1856 **June 17** The first Republican presidential nominating convention meets in Philadelphia and names California's John C. Frémont as its candidate for president. Lincoln is seriously considered as his vice-presidential running mate. When he loses, he campaigns for Frémont in Illinois.

1858 **July 16** David Glasgow Farragut commissions the Mare Island Naval Shipyard.

August–October Lincoln debates senator Stephen Douglas.

1859 **February 14** Oregon admitted to the Union.

September 13 Edward Baker acts as second to California's antislavery senator David Broderick as he engages in a duel with California's just retired, proslavery chief justice David Terry.

August 9–18 Lincoln takes his first trip west of the Mississippi, traveling across Missouri to Council Bluffs, Iowa, on the Hannibal and St. Joseph Railroad.

September 16 Broderick dies of the wound he suffered in the duel with Terry.

September 18 Edward Baker delivers impassioned eulogy over Broderick's body as it is prepared for burial on San Francisco's Lone Mountain.

November 30–December 8 Lincoln makes his second, and last, short trip across the Mississippi, traveling through St. Joseph, Missouri, to Leavenworth, Kansas.

October 2 Edward Baker is elected as U.S. senator from Oregon.

1860 **February 27** Lincoln delivers more than two-hour-long speech at Cooper Union in New York.

May 18 Lincoln receives presidential nomination of Republican Party.

June 14 Lincoln's Cooper Union speech is published in full in the *Sacramento Daily Union*, which tells its readers that the opinions he expressed were "of more consequence than those which he will utter during the campaign and under the excitement of an active Presidential contest."

October 26 On his way to Washington as Oregon's newly elected U.S. senator, Edward Baker addresses a crowd of several thousand in San Francisco's American Theatre. He condemns slavery and praises the presidential candidacy of his friend Abraham Lincoln.

November 6 Lincoln wins presidential election.

December 20 South Carolina is first state to secede.

1861 **February 18** Jefferson Davis is nominated for president of the Confederate States of America.

March 4 Senator Baker introduces Lincoln to the assembled spectators on the east front of the Capitol, after which Lincoln is inaugurated as president.

April 14 Fort Sumter surrenders.

April 15 Lincoln calls for seventy-five thousand volunteers.

April 25 Edwin V. Sumner succeeds Albert Sidney Johnston as commander of the Department of the Pacific.

May 17 Joseph Hooker is appointed brigadier general of volunteers and assigned to defense of Washington DC.

June 28 Central Pacific Railroad is legally organized, with Leland Stanford as its president.

July 21 Confederate victory at First Bull Run (Manassas).

October 21 Edward Baker is killed in the Battle of Ball's Bluff. Lincoln sobs bitterly when he learns the news.

November 6 Jefferson Davis is elected president of the Confederate States of America.

December 11 Edward Baker's body is buried on Lone Mountain in San Francisco.

1862 **January 10** Leland Stanford inaugurated as governor of California.

February 20 William Wallace Lincoln dies.

March–August Joseph Hooker commands army division in Peninsula campaign.

July 2 Lincoln signs the Morrill Act, a congressional law granting eligible states thirty thousand acres of public land for each of their U.S. senators and congressmen and authorizing that the land could be sold, with the proceedsused to establish colleges. In California, the funds raised under the act were used to help establish the University of California in Berkeley in 1868.

July 16 Congress creates rank of rear admiral, which is conferred on David Glasgow Farragut and thirteen others for the first time in U.S. history.

August 28–30 Confederates win Second Battle of Bull Run (Manassas).

September 16–18 Battle of Antietam.

September 22 Lincoln issues preliminary Emancipation Proclamation.

December 20 Readers of California's *Sacramento Daily Union* receive the first of 258 "Letters from Washington" sent by Noah Brooks, a California-based journalist who becomes one of Lincoln's best friends in the capital.

1863 **January 1** Lincoln issues final Emancipation Proclamation.

January 6 The California legislature adopts a concurrent resolution approving Lincoln's Emancipation Proclamation and pledging "the cordial and earnest support of the people of California.

January 26 Lincoln writes personal letter to Joseph Hooker.

June 28 Hooker surrenders his command to Major Gen. George Gordon Meade.

July 1–3 Union victory at Gettysburg.

Summer While in the Soldier's Home north of the White House, Lincoln speaks of Edward Baker's burial place on San Francisco's Lone Mountain, recalls Baker's eloquence, and speaks of his love for his old friend.

November 19 Lincoln delivers Gettysburg Address.

1864 **February 22** National Union Party nominates Lincoln for a second term as president.

March 4 Lincoln signs a certificate making U. S. Grant a lieutenant general, a rank previously held only by George Washington.

June 30 Lincoln signs act of Congress requiring that California's magnificent Yosemite Valley be inalienably "held for public use, resort, or reservation," making it in effect the first national park in the United States. Major General Irvin McDowell arrives in San Francisco as commander of the U.S. Army Department of the Pacific.

August 5 Farragut wins the great naval battle in Mobile Bay, Alabama.

September 1 General Sherman captures Atlanta.

November 8 Lincoln wins reelection.

December 6 Lincoln delivers his final message to Congress on the state of the Union, which, among other things, repeats his ardent support of the construction of the transcontinental railroad connecting California and its mineral riches to the rest of the nation.

December 21 General Sherman captures Savannah.

1865 **March 4** Lincoln delivers his second inaugural address.

March 18 Lincoln signs patents conveying three of California's Spanish missions and their underlying lands to Joseph S. Alemany, archbishop of San Francisco, designated in his capacity as bishop of Monterey.

April 9 U. S. Grant accepts the surrender of Robert E. Lee at Appomattox Courthouse, Virginia.

April 14 Lincoln tells Schuyler Colfax and Cornelius Cole, who are leaving for California, of his gratitude for the state's contribution to the financial strength of the Union and his wish that he could go there with them. In the evening, he goes to Ford's Theatre, where he is shot.

April 15 Lincoln dies at 7:22 a.m.

April 19 Huge procession to honor Lincoln assembles in San Francisco's Washington Square. Los Angeles Common Council declares a day of mourning for Lincoln.

June 1 California citizens present gold-encrusted sword to Joseph Hooker in appreciation for his Civil War service.

1866 **April 14** To commemorate first anniversary of Lincoln's death, a statue of him by Pietro Mezzara is dedicated in San Francisco by governor Frederick F. Low.

May 29 Winfield Scott dies at West Point, New York.

1868   **March 23** California governor Henry Haight signs a bill establishing the University of California, which receives funds derived from the Morrill Act signed by Lincoln.

1869   **August 11** David Farragut returns to a hero's welcome on Mare Island.

1870   **August 13** Farragut dies in Portsmouth, New Hampshire.

      October 12 Robert E. Lee dies in Lexington, Virginia.

1872   **January 9** Henry W. Halleck dies in Louisville, Kentucky.

1879   **October 31** Joseph Hooker dies in Garden City, New York.

1881   **February 9** Winfield Scott Hancock dies in Governors Island, New York.

1883   **January 1** William Levi Todd dies in Los Angeles.

      July 22 Edward Otho Cresap Ord dies in Havana, Cuba.

1885   **July 23** Ulysses S. Grant dies in Gansevoort, New York.

1889   **December 6** Jefferson Davis dies in New Orleans, Louisiana.

1891   **February 14** William T. Sherman dies in New York City.

1903   **August 17** Noah Brooks dies in Pasadena, California.

1907   **August 1** The Lincoln-Roosevelt League is founded to curb the political power of the Southern Pacific Railroad.

1913   **July 1** The Lincoln Highway Association is established to complete a hard-surfaced automobile road extending from New York City to San Francisco, in time for the Panama-Pacific Exposition in 1915.

1921   **February 12** Bronze cast of a Lincoln bust by Mount Rushmore sculptor Gutzon Borglum is unveiled on campus of University of California in Berkeley, commemorating Lincoln's signing of the Morrill Act of 1861.

1926   **July 4** Bronze bust of *Lincoln the Lawyer* by sculptor Julia Bracken Wendt is unveiled before eight thousand spectators in Lincoln Park in Los Angeles.

1927 **February 12** Bust of Lincoln by sculptor David Edstrom is unveiled in Bakersfield.

1928 **February 13** Granite statue of a seated Lincoln by sculptor Haig Patigian is unveiled in front of San Francisco's City Hall.

1932 **February 12** Lincoln Memorial Shrine opens in Redlands, California, becoming the only museum and research center west of the Mississippi that is exclusively devoted to Lincoln's memory.

1941 Eight-foot-tall limestone statue of Lincoln by James Lee Hansen is installed in the U.S. Courthouse in Los Angeles.

Notes

1. April 14, 1865

1. Keckley, *Behind the Scenes*, 137. Robert T. Lincoln was born on August 1, 1843, while Thomas (Tad) Lincoln was born on April 4, 1853. See Emerson, *Giant in the Shadows*, 7, 24.
2. Reck, *A. Lincoln*, 32–39.
3. Reck, *A. Lincoln*, 40.
4. Browne, *The Everyday Life of Abraham Lincoln*, 701–2.
5. Cornelius Cole was one of the founders of the Republican Party in California. He served a single term in the United States House of Representatives from 1863 to 1865 and a single term in the United States Senate from 1867 to 1873. He died in 1924 at the age of 102, thus becoming the longest-living U.S. senator in history.
6. Colfax did not mention Cole in his recollections of this morning meeting, and Cole remembered that he and Colfax met Lincoln in the afternoon. Since no schedule of Lincoln's meetings was left, it is difficult to determine the exact time of their visit and whether they came together or separately. After careful consideration of the available evidence, however, Reck has concluded that Colfax and Cole came together in the morning. See Reck, *A. Lincoln*, 3, 19.
7. Cole, *Memoirs of Cornelius Cole*, 229; Reck, *A. Lincoln*, 19.
8. Reck, *A. Lincoln*, 20; Martin, *The Life and Public Services of Schuyler Colfax*, 188.
9. Brooks, *Washington in Lincoln's Time*, 258.
10. Wilson and Davis, eds., *Herndon's Informants*, 357.
11. Cole, *Memoirs of Cornelius Cole*, 229.
12. Martin, *The Life and Public Services of Schuyler Colfax*, 179–80.
13. Martin, *The Life and Public Services of Schuyler Colfax*, 179–82; Reck, *A. Lincoln*, 21.
14. Cole, *Memoirs of Cornelius Cole*, 229–30.

2. A Western Free State Man

1. Lincoln's full statement was: "I am a Northern man, or rather, a Western free state man, with a constituency I believe to be, and with personal feelings I know to be, against the extension of slavery." Abraham Lincoln Speech, July 27, 1848, Abraham Lincoln Papers, Series 1, General Correspondence, 1833–1916, Library of Congress, Manuscript Division.
2. "Political Intelligence," *New York Daily Tribune*, June 5, 1860, 3.
3. "Letters [*sic*] from Washington," *Sacramento Daily Union*, December 2, 1864, 1.
4. California State Archives.
5. Neely, *The Abraham Lincoln Encyclopedia*, 138–39.
6. Maltby, *The Life and Public Services of Abraham Lincoln*, 34.
7. The statement was made to James Simonton and reported in San Francisco's *Bulletin*, May 15, 1863, as quoted in Burlingame, *Abraham Lincoln*, online unedited version maintained by Knox College at https://www.knox.edu/documents/LincolnStudies/BurlingameVol1chap3.pdf.
8. Maltby, *The Life and Public Services of Abraham Lincoln*, 27. The fact that Lincoln slept with men during his early working days was cited by a sexual psychiatrist as evidence that he was a homosexual, or had homosexual tendencies. See Tripp, *The Intimate World of Abraham Lincoln*. However, Tripp's argument has been persuasively controverted by many Lincoln scholars.
9. Whitney, *The Black Hawk War 1831–1832, Vol. 1, Illinois Volunteers*, 92.
10. Shutes, *Lincoln and California*, 2n1, says that Lincoln took part in at least four lawsuits against Reed in 1843 and 1844.
11. Cohen, "Lincoln Documents Accompanied Donner Party on Its Grim Journey," *Inside History*, https://www.history.com/news/lincoln-documents-accompanied-donner-party-on-its-grim-journey.
12. Wainwright, "Milestones in California History."
13. McGinty, *Lincoln's Greatest Case*, 9; Blair and Tarshis, *Lincoln's Constant Ally*, 10. Although Lincoln was formally admitted to the bar in October 1836, his actual practice began in 1837.
14. Burlingame, *Abraham Lincoln*, 1:214; Blair and Tarshis, *Lincoln's Constant Ally*, 56.
15. Blair and Tarshis, *Lincoln's Constant Ally*, 56.
16. Greenberg, *A Wicked War*, 159.
17. Greenberg, *A Wicked War*, 210.
18. Basler, *The Collected Works of Abraham Lincoln*, 1:420–22, 438; Blair and Tarshis, *Lincoln's Constant Ally*, 48–50,
19. Basler, *The Collected Works of Abraham Lincoln*, 2:54.
20. Etulain, *Lincoln and Oregon Country Politics in the Civil War Era*, 16–20.
21. Blair and Tarshis, *Lincoln's Constant Ally*, 49–57.
22. Basler, *The Collected Works of Abraham Lincoln*, 2:83–90.
23. Blair and Tarshis, *Lincoln's Constant Ally*, 59.
24. Blair and Tarshis, *Lincoln's Constant Ally*, 61–62.

25. See Lehrman, *Lincoln at Peoria*, especially 179–82, 197–98, 201, 206, 212, 253, 347.

26. Burlingame, *Abraham Lincoln*, 1:400–404; Etulain, *Lincoln and Oregon Country Politics in the Civil War Era*, 26.

27. Herr, *Jessie Benton Frémont*, 253.

28. Blair and Tarshis, *Lincoln's Constant Ally*, 69.

29. California Constitution of 1850, Art. I, Sec. 18.

30. Brief for Respondent, E. D. Baker of Counsel, Crosby and Tompkins, attorneys for Respondent, Before Geo. Pen Johnston, U.S. Commissioner, in *C.A. Stovall vs. Archy (claimed as a slave)*, Case Files of the U.S. Commissioner, RG 21, National Archives and Records Administration, San Bruno, California.

31. "Archy Discharged—Further from Puget Sound and the Gold Mines," *Sacramento Daily Union*, April 15, 1858, 2; McGinty, *Archy Lee's Struggle for Freedom*, 88. In the title to his short but well-researched book *Archy Lee: A California Fugitive Slave Case*, Rudolph M. Lapp adopts the argument of Hardy and Stovall that Archy Lee was a "fugitive slave." But the facts clearly demonstrated that Archy Lee had not fled from slavery into California, where the state constitution provided that there were no slaves, and George Pen Johnston's decision confirmed those facts. It may make some sense to argue that the legal struggle over Archy Lee's status was a "fugitive slave case," but the facts and Commissioner Johnston's decision both clearly establish that he was not a "fugitive slave," although he had been a slave in Mississippi.

32. "Obituary," *The Elevator*, June 27, 1874, 2.

33. Ethington, *The Public City*, 186.

34. *Dred Scott v. Sandford*, 60 U.S. 393, 407 (1857).

35. "Thirty-Fifth Congress, First Session," *Appendix to the Congressional Globe*, March 22, 1858, 193; *Speech of Hon. D. C. Broderick, of California, Against the Admission of Kansas, Under the Lecompton Constitution: Delivered in the Senate of the United States, March 22, 1858*, 16.

36. Blair and Tarshis, *Lincoln's Constant Ally*, 90–91, 195–200.

3. Honest Old Abe

1. Basler, *The Collected Works of Abraham Lincoln*, 3:339.

2. Stahr, *Seward*, 174–75.

3. "Republicans at Cooper Institute," *New York Times*, February 28, 1860, 1.

4. Basler, *The Collected Works of Abraham Lincoln*, 3:522–50.

5. "The Late Speech of Abraham Lincoln," *Sacramento Daily Union*, March 29, 1860, 8.

6. "Speech of Abraham Lincoln Delivered in New York City, Feb. 27" (reprinting article from *Tribune*), *Sacramento Daily Union*, June 14, 1860, 6.

7. Etulain, *Lincoln and Oregon Country Politics in the Civil War Era*, 53; Blair and Tarshis, *Lincoln's Constant Ally*, 29.

8. Etulain, *Lincoln and Oregon Country Politics in the Civil War Era*, 46–47.

9. Tutorow, *The Governor*, 1:108–9; Bancroft, *History of California*, 7:257.

10. Bancroft, *History of California*, 7:259.

11. "Proceedings of the National Republican Convention," *Sacramento Daily Union*, June 11, 1860, 2; "National Republican Convention," *Sacramento Daily Union*, June 13, 1860, 1; Untitled article, *Brooklyn Evening Star*, May 16, 1860, 2; Shutes, *Lincoln and California*, 34.

12. Proceedings of the Republican National Convention held at Chicago, May 16, 17, and 18, 1860, 79–83.

13. Basler, *The Collected Works of Abraham Lincoln*, 1:5–6.

14. McGinty, *Lincoln's Greatest Case*, 149–50.

15. *Chicago Daily Democrat*, September 26, 1846.

16. For an extended discussion of Lincoln's support for the construction of railroads, as well as his participation in the important *Effie Afton* trial, see McGinty, *Lincoln's Greatest Case*.

17. Gudde, *California Place Names*, 147.

18. Bancroft, *History of California*, 7:642–66.

19. John Wooley and Gerhard Peters, *The American Presidency Project*, at http://www.presidency.ucsb.edu/showelection.php?year=1856.

20. "The Republican Ticket for 1860," *New York Times*, May 19, 1860, 1.

21. Basler, *The Collected Works of Abraham Lincoln*, 4:52.

22. See, for example, "Honest Old Abe," *Red Bluff Beacon*, August 29, 1860, 4 (quoting from *Cleveland Plain Dealer*); "How Lincoln Received the Nomination," *Sacramento Daily Union*, June 16, 1860, 1 ("Honest Old Abe"); "Electoral Ticket," *Marysville Daily Appeal*, June 23, 1860, 2 ("Honest Old Abe"); "A Southern Tribute to Lincoln," *Sacramento Daily Union*, June 28, 1860, 3 ("Honest Old Abe," quoting from *Paris (Kentucky) Citizen, Southern Opposition*); "Lincoln Among the Children," *Red Bluff Independent*, September 11, 1860, 2 ("To know 'honest Abe' is to love him . . ."; quoting from *Chicago Tribune*). See Pratt, *Personal Finances of Abraham Lincoln*, 116: "Early in his life Lincoln came to be known as an honest man—honest, that is, beyond common honesty. There is ample evidence to show that he prized the reputation." Many Lincoln writers have stated that Lincoln hated the nickname "Abe," that he was uncomfortable with it, or that he simply disliked it. Lincoln scholar Joshua A. Claybourn has carefully researched this question and written that, because Lincoln "rooted much of his persona in the image of a common, self-made man," he did not despise the nickname and, when his associates frequently used it, "he expressed no concern about the practice." Claybourn, "Abe Lincoln: An Acceptable Nickname?," 8. See also Holst, "Another View on 'Abe,'" 4.

23. Blair and Tarshis, *Lincoln's Constant Ally*, 102–5.

24. Blair and Tarshis, *Lincoln's Constant Ally*, 106.

25. "Republican Meeting in San Francisco," *Sacramento Daily Union*, October 29, 1860, 1. The belief of many prominent opponents of slavery that "freedom is the rule, slavery is the exception" is discussed in Oakes, *The Crooked Path to Abolition*, 26–53.

26. "Republican Mass Meeting," *Daily Alta California*, October 27, 1860, 1; the full text of Baker's American Theatre Speech is set forth in Shuck, *Eloquence of the Far West. No. I. Masterpieces of E.D. Baker*, 91–127. See discussion in Matthews, *The Golden State in the Civil War*, 80.

27. Herr, *Jessie Benton Frémont*, 316.

28. Hittell, *History of California*, 4:272.

29. Spaulding, "The Attitude of California to the Civil War," 121.

30. Bancroft, *History of California*, 6:723.

31. See Waite, *West of Slavery*, quoting from the African American newspaper *National Anti-Slavery Standard*, of October 22, 1859.

32. "Political Intelligence," *New York Daily Tribune*, June 5, 1860, 3.

33. *Richmond Enquirer*, May 22, 1860, 1.

34. Bancroft, *History of California*, 7:269n27.

35. Tutorow, *The Governor*, 1:111–12.

36. "Governor's Annual Message," *Sacramento Union-Supplement*, January 10, 1860, 1; Kibby, "Union Loyalty of California's Civil War Governors," 313.

37. "Speech of W. M. Gwin," *Sacramento Daily Union*, January 12, 1860, 4.

38. Bancroft, *History of California*, 7:258–59. The Sierra Madre is the mountain chain that extends southward from the Rocky Mountains into Mexico.

39. "The Wide-Awake Parade," *New York Times*, October 3, 1860, 4.

40. See, for example, "Appropriate Name," *Visalia Weekly Delta*, November 3, 1860, 2.

41. See, for example, "A Disunionist Speaks," *Daily National Democrat* (Marysville), December 23, 1860, 2.

42. "Republican Mass Meeting," *Daily Alta California*, August 24, 1860, 1.

43. "Republican Meeting at Oakland," *Daily Alta California*, September 2, 1860, 1.

44. "Republican Meeting," *Daily Alta California*, September 29, 1860, 1.

45. "Grand Republican Demonstration," *Daly Alta California*, October 13, 1860, 1.

46. "The Barbecue at Petaluma," *Daily Alta California*, October 24, 1860, 1; "Folsom Mass Meeting," *Daily Alta California*, October 30, 1860, 2.

47. Burlingame, *Abraham Lincoln*, 1:648.

48. "The Election," *Sacramento Daily Union*, November 7, 1860, 2.

49. "Scenes and Events of the Day," *Daily Alta California*, November 7, 1860, 1.

50. John Wooley and Gerhard Peters, *The American Presidency Project*, at http://www.presidency.ucsb.edu/showelection.php?year=1860.

51. Wooley and Peters, *The American Presidency Project*.

52. Wooley and Peters, *The American Presidency Project*.

53. J. K. Morehead, interview with John G. Nicolay, Washington, May 12 and 13, 1880, in Burlingame, *An Oral History of Abraham Lincoln*, 41. Cf. Lamon, *The Life of Abraham Lincoln*, 460.

54. Burlingame, *Abraham Lincoln*, 1:679.

4. California's Future

1. For further discussion, see chapter 2.
2. Basler, *The Collected Works of Abraham Lincoln*, 2:301.
3. O'Sullivan, "Annexation," 6.
4. U.S. Constitution, Preamble. In his inaugural address on March 4, 1861, Lincoln stated that "one of the declared objects for ordaining and establishing the Constitution was 'to form a more perfect Union.'" Basler, *The Collected Works of Abraham Lincoln*, 4:265.
5. Cleveland, *Alexander H. Stephens in Public and Private*, 721.
6. California Constitution of 1850, Art. I, Sec. 18, providing that "all men are by nature free and independent" and "neither slavery nor involuntary servitude, unless for the punishment of crimes, shall ever be tolerated" in the state.
7. "Hon. John C. Burch for a Pacific Republic," *Red Bluff Independent*, January 8, 1861; Josephy, *The Civil War in the American West*, 234. For further discussion of the Bear Flag and the "California Republic," see chapter 2 of this volume.
8. "Scott of California, on the Crisis," *Sonoma County Democrat*, January 24, 1861, 4; Josephy, *The Civil War in the American West*, 234.
9. "Secession and Pacific Republic," *Sacramento Daily Union*, February 8, 1861, 2.
10. "Settlers and a Pacific Republic," *Sacramento Daily Union*, reprinting extract from *San Jose Mercury*, April 26, 1861, 4.
11. "Latham's Speech," *Mariposa Gazette*, February 12, 1861, 1.
12. Bancroft, *History of California*, 7:277–78; Roske, *Everyman's Eden*, 305; Shutes, *Lincoln and California*, 70.
13. "State Rights—State Allegiance," *Sacramento Daily Union*, April 27, 1861, 2.
14. "Union Meetings in California," *Sacramento Daily Union*, June 12, 1861, 3.
15. "It Is Consummated," *Sacramento Daily Union*, April 3, 1861, 2.
16. James Alexander McDougall was unrelated to John McDougal, an Ohio-born Democrat who came to California in 1849, served in the Constitutional Convention that met in Monterey that year, and was elected as the state's first lieutenant governor. He became governor on the resignation of Peter H. Burnett on January 9, 1851, and served until January 8, 1852.
17. Bancroft, *History of California*, 7:273–74; Shuck, *Bench and Bar in California*, 357–60; Matthews, *The Golden State in the Civil War*, 89; Blair and Tarshis, *Lincoln's Constant Ally*, 68; Williams, *David C. Broderick*, 71, 81, 95, 101, 122; Shutes, *Lincoln and California*, 57.
18. James McDougall to Abraham Lincoln, March 23, 1861, *Abraham Lincoln Papers at the Library of Congress*. This letter was written during the legislative struggle to elect a senator, when McDougall was mistakenly declared the winner. The final election occurred on April 2, 1861. See "It Is Consummated," *Sacramento Daily Union*, April 3, 1861, 2.
19. "Union Resolution," *Sacramento Daily Union*, May 22, 1861, 2; Orton, *Records of California Men in the War of the Rebellion, 1861 to 1867*, 5.

20. "Union Resolutions," *Sacramento Daily Union*, May 21, 1861, 2.

21. Roske, *Everyman's Eden*, 306–7; Matthews, *The Golden State in the Civil War*, 110; Spaulding, "The Attitude of California to the Civil War," 112–14.

22. "Mr. McConnell's Political Position," *Daily Alta California*, August 15, 1861, 2.

23. Tutorow, *The Governor*, 1:121–24.

24. Orsi, *Sunset Limited*, 7; Tutorow, *The Governor*, 1:192.

25. Tutorow, *The Governor*, 1:121–26. Newspaper reports of the vote totals varied slightly, depending on when they were counted. "XIIIth Legislature," *Sonoma Democrat*, January 16, 1862, 2, gives the total as follows: Stanford 55,935, McConnell 32,782, and Conness 30,994.

26. "Inaugural Address of Governor Stanford," *Daily Alta California*, January 11, 1862, 1.

5. The War Begins

1. See McGinty, *The Body of John Merryman*, 38.

2. "The New Administration," *New York Times*, March 5, 1861, 1.

3. Basler, *The Collected Works of Abraham Lincoln*, 4:271.

4. See, for example, "Intelligence by Pony," *Marin County Tocsin*, May 4, 1861, 3; "Arrival of Pony Express," *Daily Alta California*, May 19, 1861, 1 ("70,000 U.S. Troops at Washington"); "Arrival of the Pony Express," *Sacramento Daily Union*, May 21, 1861, 2; "News of the Morning," *Sacramento Daily Union*, July 31, 1861, 2 ("The news by Pony Express is of the highest importance"). See also Goodheart, *1861*, 218–19, 220, 250.

5. "Lincoln's Inaugural Message," *Sacramento Daily Union*, March 22, 1861, 4.

6. See McGinty, *Lincoln and the Court*, 121–25, 127–37.

7. See McGinty, *The Body of John Merryman*, 52 (Lincoln's order to Scott), 86–92 (Taney's opinion rebuking Lincoln's suspension of habeas corpus), 165–66 (constitutional views of Taney and Buchanan regarding the unconstitutionality of secession).

8. McPherson, *Battle Cry of Freedom*, 342.

9. Horace Greeley to Abraham Lincoln, July 29, 1861. Abraham Lincoln Papers, Library of Congress.

10. Burlingame, *Abraham Lincoln*, 2:208.

11. The Confiscation Act authorized Union forces to confiscate any Confederate property (including slaves) used to support the insurrection. 12 Stat. 319, Ch. 60, "An Act to confiscate Property used for Insurrectionary Purposes," August 6, 1861.

12. Burlingame, *Abraham Lincoln*, 2:210.

13. McPherson, *Tried by War*, 46.

14. Sherman, *Memoirs of General William T. Sherman*, 1:18.

15. Marszalek, *Commander of All Lincoln's Armies*, 60.

16. Marszalek, *Commander of All Lincoln's Armies*, 55.

17. Gudde, *California Place Names*, 9.

18. See Stahr, *Stanton*, 82, 83, 87, 88. Stanton opposed Lincoln's appointment of Halleck as commander in chief. Although neither Halleck nor Stanton publicly discussed their California disagreements, they harbored animosities. Stanton was quoted as saying that Halleck was "probably the greatest scoundrel and most barefaced villain in America" and a man who was "totally destitute of principal." See discussion in Marszalek, *Commander of All Lincoln's Armies*, 134.

19. See Marszalek, *Commander of All Lincoln's Armies*, 70, 73–74, 104, 111–12.
20. "By Overland Telegraph," *Sacramento Daily Union*, November 8, 1861, 2.
21. "Halleck Assigned to the Department of the West," *Daily Alta California*, November 12, 1861, 1.
22. "Gen. Halleck," *Red Bluff Independent*, November 29, 1861, 3.
23. Marszalek, *Commander of All Lincoln's Armies*, 109.
24. Utley, *The Commanders*, 129–32.
25. Utley, *The Commanders*, 132.
26. Utley, *The Commanders*, 133.
27. See Cresap, "Early California as Described by Edward O. C. Ord," 329–40; Johannsen, "Edward O. C. Ord on Frontier Defense," 23–27; Layne, "Edward Otho Cresap Ord," 139–42.
28. Sherman, *Memoirs of General William T. Sherman*, 1:58; O'Connell, *Fierce Patriot*, 36.
29. Senkewicz, *Vigilantes in Gold Rush San Francisco*, 84–85; Starr, *California*, 87, 106; McGloin, *San Francisco*, 58.
30. Williams, *David C. Broderick*, 128; McGinty, "Hung Be the Heavens with Black," 39.
31. Sherman, *Memoirs of General William T. Sherman*, 1:131.
32. Chernow, *Grant*, 55.
33. Grant, *Personal Memoirs of U. S. Grant*, 2:210.
34. See Chernow, *Grant*, 82–87, for a discussion of Grant's drinking problem at Fort Humboldt.

6. The First Californian

1. "California Matters," *Sacramento Daily Union*, May 10, 1861, 1.
2. "California Matters," *Sacramento Daily Union*, May 10, 1861, 1.
3. Newell, *The Regular Army Before the Civil War, 1845–1860*, 50.
4. Josephy, *The Civil War in the American West*, 234; Jewell, "Left Arm of the Republic," 56–57.
5. Wilkins, *The Great Diamond Hoax*, 36.
6. Jewell, "Left Arm of the Republic," 89–90; Wilkins, *The Great Diamond Hoax*, 43; Waite, "The Slave South in the Far West," 248n9.
7. Jewell, "Left Arm of the Republic," 30–35; see McGinty, "I Will Call a Traitor a Traitor," 24–31.
8. Burlingame, *Abraham Lincoln*, 2:2, 26, 36–37.
9. See discussion of Johnston in California in Bancroft, *History of California*, 7:282.

10. Bell, *On the Old West Coast*, 74; Robinson, *Los Angeles in Civil War Days, 1860–1865*, 85–86.

11. "From Rebeldom," *Los Angeles Star*, November 29, 1862, 2.

7. The Office Seekers

1. The civil service reforms that would relieve the nation's chief executive of the power (and the duty) to appoint thousands of federal officers had not yet been adopted. They would come when Congress enacted the so-called Pendleton Act in 1883, with the approval of president Chester Arthur, and created a three-man, bipartisan Civil Service Commission with the power and duty of evaluating the merits of job applicants. Stat. 403, Ch. 27, "An act to regulate and improve the civil service of the United States," January 16, 1883.

2. Burlingame, *Abraham Lincoln*, 2:70.

3. Carter, "Abraham Lincoln and the California Patronage," 495–96.

4. Carter, "Abraham Lincoln and the California Patronage," 495–96.

5. *Frank Leslie's Illustrated Newspaper*, April 6, 1861, as quoted in Burlingame, *Abraham Lincoln*, 2:70.

6. Hay, "The Heroic Age in Washington," a lecture given in 1871, quoted in Burlingame, *At Lincoln's Side*, 126. Burlingame, *Abraham Lincoln*, 2:71, offers another version of this story, in which Lincoln tells the applicant, "I'll give you an office very quick if you will undo your work!"

7. Tutorow, *The Governor*, 1:124–26.

8. See "Endorsement on Petition Concerning California Appointments," presented March 30, 1861, by Joseph A. Nunes "as spokesman of about fifty-five Californians, being present, stating it to be the expression of a majority of California Republicans now in Washington." Basler, *The Collected Works of Abraham Lincoln*, 4:302.

9. This recollection was published in the *San Francisco Call*, one of the city's leading newspapers, in 1896. See "Lincoln's Vindication of Colonel E. D. Baker: A Dramatic Scene at the White House," *San Francisco Call*, May 3, 1896, 27. David J. Staples (1824–1900), identified in this article as D. J. Staples, was a Massachusetts native, California pioneer, early-day Republican, and longtime president of the Fireman's Fund Insurance Company in San Francisco.

10. Brooks, *Abraham Lincoln and the Downfall of American Slavery*, 417; Burlingame, *Abraham Lincoln*, 2:82.

11. "News of April 3d," *Sacramento Daily Union*, April 17, 1861, 2; Blair and Tarshis, *Lincoln's Constant Ally*, 128; Kennedy, *The Contest for California in 1861*, 204–5.

12. See "Telegraphic from the East," *Marysville Daily Appeal*, August 2, 1862, 3; "News of July 31st," *Daily Alta California*, August 2, 1862, 1; "Gold and Greenbacks—Secretary Seward's Health—Markets—Arrivals—Troops for Oregon—The Obsequies," *Sacramento Daily Union*, April 19, 1865, 5.

13. Maltby, *The Life and Public Services of Abraham Lincoln*, 216. In July 1861 one copy of the Proclamation with Lincoln's signature on it was exhibited at the Reception

Headquarters of the Grand Army of the Republic in Los Angeles. A newspaper report said it was the property of "Charles Maltby of 529 Olive Street." "Reception Headquarters," *Los Angeles Herald*, July 29, 1886, 5.

14. Robert J. Stevens was married to Baker's daughter Caroline. Born in Rhode Island in 1824, Stevens died in Seattle in December 1889. He was then serving as U.S. consul in Victoria BC, Canada. See "Death of a Consul," *Daily Alta California*, December 26, 1889, 5.

15. "Federal Appointments," *The Morning Press*, October 29, 1891, 1 (Charles Maltby identified as the author).

8. The Judges

1. Tutorow, *The Governor*, 1:114, details the time required for Stanford to travel from San Francisco to New York on his way to attend Lincoln's inauguration as twenty-two days.

2. 9 Stat. 521, Ch. 86, "An Act to provide for extending the Laws and the Judicial System of the United States to the State of California," September 28, 1850.

3. The best source of biographical information about Judge Hoffman is Fritz, *Federal Justice in California*. For discussion of California land grant decisions, see chapter 11 of this volume.

4. See Johnson, *Founding the Far West*, 33–34, 106, 108, 115–17, 259.

5. Basler, *The Collected Works of Abraham Lincoln*, 4:471.

6. Gordan, *Authorized by No Law*, 5. Haight's son, an attorney named Henry Huntly Haight, was elected governor of California in 1867 and served until 1871. He was a Democrat who strongly opposed efforts to bring racial equality to the country after slaves were emancipated.

7. 10 Stat. 631, Ch. 142, "An Act to establish a Circuit Court of the United States in and for the State of California," March 2, 1855.

8. Gordan, *Authorized by No Law*, 11–13.

9. Gordan, *Authorized by No Law*, 5–6; 10 Stat. 631, Ch. 143, "An act to establish a Circuit Court of the United States in and for the State of California," March 2, 1855.

10. McAllister, *Society as I Have Found It*.

11. Swisher, *History of the Supreme Court of the United States: Volume V, The Taney Period 1836–64*, 776.

12. McGinty, *Lincoln and the Court*, 178.

13. Kens, *Justice Stephen Field*, 13–74; McGinty, "Before the Judge," 20–23, 83. An alcalde is a municipal magistrate with both judicial and administrative powers. They were the local officials in Spanish and Mexican California.

14. Field, *Personal Reminiscences*, 27.

15. Field, *Personal Reminiscences*, 40–53.

16. Field, *Personal Reminiscences*, 80.

17. Field, *Personal Reminiscences*, 75–79.

18. Bancroft, *History of California*, 7:196.

19. California Constitution of 1850, Art. XI, Sec. 2.

20. Field, *Personal Reminiscences*, 77–84.

21. Holzer, *Lincoln at Cooper Union*, 106, 147, 243.

22. Kens, *Justice Stephen Field*, 35.

23. See discussion in chapter 4.

24. Field to Lincoln, October 25, 1861, Abraham Lincoln Papers, Library of Congress.

25. McGinty, *Lincoln and the Court*, 179.

26. 12 Stat. 794, Ch. 100, "An Act to provide Circuit Courts for the Districts of California and Oregon, and for other Purposes," March 3, 1863.

27. Field, *Personal Reminiscences*, 116; Kens, *Justice Stephen Field*, 97.

28. Field, *The Life of David Dudley Field*, 196.

29. Beale and Brownsword, eds. *Diary of Gideon Welles*, 1:245.

30. Field, *Personal Reminiscences*, 116.

31. Chandler to AL, October 15, 1864; Hamlin to AL, October 15, 1864; Hale to AL, October 16, 1864; Brewster to Lincoln, October 14, 1864, Abraham Lincoln Papers, Library of Congress.

32. Niven, *Salmon P. Chase*, 374.

9. Destiny's Land

1. Alaska, with an area of 663,300 square miles, did not become a state until January 1959, making California the state with the third-largest territory.

2. See Griswold del Castillo, *The Treaty of Guadalupe Hidalgo*, 41, 42.

3. Field, *Personal Reminiscences*, 149.

4. See O'Sullivan, "Annexation," 5–6, 9–10; Pratt, "John L. O'Sullivan and Manifest Destiny," 213–34, and discussion in chapter 1.

5. See Ellison, *A Self-Governing Dominion*, 109: "Under the spell of the doctrine of 'manifest destiny' the newly arrived settlers believed California to be their 'land of promise'; . . . They noisily asserted that in the conquest of California the United States had acquired not only sovereignty over the country but ownership of the land for United States settlers."

6. See Robinson, *Land in California*, 71, referring to the rancho Suisun in Sonoma County, granted to a Christianized native named Solano, "chief of the tribes of the frontiers of Sonoma," and to a 126.6-acre rancho called Huerta de Cuati in Los Angeles County, granted to Victoria Reid, Native American wife of the Scotsman Hugo Reid.

7. See U.S. Constitution, Art VI, cl. 1: "This Constitution, and the laws of the United States which shall be made in pursuance thereof; and all treaties made, or which shall be made, under the authority of the United States, shall be the supreme law of the land; and the judges in every state shall be bound thereby, anything in the Constitution or laws of any State to the contrary notwithstanding."

8. 9 Stat. 631, Ch. 41, "An Act to ascertain and settle the private Land Claims in the State of California," March 3, 1851.

9. Marszalek, *Commander of All Lincoln's Armies*, 78.

10. Fritz, *Federal Justice in California*, 200.

11. Munro-Fraser, *History of Marin County, California*, 283.

12. Hoffman, *Reports of Land Cases*, appendix; Griswold del Castillo, *The Treaty of Guadalupe Hidalgo*, 73.

13. Basler, *The Collected Works of Abraham Lincoln*, 6:242.

14. Cain, *Lincoln's Attorney General, Edward Bates of Missouri*, 296–98.

15. Basler, *The Collected Works of Abraham Lincoln*, 6:205–6.

16. Basler, *The Collected Works of Abraham Lincoln*, 6:240.

17. "The Almaden Mine Case; The Order of Seizure by Government Revoked," *New York Times*, August 13, 1863, 8.

18. Cain, *Lincoln's Attorney General, Edward Bates of Missouri*, 300; Bates, *The Diary of Edward Bates, 1859–1866*, 354.

19. Bates, *The Diary of Edward Bates, 1859–1866*, 354, 356.

20. Bancroft, *History of California*, 6:551.

21. Basler, *The Collected Works of Abraham Lincoln*, 7:146.

22. Bancroft, *History of California*, 6:551.

23. Robinson, *Land in California*, 165–66.

24. Robinson, *Land in California*, 167–68.

25. 12 Stat. 392, Ch. 75, "An act to secure homesteads to actual settlers on the public domain," May 20, 1862.

26. Basler, *The Collected Works of Abraham Lincoln*, 4:205.

27. Basler, *The Collected Works of Abraham Lincoln*, 7:47.

28. Basler, *The Collected Works of Abraham Lincoln*, 8ed:146.

29. Etulain, *Lincoln Looks West*, 27–28.

30. Robinson, *Land in California*, 169. Riley and Etulain, *Presidents Who Shaped the American West*, 91, states that "the effects of Lincoln's homestead plan were mixed."

31. 12 Stat. 503, Ch. 130, "An act donating public lands to the several states and territories which may provide college for the benefit of agriculture and the mechanic arts," July 2, 1862.

32. The Morrill Act has been subject to modern criticism because it resulted in the loss of land that originally belonged to California's native peoples. See Royster, "This Land Is Their Land," 32–41. This is no doubt correct. But millions of acres of other lands that belonged to the native peoples were also lost because of commercial or residential development. In the fall of 2022, members of native tribes were provided full-tuition scholarships to the University of California to make up for the loss of their ancestors' lands.

33. "Letter Six," dated at San Francisco, December 1860, in King, *A Vacation among the Sierras*, 45.

34. 13 Stat. 325, June 30, 1864, "An act authorizing a grant to the State of California of the 'Yosemite Valley,' and of the land embracing the 'Mariposa Big Tree Grove.'"

35. 17 Stat. 32, March 1, 1872, "An Act to set apart a certain Tract of Land lying near the Head-waters of the Yellowstone River as a public Park."

36. See, for example, Chernow, *Grant*, 739, noting that President Grant signed the Yellowstone bill and President Lincoln signed the Yosemite bill and concluding that Grant "established Yellowstone as the first national park." For a persuasive argument that Yosemite, not Yellowstone, was the first national park of importance, see Huth, "Yosemite," 47–78.

37. 26 Stat. 478, Ch. 926, "An act to set apart a certain tract of land in the State of California as a public park," September 25, 1890.

38. 26 Stat. 650, Ch. 1263, "An act to set apart certain tracts of land in the State of California as forest reservations," October 1, 1890.

39. See "National Parks," *The Morning Call* (San Francisco), October 11, 1890, 3, reporting that President Harrison had signed the bill setting aside approximately 967,000 acres adjoining Yosemite as a national park. The law left "Yosemite proper" under its present control.

40. "Yosemite Reverts to Uncle Sam," *San Francisco Call*, August 2, 1906, 3.

41. Gudde, *California Place Names*, 89, 219.

42. See Starr, *California*, 47–49; Roske, *Everyman's Eden*, 159, 161, 167, 188, 189, 380.

43. Alemany was identified in the patents as bishop of Monterey even after he became archbishop of San Francisco because that was the capacity in which he had filed the claims.

44. The amounts covered by the patents and the dates they bear are set out in *Corrected Report of Spanish and Mexican Grants in California, Complete to February 25, 1886, Prepared by State Surveyor—General, Published as Supplement to Official Report of 1883–84*. See also Robinson, *Land in California*, 31–32.

45. For a list of patents signed by Lincoln on March 18, 1865, some for mission lands and some for other properties, see Shutes, *Lincoln and California*, 227–28.

10. Gold, Silver, and Greenbacks

1. Burlingame, "Introduction," in Brooks, *Lincoln Observed*, 3.

2. "Wealth was not the goal of his ambition. He was frank to admit that he knew nothing about money, saying that he never had enough to fret him." Pratt, *Personal Finances of Abraham Lincoln*, 25.

3. Stahr, *Salmon P. Chase*, 339–40, 353–54, 418, 439, 479, 483, 541; McPherson, *Battle Cry of Freedom*, 443.

4. Matthews, *The Golden State in the Civil War*, 157.

5. Kibby, "Union Loyalty of California's Civil War Governors," 312.

6. Richards, *The California Gold Rush and the Coming of the Civil War*, 230.

7. U.S. Constitution, Art. I, sec. 8, cl. 5.

8. 9 Stat. 59, Ch. 90, "An Act to provide for the better organization of the Treasury, and for the Collection, Safe-Keeping, Transfer, and Disbursement of the public Resources," August 6, 1846.

9. 12 Stat. 292, Ch. 45, "An Act to provide increased Revenue from Imports, to pay Interest on the Public Debt, and for Other Purposes," August 5, 1861.

10. McPherson, *Battle Cry of Freedom*, 441. See Hill, "The Civil War Income Tax," 416: "There had been no precedent for such a form of taxation in our history even in time of war."

11. Meigs, "General M. C. Meigs on the Conduct of the Civil War," 292.

12. 13 Stat. 345, Ch. 33, "An Act to authorize the Issue of United States Notes, and for the Redemption or Funding thereof, and for Funding the Floating Debt of the United States," February 25, 1862.

13. Stahr, *Salmon P. Chase*, 420.

14. Stahr, *Salmon P. Chase*, 379; Niven, *Salmon P. Chase*, 297.

15. McPherson, *Battle Cry of Freedom*, 447.

16. 12 Stat. 432, Ch. 119, "An Act to provide Internal Revenue to support the Government and to Pay Interest on the Public Debt," July 1, 1862. The federal income tax became a subject of intense constitutional debate, and in 1895 it was held unconstitutional by the U.S. Supreme Court in the case of *Pollock v. Farmers' Loan & Trust Company*, 158 U.S. 601 (1895). The Sixteenth Amendment to the Constitution, ratified in 1913, made the tax constitutional.

17. 12 Stat. 498, Ch. 120, "An Act to aid in the Construction of a Railroad and Telegraph Line from the Missouri River to the Pacific Ocean, and to secure to the Government the use of the same for Postal, Military, and Other Purposes," July 1, 1862.

18. 12 Stat. 665, Ch. 58, "An Act to provide a national Currency, secured by a Pledge of United States Stocks, and to provide for the Circulation and Redemption thereof," February 25, 1863.

19. 13 Stat. 223, Ch. 173, "An Act to provide Internal Revenue to support the Government, to Pay Interest on the Public Debt, and for other Purposes," June 30, 1864.

20. Kibby, "Union Loyalty of California's Civil War Governors," 311–12.

21. Bancroft, *History of California*, 7:295.

22. On June 13, 1861, Lincoln signed an executive order approving the commission, previously authorized by secretary of war Simon Cameron.

23. Rybczynski, *A Clearing in the Distance*, 20, 348, 409, 418.

24. Bancroft, *History of California*, 7:297–98.

25. Kibby, "Union Loyalty of California's Civil War Governors," 318.

26. Moses, "Legal Tender Notes in California," 1.

27. California Constitution, Article 14, Secs. 34 and 35.

28. Moses, "Legal Tender Notes in California," 3.

29. "Disturbance on Third Street," *Daily Alta California*, September 20, 1862, 1.

30. "Southern Characters," *Santa Cruz Sentinel*, December 13, 1862, 1.

31. "The Governor on the Greenback Question," *Marysville Daily Appeal*, October 11, 1862, 2; "Be Just, Bee," *Marysville Daily Appeal*, October 15, 1862, 2.

32. "Letter from San Francisco," *Sacramento Daily Union*, December 15, 1862, 2.

33. "News of the Morning," *Sacramento Daily Union*, January 10, 1862, 2.

34. *Evening Bulletin*, July 23, 1862.

35. *Perry v. Washburn* (1862), 20 California Reports, 318–52.

36. Statutes of California, Fourteenth Session, Ch. 421, Sec. 200.

37. Moses, "Legal Tender Notes in California," 21.

38. "Metallic Currency versus Legal Tender," *Sacramento Daily Union*, February 20, 1863, 1.

39. *Carpentier v. Atherton* (1864), 25 California Reports, 564–83; Fankhauser, *A Financial History of California*, 221.

40. Fankhauser, *A Financial History of California*, 222.

41. Hart, *Salmon Portland Chase*, 318.

42. Burlingame and Ettlinger, eds., *Inside Lincoln's White House*, 77.

43. Angle, *Abraham Lincoln*, 164–66.

11. The Native Peoples

1. The native peoples of America have been referred to as "Indians" or "Indios" since the time of Christopher Columbus, who erroneously believed that he had reached the Asian land called "India." The name has become controversial in recent years, with many of the native peoples of America preferring (even insisting) that they be called "indigenous Americans," "indigenes," "native peoples," or "native Americans." Some simply prefer to be called by their own names. This book generally describes them as "native Americans," "native peoples," "natives," or as members of individual groups.

2. This chapter cannot cover the history of the native peoples of California, nor the history of Lincoln's relations with those peoples, except in an introductory way. Rawls's *Indians of California*, Nichols's *Lincoln and the Indians*, Madley's *An American Genocide*, Lindsay's *Murder State*, Bauer's *California through Native Eyes*, and Hurtado's *Indian Survival on the California Frontier* are valuable resources for readers who wish to pursue these subjects in depth. *The Other Californians* by anthropologists Robert F. Heizer and Alan J. Almquist surveys the discrimination suffered by native peoples from the arrival of the Europeans in 1770 until 1920, including some particular discussion of differences in their treatment in the Spanish and Mexican days and after Americans came into full control of California.

3. Neely, "Pale-Faced People and Their Red Brethren," 2.

4. Madley, *An American Genocide*, 18, 22, 23; see "Controversial Cave Discoveries Suggest Humans Reached Americas Much Earlier than Thought," *Nature Brief Newsletter*, https://www.nature.com/articles/d41586-020-02190-y#ref-cr1.

5. Madley, *An American Genocide*, 38–39.

6. Madley, *An American Genocide*, 39.

7. Cook, *The Conflict between the California Indian and White Civilization*, 257.

8. For an in-depth analysis of Pablo Tac's life and writing, see Haas, *Pablo Tac, Indigenous Scholar*. Father Maynard Geiger, Franciscan historian, wrote that both Tac and his Indian companion died before reaching the priesthood. Geiger, *Franciscan Missionaries in Hispanic California, 1769–1848*, 196.

9. Salomon, *Pío Pico*, 3–9, 13.

10. Browne, *Report of the Debates*, 305; Johnson, *Founding the Far West*, 126.

11. California Constitution of 1850, Art. II, Section 1, provided as follows: "Every white male citizen of the United States, and every white male citizen of Mexico, who shall have elected to become a citizen of the United States, under the treaty of peace exchanged and ratified at Querétaro, on the 30th day of May, 1848, of the age of twenty-one years, who shall have been a resident of the State six months next preceding the election, and the county or district in which he claims his vote thirty days, shall be entitled to vote at all elections which are now or hereafter may be authorized by law: Provided, that nothing herein contained, shall be construed to prevent the Legislature, by a two-thirds concurrent vote, from admitting to the right of suffrage, Indians or the descendants of Indians, in such special cases as such a proportion of the legislative body may deem just and proper." See Heizer and Almquist, *The Other Californians*, 116–17.

12. Johnson, *Founding the Far West*, 127; Heizer and Almquist, *The Other Californians*, 131.

13. Young, *Around the World with General Grant*, 2:447–48.

14. Madley, *An American Genocide*, 3.

15. U.S. Constitution, Article IV, sec. 4: "The United States shall guarantee to every state in this union a republican form of government, and shall protect each of them against invasion; and on application of the legislature, or of the executive (when the legislature cannot be convened) against domestic violence."

16. For discussion, see chapter 11.

17. For the story of the Mariposa Battalion, see Madley, *An American Genocide*, 189–94.

18. Madley, *An American Genocide*, 164.

19. Madley, *An American Genocide*, 170.

20. Basler, *The Collected Works of Abraham Lincoln*, 2:217; Burlingame, *Abraham Lincoln*, 1:2; Wilson and Davis, eds., *Herndon's Informants*, 5, 27, 35–36, 95, 439, 675.

21. See Anderson, "Native Americans and the Origins of Abraham Lincoln's Views on Race," 14–15; also see Green, *Lincoln and Native Americans*, 6–15.

22. Wilson and Davis, eds., *Herndon's Informants*, 362.

23. See Anderson, "Native Americans and the Origins of Abraham Lincoln's Views on Race," 18.

24. Wilson and Davis, eds., *Herndon's Informants*, 18, 372. Nichols, *Lincoln and the Indians*, 3–4, speculates that this story may be a legend.

25. Basler, *The Collected Works of Abraham Lincoln*, 1:510.

26. Madley, *An American Genocide*, 290.

27. Madley, *An American Genocide*, 292.

28. Madley, *An American Genocide*, 293–94.

29. Madley, *An American Genocide*, 296.

30. Madley, *An American Genocide*, 302–3.

31. "Revenue," *Mendocino Herald*, January 9, 1863, as reprinted in *Sacramento Daily Union*, January 17, 1863, 2.

32. "Indian War at Owens River," *Sacramento Daily Union*, June 9, 1863, 2.

33. "Gold and Greenbacks—Secretary Seward's Health—Markets—Arrivals—Troops for Oregon—The Obsequies," *Sacramento Daily Union*, April 19, 1865, 5.

34. See "Report of the United States Commissioner of Indian Affairs," *Sacramento Daily Union*, December 25, 1865, 4; *Report of the Commissioner of Indian Affairs for the Year 1866*, 91–108; *Report of Indian Affairs by the Acting Commissioner for the Year 1867*, 117, 122, 130, 134, 140, 149, 150.

35. Nichols, *Lincoln and the Indians*, 78.

36. Nichols, *Lincoln and the Indians*, 79.

37. Lincoln's actions relating to the Sioux were often described as "pardons." Technically, however, he merely refused to authorize their execution. Finkelman, "Lincoln the Lawyer," 407.

38. Basler, *The Collected Works of Abraham Lincoln*, 5:550–51.

39. Basler, *The Collected Works of Abraham Lincoln*, 5:526; 6:48.

40. See *Civil Code of the State of California* (1872) and *Penal Code of the State of California* (1874).

41. The Fourteenth Amendment, prohibiting the denial of life, liberty, or property without due process of law, became part of the U.S. Constitution on July 9, 1868, but California did not ratify it until May 6, 1959. The Fifteenth Amendment, prohibiting the denial of the right to vote on the basis of race, color, or previous condition of servitude, became part of the Constitution on February 3, 1870, but California did not ratify it until April 4, 1962. Sadly, California's full assent to these basic constitutional protections of basic rights thus had to wait almost a century.

42. Prucha, *Christian Reformers and the Indians, 1865–1900*, 5, quoting John Beeson to E. P. Smith, June 25, 1873, Office of Indian Affairs, Letters Received, Miscellaneous p. 520, National Archives Record Group 75.

43. See, for example, Green, *Lincoln and Native Americans*; Rawls, *Indians of California*; Anderson, *Ethnic Cleansing and the Indian*; West, "Reconstructing Race."

44. See West, "Reconstructing Race," 9, 13, 17–18, 20, 25, 26.

45. Whipple, *Lights and Shadows of a Long Episcopate*, 137.

46. Historian David A. Nichols has commented on the "ifs" in Lincoln's statement and the questions they suggest about his real intentions. See Nichols, *Lincoln and the Indians*, 141.

12. The War Continues

1. *Official Records of the Union and Confederate Armies*, Series I, Volume L, Part 1, 623.

2. "Read and Reflect," *Los Angeles Star*, August 31, 1861, 2.

3. Josephy, *The Civil War in the American West*, 236–37; Robinson, *Los Angeles in Civil War Days, 1860–1865*, 80–81.

4. Orton, *Records of California Men in the War of the Rebellion, 1861 to 1867*, 6.

5. Hancock, *Reminiscences of Winfield Scott Hancock by His Wife*, 44–46.

6. Grant, *Personal Memoirs of U. S. Grant*, 2:383.

7. "Pregnant Truths," *Daily Alta California*, June 26, 1864, 2; "Arrival of General McDowell," *Daily Alta California*, June 30, 1864, 2.

8. See Basler, *The Collected Works of Abraham Lincoln*, 4:519 (regarding the request from senator Milton Latham to give Don Andreas [*sic*] Pico authority to raise a Cavalry Regiment of native Mexican citizens of California).

9. Newell, *The Regular Army Before the Civil War, 1845–1860*, 12.

10. "The Great Union Demonstration," *Daily Alta California*, May 12, 1861, 1.

11. "Governor Downey's Letter," *Sacramento Daily Union*, May 13, 1861, 2.

12. "Governor Downey," *The Hydraulic Press* (North San Juan, Nevada County), May 18, 1861, 1.

13. *Los Angeles Star*, May 11, 1861, as quoted in Robinson, *Los Angeles in Civil War Days, 1860–1865*, 50.

14. "List of Attorneys," *Los Angeles Star*, November 13, 1852, 2; "Charles Ducommon's Views," *Los Angeles Herald*, July 9, 1888, 1; Matthews, *The Golden State in the Civil War*, 86.

15. Richards, *The California Gold Rush and the Coming of the Civil War*, 215.

16. Robinson, *Los Angeles in Civil War Days, 1860–1865*, 47.

17. "Old California Democrats in the Rebel Army," *Sacramento Daily Union*, December 3, 1863, 2; "Californians in the Confederate Service," *Los Angeles Star*, December 12, 1863, 2.

18. "Our Letter from Los Angeles," *Daily Alta California*, October 17, 1863, 1.

19. Field and Lynch, "'Master of Ceremonies,'" 379–406; Lapp, *Blacks in Gold Rush California*, 118–19.

20. *The War of the Rebellion*, 236; see Waite, *West of Slavery*, 187–88.

21. Spaulding, "The Attitude of California to the Civil War," 115.

22. See Smith, *Freedom's Frontier*, 8; Lynch, "Southern California Chivalry," 24.

23. See "Card from Senator [Wilson] Flint," *Daily Alta California*, May 12, 1855, 3; "Benjamin Franklin Washington," *Empire County Argus*, June 23, 1855, 2; "Benjamin Franklin Washington," *Sacramento Daily Union*, June 14, 1855, 3; "O, What a Whopper!" *Trinity Journal*, January 28, 1860, 3; "For Governor," *Daily National Democrat*, March 2, 1861, 2; "Attitude of the Peaceable Secessionists in this State," *Weekly Butte Record*, June 15, 1861, 3; "A Traitorous Sheet," *The Elevator*, July 28, 1865, 2; "Death of B. F. Washington," *Grass Valley Daily Union*, January 26, 1872, 2; "John T. Washington," *Mill Valley Record*, March 1, 1929, 5; Waite, "The Lost Cause Goes West: Confederate Culture and Civil War Memory in California," 35–36.

24. Clendenin, "Dan Showalter," 309–25; Newell, *The Regular Army Before the Civil War, 1845–1860*, 15, 20, 40; Hunt, *The Army of the Pacific*, 70–75.

25. Beckert, *Empire of Cotton*, 103, 353.

26. See Waite, *West of Slavery*, 4.

27. Duffett, "Arizona Territory," 87–88.

28. Teel, "Sibley's New Mexican Campaign," 2:70.

29. See Gudde, *California Place Names*, 114. Drum Barracks was named in honor of the assistant adjutant general of the Department of the Pacific, Richard C. Drum.

30. Orton, *Records of California Men in the War of the Rebellion, 1861 to 1867*, 64–67; Josephy, *The Civil War in the American West*, 269–75.

31. Orton, *Records of California Men in the War of the Rebellion, 1861 to 1867*, 45.

32. McGinnis, "New Mexico Territory," 78; Josephy, *The Civil War in the American West*, 61–94.

33. 12 Stat. 644, Ch. 56, "An act to provide a temporary government for the Territory of Arizona, and for other purposes," February 24, 1863.

34. Duffett, "Arizona Territory," 91.

35. Basler, *The Collected Works of Abraham Lincoln*, 7:40.

36. Matthews, *The Golden State in the Civil War*, 123.

37. McPherson, *Battle Cry of Freedom*, 116.

38. Matthews, *The Golden State in the Civil War*, 185–86.

39. Wilkins, *The Great Diamond Hoax*, 47–48.

40. For discussion of Jefferson Davis's use of letters of marque and Lincoln's view of them, see McGinty, *The Rest I Will Kill*, 48–51.

41. "By Telegraph to the Union," *Sacramento Daily Union*, October 17, 1863, 1; Wilkins, *The Great Diamond Hoax*, 85–87.

42. Hunt, *The Army of the Pacific*, 305–9; see Foreman, *A World on Fire*, 418–21.

43. Basler, *The Collected Works of Abraham Lincoln*, 7:53–56. For further discussion of Asbury Harpending's Civil War conspiracy, see Roske, *Everyman's Eden*, 310–11; Matthews, *The Golden State in the Civil War*, 190–92 ("The Chapman Affair"); Hunt, *The Army of the Pacific*, 304–9; Shutes, *Lincoln and California*, 78–80.

44. Gilbert, "Kentucky Privateers in California," 256–26; Fritz, *Federal Justice in California*, 194–96.

45. Basler, *The Collected Works of Abraham Lincoln*, 7:71–72; see Foreman, *A World on Fire*, 421, 461.

46. Matthews, *The Golden State in the Civil War*, 188–89.

47. The popular belief that the slang term "hooker," referring to a prostitute, derived from Joseph Hooker's name is false. The slang term was used much before Joseph Hooker appeared. As early as 1845 it is found in North Carolina, as reported in Norman Ellsworth Eliason's *Tarheel Talk*, published in 1956. It also appears in the second edition of John Russell Bartlett's *Dictionary of Americanisms*, published in 1859, where it is defined as "a strumpet, a sailor's trull." Etymologically, it is most likely that a "hooker" is simply "one who hooks or snares clients." *American Heritage Dictionary of the English Language*.

48. Basler, *The Collected Works of Abraham Lincoln*, 6:70–71.

49. The family spelled its name "Washburn," but Elihu added the "e" to his spelling to recall an older family spelling.

50. Basler, *The Collected Works of Abraham Lincoln*, 6:540; Washburne, "Reminiscences of Abraham Lincoln," 42.

51. Basler, *The Collected Works of Abraham Lincoln*, 7:13.

52. Abraham Lincoln papers: Series 3. General Correspondence. 1837–1897: Abraham Lincoln, Tuesday, August 23, 1864 (Memorandum on Probable Failure of Reelection; endorsed by members of cabinet).

53. Bancroft, *History of California*, 7:310.

54. Bancroft, *History of California*, 7:311.

55. Basler, *The Collected Works of Abraham Lincoln*, 8:146.

56. See, for example, White, *Lincoln's Greatest Speech*.

57. Basler, *The Collected Works of Abraham Lincoln*, 7:333.

58. "News of the Day," *Daily Alta California*, April 10, 1865, 2.

13. Letters from Washington

1. Temple, *Lincoln's Confidant*, 45–49.

2. "Some Reminiscences of Abraham Lincoln," *Marysville Daily Appeal*, November 4, 1860, 1.

3. "State Election Returns," *Sacramento Daily Union*, November 7, 1860, 2.

4. Temple, *Lincoln's Confidant*, 73, 74.

5. Brooks, *Washington in Lincoln's Time*, 2.

6. Fehrenbacher, *Recollected Words of Abraham Lincoln*, 41, 517–18.

7. See Holzer, *Lincoln and the Power of the Press*, 478–82, 551–52.

8. Burlingame, "Introduction," in Brooks, *Lincoln Observed*, 1.

9. "Letter from Washington," *Sacramento Daily Union*, December 20, 1862, 1.

10. Brooks, *Washington in Lincoln's Time*, 2–3.

11. "Letter from Washington," *Sacramento Daily Union*, January 3, 1863, 4.

12. "Letter from Washington," *Sacramento Daily Union*, January 24, 1863, 1.

13. "Letters [sic] from Washington [from Our Special Correspondent]," *Sacramento Daily Union*, January 29, 1868, 1.

14. "Letter from Washington," *Sacramento Daily Union*, March 3, 1863, 3.

15. "Letter from Washington," *Sacramento Daily Union*, June 5, 1863, 1.

16. "Letter from Washington," *Sacramento Daily Union*, May 27, 1863, 1.

17. Brooks, *Washington in Lincoln's Time*, 2.

18. Brooks, *Washington in Lincoln's Time*, 57.

19. "Letters [sic] from Washington," *Sacramento Daily Union*, December 2, 1864, 1.

20. Temple, *Lincoln's Confidant*, 121.

21. "Letters [sic] from Washington," *Sacramento Daily Union*, May 8, 1865, 2.

22. "Letters [sic] from Washington," *Sacramento Daily Union*, May 8, 1865, 2.

23. Brooks, *Washington in Lincoln's Time*, 253.

24. "Letters [sic] from Washington," *Sacramento Daily Union*, May 8, 1865, 2.

25. Brooks, *Washington in Lincoln's Time*, 253–54.

26. Brooks, *Washington in Lincoln's Time*, 255.

27. Brooks, *Washington in Lincoln's Time*, 257–58.

28. "Appears to Be Confirmed," *Marysville Daily Appeal*, July 14, 1865, 2; "New Federal Officials," *Sacramento Daily Union*, August 14, 1865, 3.

29. Temple, *Lincoln's Confidant*, 135.

30. Twain, *Autobiography of Mark Twain*, 1:228.

31. Temple, *Lincoln's Confidant*, 158–60, 166, 199.

32. "Noah Brooks in Town," *San Francisco Call*, April 10, 1897, 7.

33. Temple, *Lincoln's Confidant*, 219.

34. This chapter is based in part on my article "'Castine' and Mr. Lincoln: A Reporter at the White House," which appeared in the November 1977 issue of *Civil War Times Illustrated*. An excellent source of information about Noah Brooks and his "Letters from Washington" is *Lincoln Observed*, edited by Michael Burlingame. Another, which is based upon careful and extensive research, is Temple, *Lincoln's Confidant*, which had its origin as a thesis completed at the University of Illinois in 1956. All of these sources are listed in the bibliography to this book.

14. The View from Lone Mountain

1. Reminiscences of Charles Carlton Coffin in Rice, *Reminiscences of Abraham Lincoln*, 172–73.

2. Farwell, *Ball's Bluff*, 134; Faust, *Historical Times Illustrated Encyclopedia of the Civil War*, 37, 92.

3. Burlingame, *Abraham Lincoln*, 2:82, 200.

4. Brooks, *Lincoln Observed*, 215; Brooks, *Abraham Lincoln and the Downfall of American Slavery*, 417.

5. Williams, *David C. Broderick*, 197; Lynch, *The Life of David C. Broderick*, 248, 251–52; Kennedy, *The Contest for California in 1861*, 56, 60.

6. *Mariposa Gazette*, December 17, 1861, 2.

7. Matthews, *The Golden State in the Civil War*, 104–5.

8. Blair and Tarshis, *Lincoln's Constant Ally*, 59.

9. Arnold, *The Life of Abraham Lincoln*, 240.

10. Carpenter, *The Inner Life of Abraham Lincoln*, 228.

11. Lone Mountain is today the location of the Lone Mountain campus of the University of San Francisco. Several cemeteries were situated there in the 1850s but were removed to the city of Colma, just south of San Francisco, in the 1930s and 1940s.

15. What Was Remembered

1. "The Effect in San Francisco," *Daily Alta California*, April 16, 1865, 1.

2. "The Excitement at San Francisco," *Sacramento Daily Union*, April 19, 1865, 4.

3. "The Assassination of President Lincoln," *Sacramento Daily Union*, April 17, 1865, 1.

4. "The Last Earth," *Daily Alta California*, April 20, 1865, 1.

5. "The Death of the Late President," *Sacramento Daily Union*, April 20,1865, 3.

6. "Funeral Obsequies of President Lincoln at Marysville, April 19, 1865," *Marysville Daily Appeal*, April 21, 1865, 2.

7. "Our Letter from Los Angeles," *Daily Alta California*, May 1, 1865, 1.

8. "Our Letter from Los Angeles," *Daily Alta California*, May 9, 1865, 1.

9. Robinson, *Los Angeles in Civil War Days, 1860–1865*, 161–62.

10. Warren, "Earliest Sculptors of the President," 1; Shutes, *Lincoln and California*, 194–98.

11. "Los Angeles New Briefs," *San Bernardino Sun*, July 3, 1926, 2; "Dr. Bridge's Gift," "Lincoln Statue Unveiled," and "Art in Sculpture and Poetry," newspaper clippings in "Excerpts from newspapers and other sources from the files of the Lincoln Financial Corporation."

12. Lundén, "The Rise and Fall of a Swedish-American Sculptor," 145–63; "Noted Swedish Sculptor to Visit L.A.," *Los Angeles Herald*, May 24, 1915, 1; "David Edstrom, 65, Sculptor Is Dead: Noted Creator of Memorials, Psychological Studies and Busts of Individuals," *New York Times*, Section General, August 14, 1938, 33.

13. "Heroic Model of Martyr President," *San Francisco Call*, September 26, 1909, 22.

14. The statue was dedicated on Monday, February 13, not Sunday, February 12, 1928, as public ceremonies of this kind were not then conducted on Sundays; see Elsner, "Four San Francisco Sculptors," 11; Pratt, "Haig Patigian, California's Noted Sculptor," 11; "Lincoln Day Celebration," *Organized Labor*, February 11, 1928, 2; "Refutes Stories Dwarfing Martyr," *Santa Cruz News*, February 13, 1928, 1.n.

15. Helfand, *University of California, Berkeley*, 53; "U. of C. Unveils Statue of Lincoln," *Los Angeles Herald*, February 12, 1921, A–7.

16. Great thanks to Nathan Gonzales, curator of the Lincoln Memorial Shrine, for his contributions to my research about the shrine.

17. "Unveiling of Statue Viewed by Sculptor," *San Bernardino Sun*, March 14, 1941, 9. "Young California Artist Is His Own Model for a Lincoln Statue," *Life Magazine*, September 9, 1940, 130–31.

18. Act 1471, Statutes of California, approved January 20, 1909, and Act 1471, Statutes of California, approved April 13, 1909.

19. 20 Stat. 277, Ch. 38; 23 Stat. 516, Joint Resolution No. 5.

20. *The Lincoln-Roosevelt Republican League*, 4.

21. See Bean, *Boss Ruef's San Francisco*.

22. Warren, *The Memoirs of Earl Warren*, 39.

23. See Lower, *A Bloc of One*.

24. Compston, *Earl Warren*, 60. The date upon which Lincoln made this statement about slavery is apparently unknown, although it is often given as August 1, 1858. See Basler, *The Collected Works of Abraham Lincoln*, 2:532.

25. Moke, *Earl Warren and the Struggle for Justice*, 140.

26. Warren, *The Memoirs of Earl Warren*, 149.

27. *Brown v. Board of Education of Topeka*, 347 U.S. 483 (1954), *Reynolds v. Sims*, 377 U.S. 533 (1964), and *Miranda v. Arizona*, 384 U.S. 436 (1966).

28. Wallis and Williamson, *The Lincoln Highway*, 3.

29. Large numbers of troops and freight crossed the Rock Island Bridge between Illinois and Iowa during the Civil War. It was a bridge that Lincoln had fought in court to preserve. See McGinty, *Lincoln's Greatest Case*, 183.

30. Basler, *The Collected Works of Abraham Lincoln*, 1:5.

31. See discussion in chapter 12.

32. A loop into and out of Colorado was authorized in 1913, but the Lincoln Highway Association withdrew its authorization in 1915.

33. The Lincoln Park terminus of the Lincoln Highway is now marked by a plaza and fountain in front of the Palace of the Legion of Honor, an impressive art museum that was opened to the public in 1921.

34. See Waite, "The 'Lost Cause' Goes West," 33–49, for a good review of ways in which the Confederate memory was preserved in California and gradually undermined.

35. See discussion in chapter 13.

36. "A Lincoln Forum Interview," 15.

37. See "Op-ed: Take down Chicago's Lincoln Statutes? It's Iconoclasm Gone Mad," *Chicago Tribune*, February 22, 2021.

38. On February 16, 2022, more than 70 percent of San Francisco voters voted to recall the three members of the school board, angered that they had spent time deciding whether to rename schools rather than focusing on the fundamental needs of students. *New York Times*, February 17, 2022, Sec. A, 19.

Bibliography

Archives and Manuscripts

California State Archives. Sacramento, California.

Civil Code of the State of California. Annotated by Creed Hammond and John C. Burch of the California Code Commissioners. Sacramento: H. S. Crocker, 1872.

Cohen, Jennie. "Lincoln Documents Accompanied Donner Party on Its Grim Journey." *Inside History*. https://www.history.com/news/lincoln-documents-accompanied -donner-party-on-its-grim-journey.

Corrected Report of Spanish and Mexican Grants in California, Complete to February 25, 1886, Prepared by State Surveyor–General, Published as Supplement to Official Report of 1883–84. Sacramento: James J. Ayres, Sup. State Printing, 1886.

Demaree, David. "Consuming Lincoln: Abraham Lincoln's Western Manhood in the Urban Northeast, 1848–1861." PhD diss., Kent State University, 2018.

Edwards, G. Thomas. "The Department of the Pacific in the Civil War." PhD diss., University of Oregon, 1963.

Jewell, James Robbins. "Left Arm of the Republic: The Department of the Pacific during the Civil War." PhD diss., West Virginia University, 2006.

Laws of the State of Illinois. Passed by the Fifteenth Assembly, at their Session Begun and Held in the City of Springfield, December 7, 1846. Springfield: Charles H. Lanphierjohn, Public Printer, 1847.

Laws of the State of Illinois. Passed by the Ninth General Assembly, at their Second Session, Commencing December 7, 1835, and ending January 18, 1836. Vandalia: J. Y. Sawyer, Public Printer, 1836.

Laws of the State of Illinois. Tenth General Assembly, at their Session Commencing December 5, 1836, and ending March 6, 1837. Vandalia: William Walters, Public Printer, 1837.

Lewis, Albert Lucian. "Los Angeles in the Civil War Decades, 1850–1868." PhD diss., University of Southern California, 1970.

Lincoln Papers, Manuscript Division, Library of Congress.

Lynch, Daniel. "Southern California Chivalry: The Convergence of Southerners and Californios in the Far Southwest, 1846–1866." PhD diss., University of California, Los Angeles, 2015.

Official Records of the Union and Confederate Navies in the War of the Rebellion. 30 vols. Washington: Government Printing Office, 1894–1922.

Penal Code of the State of California, Annotated by Creed Hammond and John C. Burch of the California Code Commissioners. San Francisco: A. L. Bancroft, Sumner White, 1874.

Powell, Etta Olive. "Southern Influence in California Politics before 1864." Master's thesis, University of California, 1929.

Private Laws of the State of Illinois Passed at the First Session of the Seventeenth General Assembly, Begun and Held at the City of Springfield, January 6, 1851. Springfield: Lanphier and Walker, 1851.

Report of Indian Affairs by the Acting Commissioner for the Year 1867. Washington: Government Printing Office, 1868.

Report of the Commissioner of Indian Affairs for the Year 1866. Washington: Government Printing Office, 1866.

Stowell, Daniel W., et al., eds. *Papers of Abraham Lincoln: Legal Documents and Cases.* 4 vols. Charlottesville: University of Virginia Press, 2008.

Transcript of the Proceedings, in Case No. 366, Andres Castillero, Claimant, vs. The United States, Defendant, for the Place Named New Almaden. San Francisco: Whitton, Towne, Printers, 1858.

Wainwright, Mary-Jo. "Milestones in California History: The 1846 Bear Flag Revolt: Early Cultural Conflict in California." *California History* 75, no. 2 (University of California Press, California Historical Society), 1996, https://doi.org/10.2307/25177573.

Waite, Kevin. "The Slave South in the Far West: California, the Pacific, and Proslavery Visions of Empire." PhD diss., University of Pennsylvania, 2016.

The War of the Rebellion: A Compilation of the Official Records of the Union and Confederate Armies. 128 vols. Washington: Government Printing Office, 1880–1901.

Published Works

"A Lincoln Forum Interview with Acclaimed Biographer Ronald C. White." *Lincoln Forum Bulletin* 49 (Spring 2021): 15.

American Heritage Dictionary of the English Language. 5th ed. Boston: Houghton Mifflin Harcourt, 2020.

Anderson, Christopher W. "Native Americans and the Origins of Abraham Lincoln's Views on Race." *Journal of the Abraham Lincoln Association* 37, no. 1 (Winter 2016): 11–29.

Anderson, Gary Clayton. *Ethnic Cleansing and the Indian: The Crime That Should Haunt America.* Norman: University of Oklahoma Press, 2014.

Angle, Paul M., ed. *Abraham Lincoln, by some men who knew him, being personal recollections of Judge Owen T. Reeves, Hon. James S. Ewing, Col. Richard P. Morgan, Judge Franklin Blades, John W. Bunn.* Bloomington IL: Pantagraph, 1910.

———. *"Here I Have Lived": A History of Lincoln's Springfield, 1821–1865.* New Brunswick NJ: Rutgers University Press, 1935.

Arnold, Isaac N. *The Life of Abraham Lincoln.* 11th ed. Chicago: A. C. McClurg, 1909.

Ascher, Leonard. "Lincoln's Administration and the New Almaden Scandal." *Pacific Historical Review* 5, no. 1 (1936): 38–51.

Baker memorials: consisting of a memoir, funeral sermon, and dirge, to the memory of the late Col. E. D. Baker. Compiled and published by the California regiment, and most respectfully dedicated to those who loved him. Philadelphia: Collins, 1862.

Bancroft, Hubert Howe. *History of California.* 7 vols. San Francisco: History Company, 1886–88.

Barrows, H. D. "J. Lancaster Brent." *Annual Publication of the Historical Society of Southern California* 6, no. 3 (1905): 238–41.

Bartlett, John Russell. *Dictionary of Americanisms: A Glossary of Words and Phrases Usually Regarded as Peculiar to the United States.* Boston: Little Brown, 1859.

Basler, Roy P., ed. *The Collected Works of Abraham Lincoln.* 9 vols. New Brunswick NJ: Rutgers University Press, 1953–55.

Bates, Edward. *The Diary of Edward Bates, 1859–1866.* Washington DC: U.S. Government Printing Office, 1933.

Bauer, William J., Jr. *California through Native Eyes: Reclaiming History.* Seattle: University of Washington Press, 2016.

Beale, Howard K., and Alan W. Brownsword, eds. *Diary of Gideon Welles, Secretary of the Navy under Lincoln and Johnson.* 3 vols. New York: W. W. Norton, 1960.

Bean, Walton. *Boss Ruef's San Francisco: The Story of the Union Labor Party, Big Business, and the Graft Prosecution.* Berkeley: University of California Press, 1952.

Beckert, Sven. *Empire of Cotton: A Global History.* New York: Vintage, 2015.

Bell, Horace. *On the Old West Coast: Being Further Reminiscences of a Ranger.* Edited by Lanier Bartlett. New York: Grosset & Dunlap, 1930.

Bishop, Jim. *The Day Lincoln Was Shot.* New York: Grammercy, 1983.

Bishop, William Henry. *Old Mexico and Her Lost Provinces: A Journey in Mexico, Southern California, and Arizona by Way of Cuba.* New York: Harper & Brothers, 1883.

Blair, Harry C., and Rebecca Tarshis. *Lincoln's Constant Ally: The Life of Colonel Edward D. Baker.* Portland: Oregon Historical Society, 1960.

Blumenthal, Sidney. *A Self-Made Man: The Political Life of Abraham Lincoln, 1809–1849.* New York: Simon & Schuster, 2017.

———. *All the Powers of Earth: The Political Life of Abraham Lincoln, 1856–1860.* New York: Simon & Schuster, 2019.

———. *Wrestling with His Angel: The Political Life of Abraham Lincoln, 1849–1856.* New York: Simon & Schuster, 2017.

Borneman, Walter R. *Rival Rails: The Race to Build America's Greatest Transcontinental Railroad*. New York: Random House, 2010.

Braden, Waldo W. "Lincoln's Western Travel, 1859." *Lincoln Herald* 90, no. 2 (Summer 1988): 38–43.

Brooks, Noah. *Abraham Lincoln and the Downfall of American Slavery*. New York: G. P. Putnam's Sons, 1894.

——. *Lincoln Observed: Civil War Dispatches of Noah Brooks*. Edited by Michael Burlingame. Baltimore: Johns Hopkins University Press, 1998.

——. *Washington in Lincoln's Time*. New York: Century, 1896.

Browne, Francis F. *The Everyday Life of Abraham Lincoln*. New York: Thompson, 1886.

Browne, J. Ross. *Report of the Debates in the Convention of California on the Formation of the State Constitution in September and October, 1849*. Washington DC: John T. Towers, 1850.

Buchanan, A. Russell. *David S. Terry of California: Dueling Judge*. San Marino CA: Huntington Library, 1956.

Burlingame, Michael. *Abraham Lincoln: A Life*. 2 vols. Baltimore: Johns Hopkins University Press, 2008.

Burlingame, Michael, and John R. Turner Ettlinger, eds. *Inside Lincoln's White House: The Complete Civil War Diary of John Hay*. Carbondale: Southern Illinois University Press, 1997.

Burlingame, Michael, ed. *An Oral History of Abraham Lincoln: John G. Nicolay's Interviews and Essays*. Carbondale: Southern Illinois University Press, 1996.

——. *At Lincoln's Side: John Hay's Civil War Correspondence and Selected Writings*. Carbondale: Southern Illinois University Press, 2000.

Cain, Marvin R. *Lincoln's Attorney General, Edward Bates of Missouri*. Columbia: University of Missouri Press, 1965.

Camp, Charles L., ed. *James Clyman, American Frontiersman, 1792–1881: The Adventures of a Trapper and Covered Wagon Emigrant as Told in His Own Reminiscences and Diaries*. San Francisco: California Historical Society, 1928.

Carpenter, Francis B. *The Inner Life of Abraham Lincoln: Six Months at the White House*. New York: Hurd and Houghton, 1868.

Carr, John. *Pioneer Days in California: Historical and Personal Sketches*. Eureka CA: Times, 1891.

Carter, John Denton. "Abraham Lincoln and the California Patronage." *American Historical Review* 58 (1943): 495–506.

Chadwick, Bruce. *1858: Abraham Lincoln, Jefferson Davis, Robert E. Lee, Ulysses S. Grant, and the War They Failed to See*. Naperville IL: Sourcebooks, 2008.

Chandler, Robert J. "Friends in Time of Need: Republicans and Black Civil Rights in California during the Civil War Era." *Arizona and the West* 24, no. 4 (Winter 1982): 319–40.

Chernow, Ron. *Grant*. New York: Penguin, 2017.

Claybourn, Joshua A. "Abe Lincoln: An Acceptable Nickname?" *For the People, A Newsletter of the Abraham Lincoln Association* 20, no. 3–4 (Fall–Winter 2018): 8.

Clendenin, Clarence C. "Dan Showalter: California Secessionist." *California Historical Society Quarterly* 40 (December 1961): 309–25.

Cleveland, Henry. *Alexander H. Stephens in Public and Private.* Philadelphia: National, 1866.

Cole, Cornelius. "The Lincoln I Knew." As told to Mabel Sherman. *Colliers* 71 (February 10, 1923): 29.

———. *Memoirs of Cornelius Cole, Ex-Senator of the United States from California.* New York: McLoughlin Brothers, 1908.

Compston, Christine L. *Earl Warren: Justice for All.* New York: Oxford University Press, 2001.

Conness, John. "Reminisces of Abraham Lincoln." In *Reminiscences of Abraham Lincoln by Distinguished Men of His Time*, edited by Allen Thorndike Rice, 559–71. New York: North American Review, 1888.

Cook, Sherburne F. *The Conflict between the California Indian and White Civilization.* Berkeley: University of California Press, 1976.

Costello, Mary Charlotte Aubry. *Climbing the Mississippi River Bridge by Bridge.* Vol. 2. *All the Minnesota Bridges across the Mississippi River from the Iowa Border to the Lake Itasca, the Source of the Mississippi River.* Davenport IA: Mary C. Costello, 2002.

Cresap, Bernarr. "Early California as Described by Edward O. C. Ord." *Pacific Historical Review* 21 (November 1952): 329–40.

Davis, William C. *Jefferson Davis: The Man and His Hour.* New York: HarperCollins, 1991.

Davis, Winfield J. *History of Political Conventions in California, 1849–1892.* Sacramento: California State Library, 1893.

De Wolk, Roland. *American Disruptor: The Scandalous Life of Leland Stanford.* Oakland: University of California Press, 2019.

Denning, Robert. "A Fragile Machine: California Senator John Conness." *California History* 85 (2008): 26–49, 71–73.

Dickson, Edward A. "Lincoln and Baker: The Story of a Great Friendship." *Historical Society of Southern California Quarterly* 34 (September 1952): 229–42.

Dixon, Kelly J., Julie M. Schablitsky, and Shannon A. Novak, eds. *An Archaeology of Desperation: Exploring the Donner Party's Alder Creek Camp.* Norman: University of Oklahoma Press, 2011.

Dodge, Grenville M. *Personal Recollections of President Abraham Lincoln, General Ulysses S. Grant, and General William T. Sherman.* Council Bluffs IA: Monarch, 1914.

Donald, David Herbert. *Lincoln.* New York: Simon & Schuster, 1995.

Duffett, Walter N. "Arizona Territory." In *Abraham Lincoln and the Western Territories*, edited by Ralph Y. McGinnis and Calvin N. Smith, 84–96. Chicago: Nelson-Hall, 1994.

Dwinelle, John W. *A Funeral Oration upon David C. Broderick, Late Senator from California, Delivered at the Chapel of the New York University, on Sunday Evening, Nov. 20th, 1859.* Rochester NY: Benton & Andrews, 1859.

Eliason, Norman Ellsworth. *Tarheel Talk: An Historical Study of the English Language in North Carolina to 1860.* Chapel Hill: University of North Carolina Press, 1956.

Ellison, Joseph. "Designs for a Pacific Republic, 1843–62." *Oregon Historical Quarterly* 31, no. 4 (December 1930): 319–42.

Ellison, William Henry. *A Self-Governing Dominion: California, 1849–1860.* Berkeley: University of California Press, 1950.

Elsner, William H. "Four San Francisco Sculptors." *Bulletin of the California Palace of the Legion of Honor* 25 (May–June 1967): 11.

Emerson, Jason. *Giant in the Shadows: The Life of Robert T. Lincoln.* Carbondale: Southern Illinois University Press, 2012.

Ethington, Philip J. *The Public City: The Political Construction of Urban Life in San Francisco, 1850–1900.* New York: Cambridge University Press. 1994.

Etulain, Richard W. *Abraham Lincoln: A Western Legacy.* Pierre: South Dakota Historical Society Press, 2020.

———. "Abraham Lincoln and the Oregon Country." *Lincoln Lore* 1899 (Spring 2012): 12–20.

———. "Abraham Lincoln: Political Founding Father of the American West." *Montana: The Magazine of Western History* 59 (Summer 2009): 3–22.

———. *Beyond the Missouri: The Story of the American West.* Albuquerque: University of New Mexico Press, 2006.

———. *Lincoln and Oregon Country Politics in the Civil War Era.* Corvallis: Oregon State University Press, 2013.

———. *Lincoln Looks West: From the Mississippi to the Pacific.* Edited by Richard W. Etulain. Carbondale: Southern Illinois University Press, 2010.

Fairman, Charles. *Reconstruction and Reunion, 1864–88, Part One.* New York: Macmillan, 1971.

Fankhauser, William C. *A Financial History of California: Public Revenues, Debts, and Expenditures.* Berkeley: University of California Press, 1913.

Faragher, John Mack. *Eternity Street: Violence and Justice in Frontier Los Angeles.* New York: W. W. Norton, 2016.

Farwell, Byron. *Ball's Bluff: A Small Battle and Its Long Shadow.* McLean VA: EPM, 1990.

Fatout, Paul. "The California Regiment, Colonel Baker, and Ball's Bluff." *California Historical Society Quarterly* 31, no. 3 (1952): 229–40.

Faust, Patricia L., ed. *Historical Times Illustrated Encyclopedia of the Civil War.* New York: Harper & Row, 1986.

Fehrenbacher, Don E. *The Dred Scott Case: Its Significance in American Law and Politics.* New York: Oxford University Press, 1978.

———. *Recollected Words of Abraham Lincoln.* Edited by Don E. Fehrenbacher and Virginia Fehrenbacher. Stanford CA: Stanford University Press, 1996.

Field, Henry M. *The Life of David Dudley Field*. New York: Charles Scribner's Sons, 1898.

Field, Kendra, and Daniel Lynch. "'Master of Ceremonies': The World of Peter Biggs in Civil War–Era Los Angeles." *Western Historical Quarterly* 47, no. 4 (2016): 379–406.

Field, Stephen J. *Personal Reminiscences of Early Days in California with Other Sketches. By Stephen J. Field. Printed for a few friends.* Not published. Copyright 1893 by Stephen J. Field.

Finkelman, Paul. *An Imperfect Union: Slavery, Federalism, and Comity*. Chapel Hill: University of North Carolina Press, 1981.

———. *Dred Scott v. Sandford: A Brief History with Documents*. Boston: Bedford/ St. Martin's, 1997.

———. "The Law of Slavery and Freedom in California 1848–1860." *California Western Law Review* 17, no. 3 (1980–1981): 437–64.

———. "Lincoln, Emancipation, and the Limits of Constitutional Change." *Supreme Court Review* 2008, no. 1 (2008): 349–87.

———. "Lincoln the Lawyer, Humanitarian Concerns, and the Dakota Pardons." *William Mitchell Law Review* 39, no. 2 (2013): 409–49.

———. *The Political Lincoln: An Encyclopedia*. Edited by Paul Finkelman and Martin J. Hershock. Washington DC: CQ Press, 2008.

———. *Supreme Injustice: Slavery and the Nation's Highest Court*. Cambridge MA: Harvard University Press, 2018.

Fischetti, Peter B. "Redlands: History lives at Lincoln Memorial Shrine." *The Press— Enterprise*. February 15, 2015.

Foote, H. S. *War of the Rebellion; or, Scylla and Charybdis, Consisting of Observations upon the Causes, Course, and Consequences of the Late Civil War in the United States*. New York: Harper & Brothers, 1866.

Foreman, Amanda. *A World on Fire: Britain's Crucial Role in the American Civil War*. New York: Random House, 2012.

Frey, Robert L., ed. *Encyclopedia of American Business History and Biography: Railroads in the Nineteenth Century*. New York: Facts on File, 1988.

Fritz, Christian G. *Federal Justice in California: The Court of Ogden Hoffman, 1851– 1891*. Lincoln: University of Nebraska Press, 1991.

Gates, Paul W. *Land and Law in California: Essays on Land Policies*. Ames: Iowa State University Press, 1991.

Geiger, Maynard, OFM. *Franciscan Missionaries in Hispanic California 1769–1848: A Biographical Dictionary*. San Marino CA: Huntington Library, 1969.

Gilbert, Benjamin Franklin. "Kentucky Privateers in California." *Kentucky State Historical Society Register* 30 (1940): 256–66.

Goodheart, Adam. *1861: The Civil War Awakening*. New York: Alfred A. Knopf, 2011.

Gordan, John D., III. *Authorized by No Law: The San Francisco Committee of Vigilance of 1856 and the United States Circuit Court for the Districts of California*. Pasadena CA: Ninth Judicial Circuit Historical Society, and San Francisco:

United States District Court for the Northern District of California Historical Society, 1987.

Graebner, Norman. *Empire on the Pacific: A Study in American Continental Expansion*. Santa Barbara CA: ABC-Clio, 1983.

Grant, U. S. *Personal Memoirs of U. S. Grant*. 2 vols. New York: Charles L. Webster, 1885.

Greenberg, Amy S. *A Wicked War: Polk, Lincoln, and the 1846 U.S. Invasion of Mexico*. New York: Alfred A. Knopf, 2012.

Green, Michael S. *Lincoln and Native Americans*. Carbondale: Southern Illinois University Press, 2021.

——— . *Lincoln and the Election of 1860*. Carbondale: Southern Illinois University
Press, 2011.

——— . "Lincoln, the West, and the Antislavery Politics of the 1850s." In *Lincoln
Looks West: From the Mississippi to the Pacific*, edited by Richard W. Etulain,
90–112. Carbondale: Southern Illinois University Press, 2010.

Grinspan, Jon. "'Young Men for War': The Wide Awakes and Lincoln's 1860 Presidential Campaign." *Journal of American History* 96, no. 2 (2009): 357–78.

Griswold del Castillo, Richard. *The Treaty of Guadalupe Hidalgo: A Legacy of Conflict*. Norman: University of Oklahoma Press, 1990.

Gudde, Erwin G. *California Place Names: The Origin and Etymology of Current Geographical Names*, 4th ed. Rev. and enlarged by William Bright. Berkeley: University of California Press, 1998.

Haas, Lizbeth. *Pablo Tac, Indigenous Scholar: Writing on Luiseno Language and Colonial History, c. 1840*. Berkeley: University of California Press, 2011.

Hancock, Almira Russell. *Reminiscences of Winfield Scott Hancock by His Wife*. New
York: Charles L. Webster, 1887.

Hart, Albert Bushnell. *Salmon Portland Chase*. Boston: Houghton Mifflin, 1899.

Hastings, Lansford W. *The Emigrants' Guide to Oregon and California*. Cincinnati:
George Conclin, 1845.

Heidler, David S., and Jeanne T. Heidler. *Henry Clay: The Essential American*. New
York: Random House, 2010.

Heizer, Robert F., and Alan J. Almquist. *The Other Californians: Prejudice and Discrimination under Spain, Mexico, and the United States to 1920*. Berkeley: University of California Press, 1977.

Helfand, Harvey. *University of California, Berkeley: An Architectural Tour and Photographs*. New York: Princeton Architectural Press, 2002.

Herndon, William H., and Jesse W. Weik. *Herndon's Lincoln*. Edited by Douglas L.
Wilson and Rodney O. Davis. Urbana: Knox College Lincoln Studies Center
and the University of Illinois Press in association with the Abraham Lincoln
Bicentennial Commission, 2006.

Herr, Pamela. *Jessie Benton Frémont: A Biography*. Norman: University of Oklahoma
Press, by arrangement with Franklin Watts, 1988.

Hershock, Martin J. *The Political Lincoln: An Encyclopedia*. Edited by Paul Finkelman and Martin J. Hershock. Washington DC: CQ Press, 2008.

Hill, Joseph A. "The Civil War Income Tax." *Quarterly Journal of Economics* 8, no. 4 (1894): 416–52.

Hiltzik, Michael. *Iron Empires: Robber Barons, Railroads, and the Making of Modern America*. New York: Houghton Mifflin Harcourt, 2020.

Hittell, Theodore Henry. *The General Laws of the State of California, from 1850 to 1864 Inclusive*. 2 vols. 2nd ed. San Francisco: H. H. Bancroft, 1870.

——. *History of California*. 4 vols. San Francisco: N. J. Stone, 1897.

Hoffman, Ogden. *Reports of Land Cases Determined in the United States District Court for the Northern District of California: June term, 1853, to June term, 1858, inclusive*. Vol. 1. San Francisco: Numa Herbert, 1862.

Holst, Erika. "Another View on 'Abe.'" *For the People, A Newsletter of the Abraham Lincoln Association* 21, no. 2 (Summer 2019): 4.

Holzer, Harold. *Lincoln and the Power of the Press*. New York: Simon & Schuster, 2014.

——. *Lincoln at Cooper Union: The Speech That Made Abraham Lincoln President*. New York: Simon & Schuster, 2004.

Howe, Daniel Walker. "American Victorianism as a Culture." *American Quarterly* 27, no. 5 (1975): 507–32.

Howe, M. A. DeWolfe. *Home Letters of General Sherman*. New York: Charles Scribner's Sons, 1909.

Hull, Dorothy. "The Movement in Oregon for the Establishment of a Pacific Coast Republic." *Oregon Historical Quarterly* 17, no. 3 (1916): 177–200.

Hunt, Aurora. *The Army of the Pacific: Its Operations in California, Texas, Arizona, New Mexico, Utah, Nevada, Oregon, Washington, Plains Region, Mexico, etc., 1860–1866*. Rev. ed. with a new introduction by Robert A. Clark. Harrisburg PA: Stackpole, 2004.

Hurtado, Albert L. *Indian Survival on the California Frontier*. New Haven CT: Yale University Press, 1988.

Huth, Hans. "Yosemite: The Story of an Idea." *Sierra Club Bulletin* 33 (1947): 47–78.

"The Iron Horse." *Hutchings' California Magazine* 14 (1856): 175–76.

Jackson, Donald, ed. *Black Hawk: An Autobiography*. Urbana: University of Illinois Press, 1956.

Johannsen, Robert W. "Edward O. C. Ord on Frontier Defense." *California Historical Society Quarterly* 35, no. 1 (March 1956): 23–27.

Johnson, David Alan. *Founding the Far West: California, Oregon, and Nevada, 1840–1890*. Berkeley: University of California Press, 1992.

Johnson, J. Edward. "E. B. Crocker." *Journal of the State Bar of California* 24, no. 5 (1949): 338–42.

Johnson, Reinhard O. *The Liberty Party, 1840–1848: Antislavery Third-Party Politics in the United States*. Baton Rouge: Louisiana State University Press, 2009.

Johnson, Robert Underwood, and Clarence Clough Buel, eds. *Battles and Leaders of the Civil War*. 4 vols. New York: Century, 1884–88.

Johnston, Andrew Scott. *Mercury and the Making of California Mining, Landscape, and Race*. Boulder: University Press of Colorado, 2013.

Josephy, Alvin M., Jr. *The Civil War in the American West*. New York: Alfred A. Knopf, 1991.

Judah, Theodore D. *A Practical Plan for Building the Pacific Railroad*. Washington DC: H. Pilkinhorn, 1857.

Judson, Isabella Field. *Cyrus W. Field: His Life and Work*. New York: Harper & Brothers, 1896.

Keckley, Elizabeth. *Behind the Scenes: Or, Thirty Years a Slave, and Four Years in the White House*. New York: G. W. Carleton, 1868.

Kennedy, Elijah R. *The Contest for California in 1861: How Colonel E. D. Baker Saved the Pacific States to the Union*. Boston: Houghton Mifflin, 1912.

Kennett, Lee. *Sherman: A Soldier's Life*. New York: Harper Collins, 2001.

Kens, Paul. *Justice Stephen Field: Shaping Liberty from the Gold Rush to the Gilded Age*. Lawrence: University Press of Kansas, 1997.

Kibby, Leo P. "Union Loyalty of California's Civil War Governors." *California Historical Society Quarterly* 44, no. 4 (December 1965): 311–21.

King, Thomas Starr. *A Vacation among the Sierras: Yosemite in 1860*. Edited by John A. Hussey. San Francisco: Book Club of California, 1962.

Kiser, William S. *Coast-to-Coast Empire: Manifest Destiny and the New Mexico Borderland*. Norman: University of Oklahoma Press, 2018.

Lamon, Ward Hill. *The Life of Abraham Lincoln: From His Birth to His Inauguration as President*. Boston: Osgood, 1872.

Langley, Henry G. *San Francisco Directory for the Year 1858*. San Francisco: S. D. Valentine, 1858.

Lapp, Rudolph M. *Blacks in Gold Rush California*. New Haven CT: Yale University Press, 1977.

Layne, J. Gregg. "Edward Otho Cresap Ord: Soldier and Surveyor." *Quarterly Publication of the Historical Society of Southern California* 17 (December 1935): 139–42.

Lehrman, Lewis E. *Lincoln at Peoria: The Turning Point*. Mechanicsburg PA: Stackpole, 2008.

Leroy, David H. *Mr. Lincoln's Book: Publishing the Lincoln-Douglas Debates*. New Castle DE: Oak Knoll, 2009.

The Lincoln-Roosevelt Republican League. Los Angeles: Los Angeles County Central Committee and Lincoln-Roosevelt Republican League, 1908.

Lindsay, Brendan C. *Murder State: California's Native American Genocide, 1846–1873*. Lincoln: University of Nebraska Press, 2012.

Long, E. B., with Barbara Long. *The Civil War Day by Day: An Almanac, 1861–1865*. Garden City NY: Da Capo, 1971.

Loosley, Allyn C. *Foreign Born Population of California, 1848–1920*. San Francisco: R and E Research Associates, 1971.

Lowenstein, Roger. *Ways and Means: Lincoln and His Cabinet and the Financing of the Civil War*. New York: Penguin, 2022.

Lower, Richard Coke. *A Bloc of One: The Political Career of Hiram W. Johnson*. Stanford CA: Stanford University Press, 1993.

Lundén, Rolf. "The Rise and Fall of a Swedish-American Sculptor: The Case of David Edstrom." *Swedish-American Historical Quarterly* 54, no. 3 (2003): 145–63.

Lynch, Daniel. "Southern California Chivalry: Southerners, Californios, and the Forging of an Unlikely Alliance." *California History* 91, no. 3 (Fall 2014): 60–62.

Lynch, Jeremiah. *The Life of David C. Broderick, a Senator of the Fifties*. New York: Baker & Taylor, 1911.

Madley, Benjamin. *An American Genocide: The United States and the California Indian Catastrophe*. New Haven CT: Yale University Press, 2016.

Maltby, Charles. *The Life and Public Services of Abraham Lincoln*. Stockton CA: Daily Independent Steam Power Print, 1884.

Marszalek, John F. *Commander of All Lincoln's Armies: A Life of General Henry W. Halleck*. Cambridge MA: Belknap Press of Harvard University Press, 2004.

Martin, Edward Winslow. *The Life and Public Services of Schuyler Colfax, Together with His Most Important Speeches*. San Francisco: H. H. Bancroft, 1868.

Masich, Andrew E. *Civil War in the Southwest Borderlands, 1861–1867*. Norman: University of Oklahoma Press, 2017.

Mattes, Merrill J. *Platte River Road Narratives: A Descriptive Bibliography of Travel Over the Great Central Overland Route to Oregon, California, Utah, Colorado, Montana, and Other Western States and Territories, 1812–1866*. Urbana: University of Illinois Press, 1988.

Matthews, Glenna. *The Golden State in the Civil War: Thomas Starr King, the Republican Party, and the Birth of Modern California*. New York: Cambridge University Press, 2012.

McAfee, Ward M. "California's House Divided," *Civil War History* 33, no. 2 (1987): 115–30.

McAllister, Ward. *Society as I Have Found It*. New York: Cassell, 1896.

McClain, Charles J. "Pioneers on the Bench: The California Supreme Court, 1849–1879." In *Constitutional Governance and Judicial Power: The History of the California Supreme Court*, 1–4. Berkeley: Berkeley Public Policy Press, Institute of Governmental Studies, University of California, Berkeley, 2016.

McCurdy, Charles W. "Prelude to Civil War: A Snapshot of the California Supreme Court at Work in 1858." *California Supreme Court Historical Society Yearbook* 1 (1994): 33–54.

McGinnis, Ralph Y. "New Mexico Territory." In *Abraham Lincoln and the Western Territories*, edited by Ralph Y. McGinnis and Calvin N. Smith, 71–83. Chicago: Nelson-Hall, 1994.

McGinnis, Ralph Y., and Calvin N. Smith, eds. *Abraham Lincoln and the Western Territories*. Chicago: Nelson-Hall, 1994.

McGinty, Brian. *Archy Lee's Struggle for Freedom: The True Story of California Gold, the Nation's Tragic March Toward Civil War, and a Young Black Man's Fight for Liberty*. Guilford CT: Lyons, 2019.

———. "Before the Judge." *Westways* 71, no. 5 (May 1979): 20–23, 83.

———. *The Body of John Merryman: Abraham Lincoln and the Suspension of Habeas Corpus*. Cambridge MA: Harvard University Press, 2011.

———. "'Castine' and Mr. Lincoln: A Reporter at the White House." *Civil War Times Illustrated* 16, no. 7 (November 1977): 2–35.

———. "The Green and the Gold: The Irish in Early California." *The American West* 15, no. 2 (March/April 1978): 18–21, 65–69.

———. "Hung Be the Heavens with Black." *American History Illustrated* 17, no. 10 (February 1983): 31–39.

———. "I Will Call a Traitor a Traitor: Albert Sidney Johnston in San Francisco." *Civil War Times Illustrated* 22, no. 3 (June 1981): 24–31.

———. *John Brown's Trial*. Cambridge MA: Harvard University Press, 2009.

———. *Lincoln and the Court*. Cambridge MA: Harvard University Press, 2008.

———. *Lincoln's Greatest Case: The River, the Bridge, and the Making of America*. New York: Liveright, 2015.

———. "'Old Brains' in the New West: A Profile of Henry W. Halleck." *American History Illustrated* 13, no. 2 (May 1978): 10–19.

———. "Portrait for a Western Album. Maria Ignacia Bonifacio: The Legend of the Sherman Rose." *The American West* 16, no. 6 (November/December 1979): 28–29.

———. "Search for Nova Albion: Sir Francis Drake—Hero, God & Pirate." *Oceans* 12, no. 4 (July–August 1979): 21–27.

———. "Stephen J. Field: California's Superjudge." *Old West* 20, no. 2 (Winter 1983): 36–40, 60.

———. *The Rest I Will Kill: William Tillman and the Unforgettable Story of How a Free Black Man Refused to Become a Slave*. New York: Liveright, 2016.

McGloin, John B., S. J. *San Francisco: The Story of a City*. San Rafael CA: Presidio, 1978.

McPherson, James M. *Battle Cry of Freedom: The Civil War Era*. New York: Oxford University Press, 1988.

———. *Tried by War: Abraham Lincoln as Commander in Chief*. New York: Penguin, 2008.

Meigs, Montgomery C. "General M. C. Meigs on the Conduct of the Civil War." *American Historical Review* 26 (1921): 285–303.

Merk, Frederick. *Manifest Destiny and Mission in American History: A Reinterpretation*. Cambridge MA: Harvard University Press, 1963.

Moke, Paul. *Earl Warren and the Struggle for Justice*. Lanham MD: Lexington, 2015.

Morgan, James A., III. *A Little Short of Boats: The Battles of Ball's Bluff & Edwards Ferry, October 21–22, 1861*. New York: Savas Beattie, 2011.

Morris, Richard B. *Encyclopedia of American History*. 6th ed. New York: Harper & Row, 1982.

Moses, Bernard. "Legal Tender Notes in California." *Quarterly Journal of Economics* 7, no. 1 (1892): 1–25.

Munro-Fraser, J. P. *History of Marin County, California*. San Francisco: Alley, Bowen, 1880.

Murphy, Virginia Reed. "Across the Plains in the Donner Party: A Personal Narrative of the Overland Trip to California." *Century Magazine* 42 (1891): 409–26.

Murray, Keith. "The Movement for Statehood in Washington." *Pacific Northwest Quarterly* 32, no. 4 (1914): 349–84.

National Cyclopedia of American Biography. Vol. 13. New York: James T. White, 1906.

Neely, Mark E., Jr. *The Abraham Lincoln Encyclopedia*. New York: McGraw-Hill, 1982.

———. "Lincoln and the Mexican War: An Argument by Analogy." In *Lincoln Looks West: From the Mississippi to the Pacific*, edited by Richard W. Etulain, 68–89. Carbondale: Southern Illinois University Press, 2010.

———. "Pale-Faced People and Their Red Brethren," *Lincoln Lore*, no. 1686 (August 1978): 1–4.

Nelson, Megan Kate. "The Civil War from Apache Pass." *Journal of the Civil War Era* 6, no. 4 (2016): 510–35.

———. *The Three-Cornered War: The Union, the Confederacy, and Native People in the Fight for the West*. New York: Scribner, 2020.

Nevins, Allan, and Milton Halley Thomas, eds. *The Diary of George Templeton Strong*. Vol. 2. New York: Macmillan, 1953.

Newell, Clayton R. *The Regular Army Before the Civil War, 1845–1860*. Washington DC: Center of Military History, United States Army, 2014.

Nichols, David A. *Lincoln and the Indians: Civil War Policy and Politics*. St. Paul: Minnesota Historical Society Press, 2012.

———. "The Other Civil War: Lincoln and the Indians." *Minnesota History* 44, no. 1 (Spring 1974): 2–15.

Niven, John. *Salmon P. Chase: A Biography*. New York: Oxford University Press, 1995.

Nugent, Walter. *Habits of Empire: A History of American Expansion*. New York: Knopf, 2008.

Oakes, James. *The Crooked Path to Abolition: Abraham Lincoln and the Antislavery Constitution*. New York: W. W. Norton, 2021.

———. *Freedom National: The Destruction of Slavery in the United States, 1861–1865*. New York: W. W. Norton, 2013.

O'Connell, Robert L. *Fierce Patriot: The Tangled Lives of William Tecumseh Sherman*. New York: Random House, 2014.

O'Dowd, Niall. *Lincoln and the Irish: The Untold Story of How the Irish Helped Abraham Lincoln Save the Union*. New York: Skyhorse, 2018.

O'Sullivan, John L. "Annexation." *The United States Magazine and Democratic Review* 17 (1845): 5–6, 9–10.

Ord, Edward Otho Cresap. *Plan de la Ciudad de Los Angeles*. Surveyed & drawn by E. O. C. Ord, Lt., U.S.A. and Wm. Hutton, asst., August 29, 1848.

Orsi, Richard J. *Sunset Limited: The Southern Pacific Railroad and the Development of the American West, 1850–1930.* Berkeley: University of California Press, 2005.

Orton, Richard H. *Records of California Men in the War of the Rebellion, 1861 to 1867.* Sacramento: J. D. Young, Supt. State Printing, 1890.

Plummer, Mark A. *Lincoln's Rail-Splitter: Governor Richard J. Oglesby.* Urbana: University of Illinois Press, 2001.

Pratt, Harry E. "Abraham Lincoln's First Murder Trial." *Journal of the Illinois State Historical Society* 37, no. 2 (September 1944): 242–48.

———. *Personal Finances of Abraham Lincoln.* Chicago: Lakeside Press, 1943.

Pratt, Harry Noyes. "Haig Patigian, California's Noted Sculptor." *Overland Monthly and Out West Magazine* 81 (August 1923): 11.

Pratt, Julius W. "John L. O'Sullivan and Manifest Destiny." *New York History* 14 (1933): 213–34.

Prucha, Francis Paul. *Christian Reformers and the Indians, 1865–1900.* Norman: University of Oklahoma Press, 1976.

Rawls, James J. *Indians of California: The Changing Image.* Norman: University of Oklahoma Press, 1984.

Reck, W. Emerson. *A. Lincoln: His Last 24 Hours.* Columbia: University of South Carolina Press, 1994.

Reynolds, David S. *Abe: Abraham Lincoln in His Times.* New York: Penguin, 2020.

Rice, Allen Thorndike, ed. *Reminiscences of Abraham Lincoln by Distinguished Men of His Time.* New York: North American Review, 1888.

Richards, Leonard L. *The California Gold Rush and the Coming of the Civil War.* New York: Vintage, 2008.

Ridge, Martin. "Reflections on the Pony Express." *Montana: The Magazine of Western History* 46, no. 3 (Autumn 1996): 2–13.

Riley, Glenda, and Richard W. Etulain. *Presidents Who Shaped the American West.* Norman: University of Oklahoma Press, 2018.

Robinson, John W. *Los Angeles in Civil War Days, 1860–1865.* Norman: University of Oklahoma Press, 2013.

Robinson, W. W. *Land in California: The Story of Mission Land, Ranchos, Squatters, Mining Claims, Railroad Grants, Land Scrip, Homesteads.* Berkeley: University of California Press, 1948.

Roske, Ralph J. *Everyman's Eden: A History of California.* New York: Macmillan, 1968.

Rowland, Dunbar, ed. *Jefferson Davis, Constitutionalist: His Letters, Papers, and Speeches.* Vol. 3. Jackson: Mississippi Department of Archives and History, 1923.

Royster, Hayden. "This Land Is Their Land." *California* (Summer 2022): 32–41.

Rybczynski, Witold. *A Clearing in the Distance: Frederick Law Olmsted and America in the Nineteenth Century.* New York: Scribner, 2000.

Salomon, Carlos Manuel. *Pío Pico: The Last Governor of Mexican California.* Norman: University of Oklahoma Press, 2010.

Scheiber, Harry N., ed. *Constitutional Governance and Judicial Power: The History of the California Supreme Court.* Berkeley: Berkeley Public Policy Press, Institute of Governmental Studies, University of California, Berkeley, 2016.

Schneller, Robert J., Jr. *Farragut, America's First Admiral.* Washington DC: Potomac, 2002.

Senkewicz, Robert M. *Vigilantes in Gold Rush San Francisco.* Stanford CA: Stanford University Press, 1985.

Shafter, Oscar Lovell. *Life, Diary, and Letters of Oscar Lovell Shafter.* San Francisco: Blair-Murdock, 1915.

Sherman, William T. *Memoirs of General William T. Sherman.* 2 vols. New York: D. Appleton, 1875.

Shuck, Oscar T. *Bench and Bar in California.* San Francisco: Occident, 1889.

———. *The California Scrap-Book: A Repository of Useful Information and Select Reading.* San Francisco: H. H. Bancroft, 1869.

———. *Eloquence of the Far West. No. I. Masterpieces of E. D. Baker.* San Francisco: self-published, 1899.

Shutes, Milton H. *Colonel E. D. Baker.* San Francisco: s.n., 1938; repr. from *California Historical Society Quarterly*, December 1938.

———. "'Fighting Joe' Hooker." *California Historical Society Quarterly* 16, no. 4 (1937): 304–20.

———. *Lincoln and California.* Stanford CA: Stanford University Press, 1943.

Smith, Stacey L. *Freedom's Frontier: California and the Struggle over Unfree Labor, Emancipation, and Reconstruction.* Chapel Hill: University of North Carolina Press, 2013.

———. "Remaking Slavery in a Free State: Masters and Slaves in Gold Rush California." *Pacific Historical Review* 80, no. 1 (February 2011): 28–63.

Spaulding, Imogene. "The Attitude of California to the Civil War." *Annual Publication of the Historical Society of Southern California* 9, no. 1 and 2 (1912–1913): 104–31.

Spence, Mark David. *Dispossessing the Wilderness: Indian Removal and the Making of the National Parks.* New York: Oxford University Press, 1999.

Stahr, Walter. *Salmon P. Chase: Lincoln's Vital Rival.* New York: Simon & Schuster, 2022.

———. *Seward: Lincoln's Indispensable Man.* New York: Simon & Schuster, 2012.

———. *Stanton: Lincoln's War Secretary.* New York: Simon & Schuster, 2017.

Starr, John W., Jr. *Lincoln & the Railroads: A Biographical Study.* New York: Dodd, Mead, 1927.

———. *Lincoln's Last Day.* New York: Frederick A. Stokes, 1922.

Starr, Kevin. *Americans and the California Dream, 1850–1915.* New York: Oxford University Press, 1973.

———. *California: A History.* New York: Modern Library, 2005.

Steiner, Mark E. *An Honest Calling: The Law Practice of Abraham Lincoln.* DeKalb: Northern Illinois University Press, 2006.

———. *Lincoln and Citizenship.* Carbondale: Southern Illinois University Press, 2021.

Stover, John F. *The Routledge Historical Atlas of the American Railroads*. New York: Routledge, 1999.

Stowell, Daniel, et al., eds. *The Papers of Abraham Lincoln: Legal Documents and Cases*. 4 vols. Charlottesville: University of Virginia Press, 2008.

Swisher, Carl B. *History of the Supreme Court of the United States: Volume V, The Taney Period 1836–64*. New York: Macmillan, 1974.

Symonds, Craig L. *Lincoln and His Admirals: Abraham Lincoln, the U.S. Navy, and the Civil War*. New York: Oxford University Press, 2008.

Talbott, Laurence Fletcher. *California in the War for Southern Independence*. Glendale CA: Hall, 1996.

Teel, T. T. "Sibley's New Mexican Campaign,—Its Objects and the Causes of Its Failure." In *Battles and Leaders of the Civil War*, edited by Robert Underwood Johnson and Clarence Clough Buel, 2: 70.

Temple, Wayne C. *Lincoln's Confidant: The Life of Noah Brooks*. Edited by Douglas L. Wilson and Rodney O. Davis. Urbana: University of Illinois Press, 2019.

———. "Lincoln's Fence Rails." *Journal of the Illinois State Historical Society (1908–1984)* 47, no. 1 (1954): 20–34.

Tripp, C. A. *The Intimate World of Abraham Lincoln*. New York: Free Press, 2005.

Tutorow, Norman E. *The Governor: The Life and Legacy of Leland Stanford, A California Colossus*. 2 vols. Spokane WA: Arthur H. Clark, 2004.

Twain, Mark. *Autobiography of Mark Twain*. Vol. 1. Edited by Harriet Elinor Smith. Berkeley: University of California Press, 2010.

Utley, Robert M. *The Commanders: Civil War Generals Who Shaped the American West*. Norman: University of Oklahoma Press, 2018.

Vandenhoff, Anne. *Edward Dickinson Baker: Western Gentleman, Frontier Lawyer, American Statesman*. Auburn CA: Anne Vandenhoff, 1979.

VanderVelde, Lea. *Mrs. Dred Scott: A Life on Slavery's Frontier*. New York: Oxford University Press, 2009.

Waite, Kevin. "Jefferson Davis and Proslavery Visions of Empire in the Far West." *Journal of the Civil War Era* 6, no. 4 (2016): 536–65.

———. "The Lost Cause Goes West: Confederate Culture and Civil War Memory in California." *California History* 97, no. 1 (2020): 33–49.

———. *West of Slavery: The Southern Dream of a Transcontinental Empire*. Chapel Hill: University of North Carolina Press, 2021.

Wallace, Joseph. *Sketch of the life and public services of Edward D. Baker, United States senator from Oregon, and formerly representative in Congress from Illinois, who died in battle near Leesburg, Va., October 21 AD, 1861*. Springfield IL: Journal Company, 1870.

Wallis, Michael. *The Best Land Under Heaven: The Donner Party in the Age of Manifest Destiny*. New York: Liveright, 2017.

Wallis, Michael, and Michael S. Williamson. *The Lincoln Highway: Coast to Coast from Times Square to the Golden Gate*. New York: W. W. Norton, 2007.

Walters, Helen B. "Confederates in Southern California." *Historical Society of Southern California Quarterly* 35 (March 1953): 41–54.

Warren, Earl. *The Memoirs of Earl Warren.* Garden City NY: Doubleday, 1977.

Warren, Louis A., ed. "Earliest Sculptors of the President." *Lincoln Lore,* July 1, 1946.

Washburne, Elihu B. "Reminisces of Abraham Lincoln." In *Reminiscences of Abraham Lincoln by Distinguished Men of His Time,* edited by Allen Thorndike Rice, 5–45. New York: North American Review, 1888.

Waugh, John C. *One Man Great Enough: Abraham Lincoln's Road to Civil War.* New York: Harcourt, 2007.

West, Elliott. "Reconstructing Race." *Western Historical Quarterly* 34, no. 1 (Spring 2003): 6–26.

Wheeler, Samuel P. "Solving a Lincoln Literary Mystery: 'Little Eddie.'" *Journal of the Abraham Lincoln Association* 33, no. 2 (2012): 34–46.

Whipple, Henry Benjamin. *Lights and Shadows of a Long Episcopate.* New York: Macmillan, 1899.

White, Richard. *Railroaded: The Transcontinentals and the Making of Modern America.* New York: W. W. Norton, 2011.

White, Ronald C., Jr. *Lincoln in Private: What His Most Personal Reflections Tell Us about Our Greatest President.* New York: Random House, 2021.

———. *Lincoln's Greatest Speech: The Second Inaugural.* New York: Simon & Schuster, 2002.

Whitney, Ellen M., ed. *The Black Hawk War 1831–1832, Vol. 1, Illinois Volunteers.* Springfield: Illinois State Historical Society, 1970.

Wiecek, William M. "*Somerset:* Lord Mansfield and the Legitimacy of Slavery in the Anglo-American World." *University of Chicago Law Review* 42 (1974): 86–146.

Wilkins, James H., ed. *The Great Diamond Hoax and Other Stirring Incidents in the Life of Asbury Harpending.* San Francisco: James H. Barry, 1913.

Williams, David A. *David C. Broderick: A Political Portrait.* San Marino CA: Huntington Library, 1969.

Williams, T. Harry. *Lincoln and His Generals.* New York: Alfred A. Knopf, 1952.

Wilson, Douglas L., and Rodney O. Davis, ed. *Herndon's Informants: Letters, Interviews, and Statements about Abraham Lincoln.* Urbana: University of Illinois Press, 1998.

Woodward, Walter Carleton. *The Rise and Early Political Parties in Oregon, 1843–1868.* Portland: J. K. Gill, 1914.

Woolsey, Ronald C. "Disunion or Dissent? A New Look at an Old Problem in Southern California Attitudes toward the Civil War." *Southern California Quarterly* 66, no. 3 (1984): 185–205.

———. "The Politics of a Lost Cause: 'Seceshers' and Democrats in Southern California during the Civil War." *California History* 69, no. 4 (Winter 1990–1991): 372–83.

Young, John Russell. *Around the World with General Grant.* Vol. 2. New York: American News, 1879.

Index

coln, xiv, 14, 26, 152, 189; and Kansas-
Nebraska Act, 13; and Lecompton
constitution, 31; and popular sovereignty, 13, 19, 29–30; as presidential candidate, 30–31, 34–35, 40–41, 51–52, 153;
supported by Grant, 67

Downey, John G.: Breckinridge supporter,
45; governor of California, 28, 46, 87,
108, 130; and Henry W. Halleck, 60; and
Los Angeles Mounted Rifles, 132; and
secession, 131

Drake, Francis, 114

Dred Scott (Dred Scott v. Sandford) (1857),
16, 19, 22, 88, 93, 181

Drum Barracks, 134, 137–38, 171

Edstrom, David, 173

Edwards, Ninian, 9–10

Edwards, Ninian W., 10

the *Effie Afton*, 22–23

Eisenhower, Dwight D., 183–84

Emancipation Proclamation, 109, 157, 172,
192

Ethington, Philip J., 16

Etulain, Richard W., 98

Everett, Edward, 31

Ewing, Thomas, 63

Farragut, David Glasgow: arrival in California, 189; and attack on New Orleans,
68; early career of, 68; and Mare Island,
63, 189, 194; and Mobile Bay, 193; as rear
admiral, 191; request for help in suppressing vigilantes, 64

Fay, Caleb T., 157

Fehrenbacher, Don, 154

Fessenden, William P., 89

Field, David Dudley, 19, 84, 85, 86–87, 88

Field, Henry Martyn, 88

Field, Stephen J.: and abolitionism, 87;
appointment to U.S. Supreme Court
by Lincoln, 87–88; and California land
grants, 91; as California Supreme Court
chief justice, 19, 84; conflict with Benjamin F. Moore, 86; conflict with William
Turner, 85; early life and career, 84–85;

and Asbury Harpending, 142; as member of California State Assembly, 85–86;
and *Perry v. Washburn* (1862), 111; and
Alfred Rubery, 143; and telegraph, 87

Fillmore, Millard: and California's first
state constitution, 15; and California
judges, 82; and 1856 reelection effort, 25;
as U.S. president, 15, 63, 118;

Fisher, Carl G., 181, 182

Fort Colville, 71

Fort Humboldt, 66, 120, 121, 189

Fort Laramie, 130, 152

Fort Mojave, 129

Fort Point, 58, 71

Fort Ross, 114

Fort Sumter, 43, 52, 53, 67, 130, 131, 132, 190

Fort Tejon, 129

Fort Vancouver, 66

Fort Yuma, 71, 135, 138, 139

Frémont, Jessie Benton, 19, 28, 54, 55

Frémont, John C.: and "Bear Flag" uprising,
9; and campaign for president in 1856, xv,
14, 151–52, 189; career in California and
with Lincoln, xv; and Department of the
West, 55, 56; and "The Golden Gate," 25;
and Lincoln's speech at Cooper Union
19; and Mariposa land grant, 54; and the
Mountain Department, 56; "The Pathfinder," xv; and San Francisco speech of
Edward D. Baker, 28; and slavery in Missouri free, 55; as U.S. senator, xv, 25, 58

Fritz, Christian G., 93

Garnett, Robert S., 183

Garrison, Cornelius K., 69

Grant, Ulysses S.: animosity toward, 184;
and California gold, 105; death of, 194;
hotel named for in San Diego, 183; as
lieutenant general, 145; with Lincoln
on April 14, 1865, 1; Mexican conflict
as a "wicked war," xiv, 116; military service in prewar California, xv, 65–67, 18,
189; praise by Noah Brooks, 160, 162;
resumption of military duties, 65, 67;
and surrender of Robert E. Lee, 149; as
U.S. president, 161

King of William, James, 15
Kirkwood, Samuel J., 123
Knights of the Columbian Star, 46
Knights of the Golden Circle, 45–46, 141
Knowlton, Ebenezer, 171
Know-Nothings, 29, 31
Kuskov, Ivan Alexander, 114

Lane, Joseph, 27, 35
Lassik, 122
Latham, Milton: as governor of California, 28; and Pacific Republic, 32, 43–43; and secession, 131; as U.S. senator, 29, 32
Lecompton constitution, 30, 31
Lee, Archy, 15–16
Lee, Robert E.: at Battle of Gettysburg, 130; death of, 194; portrait of viewed by Lincoln, 1; resignation from U.S. Army, 52; revered memory of, 183; surrenders to Ulysses S. Grant, 193
Levertin, Oscar, 173
Lincoln, Abraham: and April 14, 1865, 1–4; and Arizona territorial status, 139; birth, 6; as a "Black Republican," 26, 45; and California's Native Americans, xvi, 113–27; Cooper Union speech, 18–19; death of, 4, 193; debates with Stephen A. Douglas, xiv, 14, 26, 152, 189; and division of California, 38–39; and Dred Scott decision, 16; duty to appoint officeholders, 74–89; and Effie Afton case, 24; and election of 1860, 34–36; and federal bonds, 106, 107–8; and federal taxes, 107; and first federal income tax law, 106; as "Honest Old Abe," 27, 28; and Kansas and Nebraska, xiv, 13, 38; and national banking system, 107–8; and New Almaden, 95–96; and Oregon, xiii–xiv, 11–12; "The Rail Candidate for President in 1860," 19; and Spanish missions in California, 102–3; sculptures of in California; xvii; as U.S. congressman, 10–11; and war with Mexico, xiv, 11; as "western free state man," xiii, 5–17; wish to reside in California, xiii, xvi, xvii, 5, 166, 168, 182, 184

Lincoln, Edward Baker (Eddie), 6, 10, 187, 188
Lincoln, Mary Todd, 1–4, 6, 9, 12, 166, 187
Lincoln, Mordecai, 119
Lincoln, Nancy Hanks, 6
Lincoln, Robert Todd, 1, 6, 187
Lincoln, Thomas (Tad), 1, 189
Lincoln, William Wallace (Willie), 167
Lincoln Highway, xii, xvii, 173, 181–83, 184
Lincoln Highway Association, 194
Lincoln Memorial Shrine and Library, xii, xvii, 173, 175–76, 195
Lincoln Park (Los Angeles), 172–73, 194
Lincoln Park (San Francisco), xvii, 182, 184
Lincoln-Roosevelt League, xvii, 178–79, 194
Lippitt, Francis, 121
Lone Mountain, xvi, 17, 166, 167, 168, 170, 182, 190, 191, 192
Los Angles Mounted Rifles, 132
Loughery, Andrew S., 117–18
Lovell, Charles S., 120–21
Low, Frederick F., 95, 170, 193
Lucas, Turner & Co., 63
Lummis, Charles Fletcher, 172
Lyon, Nathaniel, 54

Magruder, John B., 133
Maltby, Charles: biographer of Lincoln, xv; and Black Hawk War, 7; in California, xv, 8, 79; as collector of internal revenue, 79; and Lincoln's wish to visit California, 5; in New Salem with Lincoln, xiv, 7–8, 79; and public offices in California, xv, 78–79, 80, 123; and testimony about Robert J. Stevens, 80
Maltby, Charlotte, 79–80
manifest destiny, 39–40, 91
Mare Island, 63, 68 141–42
Mariposa Battalion, 117
Marszalek, John F., 93
Mason, John, 141
Mason, Richard B., 57, 61, 62, 188
Matteson, Joel, 13
Matthews, Glenna, 167
McAllister, Hall, 83
McAllister, Matthew Hall, 82, 83–85, 87

McAllister, Ward, 83–84

McClellan, George B.: appointment by Lincoln, 56; battles Robert E. Lee, 143; and death of Edward D. Baker, 165–66; described by Noah Brooks, 156; meeting with Ulysses S. Grant, 66; and Henry W. Halleck, 60; and general reconnaissance of Potomac Valley, 165; as "Little Mac," 56–57; presidential candidacy of, 147–48

McConnell, John R., 46

McDougall, James A., xv, 28–29, 44, 77, 158

McDowell, Irvin, 53, 130, 143, 156, 169–70, 192

McKee, Redick, 118

McKinley, William, 174

McLaughlin, Moses A., 122

McLean, John, 24

McPherson, James M., 57, 107

Meade, George Gordon, 145, 160, 192

Mechanics' Pavilion, 171

Meigs, Montgomery C., 106

Meunier, Constantin, 173

Mezzara, Pietro, 172

Mezzofanti, Giuseppe, 115

Miranda v. Arizona (1966), 180

Mission San Juan Capistrano, 102

Mission San Luis Rey de Francia, 103

Mission San Rafael Arcángel, 102

Mission Santa Barbara, 102, 103

Moore, Benjamin F., 86

Mormon Battalion, 133

Morrill, Justin, 98

Morrill Act, 98, 175, 191, 194

Moses, Bernard, 111

National Union Party, 146

Native Peoples (Indians): and Black Hawk War, 6, 119–20; Cherokees, 120; and Civil War, 120; and Millard Fillmore, 118; Lincoln and the Sioux, xvi, 123–27, 184–85; Lincoln's early knowledge of, 119–20; Lincoln's failure to better their conditions, xvi, 112–14, 127; and "military reservations," 118; and mission fathers, 92, 101–2, 114, 115; and New Almaden, 58; and Edward Otho Cresap Ord, 61; population in California, 114–16, 117, 119, 125; and racial mixtures, 115–16; regret expressed by Lincoln, 127; and the Sioux, 123–24; and Superintendent of Indian Affairs for California, 118–19; and Yosemite, 99

Neely, Mark E., Jr., 113

Nelson, Samuel, 96

Nesmith, James W., 27, 72

New Almaden mine, 58, 59, 75, 94–96

Nicolay, John G., 34, 50, 161

Nunes, Joseph A., 78

Offutt, Denton, 7

Ogier, Isaac S. K., 82

Oglesby, Richard J., xv, 20

Olmsted, Frederick Law, 108

Ord, Edward Otho Cresap, 57, 60–61, 188, 194

Ord, James L., 61

O'Sullivan, John L., 53

Overland Monthly, 163

Pacific Republic, 32, 40, 41–42, 43

Packard Motor Car Company, 181

paper currency, 109

Patigian, Haig, 174–75

Pearce, James A., 50

Pendleton, George H., 147

Perry v. Washburn (1862), 111

Peyri, Antonio, 115

Pickett, George E., 183

Pico, Andrés, 130

Pico, José Ramon, 130–31

Pico, Pío, 115, 130

Pierce, Franklin, 82, 83, 96

Piercy, Charles, 135

Polk, James Knox: and discovery of gold in California, 62; and Mexican War, xiv, 11, 188

Pony Express, 26, 43, 51, 54

Pope, John C., 56, 123–24, 155

Porter, David Dixon, 68

Porter, Fitz John, 153

Portolá, Gaspar de, 114

Poston, Charles, 139